30
67

MUSICAL INSTRUMENTS

by Karl Geiringer

BRAHMS

HIS LIFE AND WORK

THE BACH FAMILY

Angel playing the Lute. By Melozzo da Forli. Fifteenth century.
Rome, Vatican Museum

KARL GEIRINGER

Musical
Instruments

Their History in Western Culture
from the Stone Age to the
Present Day

Translated by BERNARD MIALL

Edited by W. F. H. BLANDFORD

NEW YORK
OXFORD UNIVERSITY PRESS

FIRST PUBLISHED IN 1943
SECOND EDITION 1945
THIRD IMPRESSION 1949
FOURTH IMPRESSION 1959

To
EDITH W. HOMANS
in respect and admiration

PRINTED IN GREAT BRITAIN
in 12-point Fournier Type
BY UNWIN BROTHERS LIMITED
WOKING

PREFACE

The arrangement and presentation of material in this book may surprise the reader. Textbooks on musical instruments usually deal with the different types in systematic order, starting with the percussion and ending with the stringed and wind instruments. For this book, however, a historical method has been chosen. In seven chapters the instruments of the West are treated within the great epochs of history, from the Stone Age to our present day. A period of about twenty-five thousand years is thus covered, beginning with the whirring bones and clay drums of the earliest men, and traced up to the most refined electrical instruments of our time. This method enables the instruments' connexion with the art and culture of the several periods to be brought out, and makes the book kind of a supplement to any History of Music. The student interested in the music of the "Ars antiqua" will learn about the instruments of that period in the chapter on the Early Middle Ages. He who looks for information on the orchestra of Bach and Handel will consult the chapter on the Baroque period. The final chapter, which reviews the gigantic development of instrumental resources during the last hundred years, is necessarily the most extensive.

Each chapter starts with an introduction summarizing the cultural and artistic trends of the period. Then follows a discussion of the different instruments which, as far as possible, are dealt with in the same order in all chapters. This arrangement, although far from orthodox, has stood the test of some twenty years of teaching experience; but the reader, however, who prefers to follow the course of an instrument through the centuries can do so with the help of the table of contents and index.

Acoustical and technical principles have been summarized in an introduction in order to relieve the text from too many definitions and figures. This introduction can, without detriment to the understanding of the historical chapters, be passed over by those not interested in these problems.

In selecting the illustrations I have aimed primarily at showing the instruments in actual use in contemporary pictures and not as lifeless pieces of wood or brass. Several pictures, especially of the oldest and modern periods, are here reproduced for the first time.

I have not been able to limit myself to the literature mentioned in the Bibliography. The unusual viewpoint adopted in this book called for special research into many details, notably as regards the Middle Ages and the Renaissance. In order not to interrupt the continuity of the story, this new material has not been given special mention. Footnotes are uninteresting for the amateur, and the expert does not require them.

The manuscript of the book was begun in 1936 in Vienna. Work on it was continued through 1938 and 1939 in London and finished in New York in August 1940. The production has then required another two years. I consider it a miracle of determination and idealism on the part of the publishers that in spite of the endless obstacles caused through the war, a book of this kind can appear at all. There are several English and American scholars and friends to whom I feel deeply indebted, for without their active help and encouragement I should never have succeeded in finishing the work at a time that is anything but favourable to scientific research. I should like to mention in this respect Dr. H. C. Colles, first music critic of the London *Times* and Editor of Grove's *Dictionary of Music and Musicians*; Sir George Dyson, Director of the Royal College of Music, London; Adam Carse, Professor at the Royal Academy of Music, London; Paul Hirsch, Cambridge; Sir Adrian Boult, Music Director of the B.B.C.; Ralph Hill, Music Editor of the *Radio Times*, and my other friends in the British Broadcasting Corporation. In the United States it is mainly Alfred H. Meyer, Dean of the College of Music of Boston University and Berrian R. Shute, Professor of Music at Hamilton College, Clinton, N.Y., to whom I feel grateful for the opportunity they have afforded me of finishing this work. I have also to thank Mr. Carse for having drawn Figure 13 specially for this work, Messrs. Boosey & Hawkes Ltd. for the loan of blocks, and the owners whose permission to reproduce photographs of objects in their possession is acknowledged under the illustrations. Last, but certainly not least, my sincere thanks are due to my friend, Mr. W. F. H. Blandford, London, who has placed his knowledge and experience fully at my disposal. At a time when a letter from the United States to England required a month or more and the work of correction threatened to extend over an indefinite period, he took charge of the greatest part of it and thus rendered an invaluable service to the book.

KARL GEIRINGER

Professor of Music
Boston University

Boston
December 1941

PREFACE TO THE SECOND EDITION

The text of this edition differs from that of the first edition only in a few minor amendments and additions. The original Plate LXII, which had been accepted for many years without question as representing the Distin family quintet, has been found to represent another unidentified quintet, and has therefore been withdrawn. Its place has been taken by the reproduction of a print, of the authenticity of which there can be no question.

CONTENTS

CHAPTER VI

THE CLASSICAL PERIOD (1750–1810) . . . 192–231

LIST OF PLATES

Angel playing the Lute. By Melozzo da Forli.
Fifteenth century. Rome, Vatican Museum.

Frontispiece

B

FIGURES IN THE TEXT

INTRODUCTION

THE ACOUSTICS OF MUSICAL INSTRUMENTS

THE common purpose of all musical instruments is to create sound. Sound, therefore, must be the first object of our enquiry.

Sound

Musical sound (as distinct from noise) is produced by the vibrations of an elastic body. If an ordinary knitting-needle is clamped to the top of a table with the greater part of it projecting beyond the edge—the part between A and B in Figure 1—and if the end B is then pressed sideways (phase 1) and suddenly released, it will at once begin to vibrate in the manner of a pendulum. Because of its elasticity it will immediately return to the point of rest (phase 2), but, instead of remaining there, it will swiftly travel to the opposite extreme (phase 3); and from here once more, because of its elasticity, the needle will return to phase 1. This process would repeat itself to infinity did not the manifold hindrances to free movement— internal friction, and above all the resistance of the air itself—gradually absorb the initial effective impulse.

FIG. 1.—Diagram of a vibration

The path from phase 1 to phase 3 and back again is a double, or *complete vibration*. By the word *frequency* we understand the sum of complete vibrations effected in one second.

If we leave a very large portion of the needle projecting into the air the vibrations will be slow. and we shall hear no musical sound. If, on the contrary, we shorten the free part of the needle (i.e. A–B) it will vibrate more rapidly, and a musical sound will be audible. And if the needle is gradually drawn farther on to the table, so that the vibrating portion is correspondingly curtailed, the vibrations will become more and more rapid, while simultaneously the pitch of the sound will be raised. From this experiment we learn (1) that for sound to be audible the vibrations must have a certain minimum frequency; (2) that the frequency increases as the length of the vibrating body is decreased; and (3) that as the frequency increases the pitch is raised. Actually the human ear will not respond to fewer than 16 complete vibrations per second. At the other extreme an analogous limit is established, for the human ear cannot discern more than 20,000 vibrations per second. Music, however, does not make use of the whole of this immense range. Usually it is content with a middle position, between 30 and 4,000 vibrations. This, musically speaking, embraces a range of some seven octaves, i.e. C_1–c^5.

The sound-impulses which are set up by the sound-producer (in our case the metallic needle) are imparted to the surrounding air, and by it are transmitted farther. The process is as follows:

Longitudinal and Transverse Vibrations

When the needle (Fig. 1) reaches phase 3 at the end of its first vibration the air-molecules at this spot are pushed and hustled against the neighbouring molecules. There ensues a condensation of the air. But the needle at once swings back to phase 1, and since it drags the adjacent air-molecules back with it, the pressure is reduced, and rarefaction of the air results. This phenomenon of condensation and rarefaction, which is the characteristic of vibrations in air, repeats itself as long as the needle is in motion. The vibrations of the air, however, are not confined to the immediate neighbourhood of the initial impulse; they are taken up by the adjacent air-molecules, and by them are transmitted still farther. Nor does the sound travel in one direction only; it is propagated in all three dimensions, in the form of spherical surfaces.

It should be clearly understood that the individual air-molecules are not themselves transmitted; they merely swing to and fro on the spot, as it were; what is transmitted is simply the local *movement*. Thus, an object floating in water is not carried forward by the motion of the waves, but is merely raised and lowered in a vertical plane.

The example of waves in water may well be adduced in order to throw some further light on the fundamental principles of acoustics. Watching the waves by the seashore, we see that wave-crests alternate with troughs or hollows: the individual particles of water are rising and falling in a vertical plane, while at the same time the wave-movement is progressing in a horizontal plane. A similar image may be obtained if we take one end of a rope and vigorously swing it to and fro in the manner of a pendulum. Here, too, a wave-movement is set up, which travels along the length of the rope in a horizontal plane, while the rope

itself, at any point, is moving vertically up and down. The
pendulum-like vibrations of the separate points are thus
set up in a direction at right angles to the direction in
which the waves are proceeding. Vibrations of this kind
are called *transverse vibrations*. On the other hand, in the
case of waves transmitted by alternate condensations and
rarefactions of the air, the separate molecules vibrate in
the same direction as that in which the waves are travelling.
Vibrations of this kind are called *longitudinal vibrations*.
Since the conception of longitudinal waves may at first
present a certain difficulty, we shall try to illustrate it by an
image from another sphere (Fig. 2). Think of a long tube
in which elastic rubber balls lie at regular intervals, being
connected by an elastic thread (Fig. 2, stage I). If the ball *a*
is knocked against the ball *b* (stage II) this impact will be
transmitted, step by step, through the whole series—to
ball *c* (stage III), ball *d* (stage IV), ball *e* (stage V), and so on.
But each ball, because of its elasticity, will rebound to its
starting-point, and beyond this, to the opposite extreme,
in a pendulum-like motion. In stages IV–VII we see the ball *a*
in reverse motion, in stages V–VIII the ball *b*, in stages VI–IX
the ball *c*, and so on. But on their way back the balls will
be checked by the elastic pull of the rubber thread. After
each ball has returned, past its point of first departure, to
a point corresponding to that reached in its initial forward
movement (the ball *a* has reached this point in stage VII,
the ball *b* in stage VIII, and so on), it will be returned again
to the starting-point by the rubber thread, again moving
forward, so that the whole vibration is repeated.

And if, instead of rubber balls, we imagine the separate
air-molecules which have been set in vibration by the
sound-producer—our knitting-needle, for instance—we
can visualize the progress of an air-wave of the longitudinal
kind. The molecule *a* is pushed toward *b* by the vibration

of the elastic needle; but is immediately drawn back again from *b* by the return movement of the needle, only to be pushed forward again toward *b*, and so on, for as long as the needle continues to vibrate. In this case the air-molecules *b, c, d*, etc., behave in precisely the same way as the balls in Fig. 2; and thus we see quite clearly the various stages in the progressive compression of the air (as in stage II at *a* and *b*, or in stage XIII at *d, e* and *f*), and the consequent rarefaction (as in stage VI at *a, b* and *c*, or in stage XII at *g, h* and *i*).

Transverse and longitudinal vibrations both play their part in the functioning of musical instruments. Here we are dealing, not with a progression of waves, as in the sea or the air, but with static waves. Longitudinal vibrations are restricted to wind instruments (aerophones); while transverse vibrations occur in the stringed instruments (chordophones), in drums (membranophones), and other percussion instruments (idiophones).

Tone and Noise

Both the sound produced by a vibrating string and the sound produced by blowing into a wind instrument cause in the human ear a smooth, harmonious sensation. A sound of this kind we shall call a *tone*. But the crunching of a cart-wheel or the clash of cymbals produces a rough, inharmonious sound-sensation in the ear. A sound of this kind we shall call a *noise*.

Both tones and noises are composed of various components, called *partial tones*, or shortly, *partials*.

Listen to the ringing of a bell, and you will hear, pretty clearly, that the sound which determines, to our ears, the pitch of the bell, and is called the "strike note," is accompanied by the simultaneous sounds of a whole series of higher notes, known as *overtones* or *upper partials*. In other sounds the overtones are fused into a single composite sound which can be dissected only with the aid of acoustic apparatus; but even in these cases their existence can be objectively established, and they play an important part in determining the colour of the sound. The difference between tones and noises, physically speaking, is simply that in a tone the frequencies of the overtones stand in a simple and unalterable relation to one another, while in a noise the frequencies of the overtones stand in a complicated relationship to one another, which, moreover, can be subject to unlimited variation.

When the frequencies of the partials constituting a sound are in the ratio of $1 : 2 : 3 : 4 : 5 : 6 : 7$, etc., the partials are called *harmonics* and we speak of a "natural series of harmonics." In the natural series of harmonics the first harmonic or *fundamental tone* can have any frequency you like, and invariably the second harmonic will have double that frequency, the third three times, the fourth four times, and so on. Let us take it, then, that the fundamental tone has 435 double or complete vibrations per second. Then:

the 2nd harmonic will have $2 \times 435 = \quad$ 870 vibrations
the 3rd harmonic will have $3 \times 435 = $ 1,305 vibrations
the 4th harmonic will have $4 \times 435 = $ 1,740 vibrations
the 5th harmonic will have $5 \times 435 = $ 2,175 vibrations

per second, and so on. Musically speaking, a tone of 435 double vibrations per second has the pitch a^1, a tone of 870 vibrations the pitch a^2, a tone of 1,305 vibrations the pitch e^3, a tone of 1,740 vibrations the pitch a^3, a tone of 2,175 vibrations the pitch $c\sharp^4$. If we write down this series in musical notation, as far as the 16th harmonic, we have the following:

The 7th, 11th, 13th and 14th harmonics, written here within brackets, are out of tune in any musical scale

(For easier reading every note is put two octaves lower than it really sounds.)

Thus, between the first and the second harmonics there is an interval of an octave; between the 1st and 3rd an octave and a fifth; between the 1st and 4th a double octave; between the 1st and 5th a double octave and a major third; and so on. This series of harmonic overtones may be built up on any other fundamental note; so if we take C as our first harmonic, or fundamental note, the series will follow thus:

This series of harmonics is of the greatest importance, and we shall often find ourselves returning to it.

Tone-Colour

As we have already established, in tones, as distinct from noises, the frequencies of the harmonics stand in a simple and straightforward relationship to one another. On the other hand, no single tone comprises the whole series of harmonics, and those represented are not equal in strength. These variations in the structure of tones are the most important causes of the differences of sound-colour—or, since we are now speaking of tones, let us say tone-colour. A few examples may serve to illustrate this fact.

In the tone of a tuning-fork or of a Flute gently blown, only the first harmonic—the fundamental note—is present. The effect is soft and pleasant to the ear, but at the same time uncharacteristic and wearisome. A tone of such simplicity is exceptional in music. Combinations of harmonics are much more frequent.

In the tone of a gently-blown Horn or a softly-struck Piano note the first five or six harmonics are present. The tone is now fuller and more powerful, but still comparatively expressionless.

A strongly-blown Horn or a powerfully-struck Piano note comprises a whole series of soft harmonics in addition to the first six strongly sounding overtones. The effect is more solid and vigorous. In the Violin, the Oboe, and the human voice, a whole series of harmonics is present besides the first six. All these harmonics serve to produce a strong and characteristic effect.

If, as in the Trumpet, the higher harmonics (above the sixth or seventh) are more strongly accentuated than the lower, the tone will be particularly sharp, penetrating and brilliant. If, as in the Clarinet, the even-numbered harmonics are missing and only the odd-numbered (1, 3, 5, 7) are represented, the effect will be a rather hollow-sounding tone.

Pitch

Another quality of every tone is the *pitch*. In tones, as distinct from noises, the pitch of the first harmonic, the fundamental note, is always the decisive factor in the pitch of the whole tone. This is the case not only when the first harmonic is heard as a dominant feature of the whole tone, but also when it is weak. Even when it is physically imperceptible, it nevertheless determines the human perception of the pitch of a given tone. In short, the pitch of the fundamental note is invariably the pitch of the whole tone. In noises with a complicated and unstable relationship of overtones there is really no question of a definite pitch. But if in these sounds, together with the overtones of an unstable relationship, there are also harmonics which stand in a simple relation, and remain constant for some time (as e.g. in the Kettledrum), then even a noise may have its pitch established.

Intervals

In our discussion of overtones we saw that the frequencies of two tones separated by the interval of an octave stand in the ratio of 1 : 2—just as the frequencies of two tones separated by the interval of an octave and a fifth are as 1 : 3, while the double octave is expressed by the ratio 1 : 4, the double octave and a major third by the ratio 1 : 5, and so on. From the series of overtones in the example on page 23 we are able to draw further conclusions as to the relationship between the frequencies of two tones. Between the second and third harmonics of this example— i.e. between *c* and *g*—there lies the interval of a perfect fifth. The ratio of these two frequencies is 2 : 3. As we have already seen, the series of harmonic overtones can be built up on any fundamental note, and this helps us to realize the significant point, that when two tones are separated by the interval of a fifth their frequencies stand in the ratio of 2 : 3. Similarly, the frequency-ratio of a further series of important intervals can be established. Between

the third overtone (g) and the fourth (c^1) lies the interval
of a perfect fourth. Thus, the frequency-ratio of a fourth
is 3 : 4. Between the fourth and fifth overtones there lies a
major third, the ratio accordingly being 4 : 5. Similarly we
can determine the ratio of the major sixth as 3 : 5, of the
minor third as 5 : 6, of the major second as 8 : 9, of the
major seventh as 8 : 15, of the minor sixth as 5 : 8. And thus
we have established the relative frequencies of every interval
met with in a major or a harmonic minor scale. If we now
call the frequency of the tonic of a major scale 1, then to
obtain the second note 1 must be multiplied by 9/8, by 5/4
to obtain the third note, by 4/3 to obtain the fourth note,
etc. Thus, for the individual notes of a major scale we
have the following ratios :

$$1, \ 9/8, \ 5/4, \ 4/3, \ 3/2, \ 5/3, \ 15/8, \ 2.$$

Similarly, in a harmonic minor scale, we have the following :

$$1, \ 9/8, \ 6/5, \ 4/3, \ 3/2, \ 8/5, \ 15/8, \ 2.$$

Just Intonation

In this case any frequency may be chosen for the fundamental note of the scale, and the frequencies of every stage
in the major or harmonic minor scale built up upon it
may always be determined by multiplying it by the suitable
proportional value. Thus, if we require to determine the
frequencies of, say, the A major scale, beginning with a^1,
with its 435 double vibrations per second, we find that
b^1 has $435 \times 9/8$ vibrations, or approximately 489.4
vibrations per second, while $c\#^2$ has $435 \times 5/4$, or 543.75;
d^2 $435 \times 4/3$, or 580; e^2 $435 \times 3/2$, or 652.5; $f\#^2$ $435 \times 5/3$,
or 725; $g\#^2$ $435 \times 15/8$, or approximately 815.6; and a^2
435×2, or 870 vibrations per second.

This natural acoustic system of "Just Intonation" is useful only as long as we keep to one key; the moment we try to modulate to another key we encounter serious difficulties. If we want to form the scale of B major, and take b^1 to be 489.4 double vibrations per second, as previously calculated from the A major scale, we shall immediately find ourselves with quite another frequency for $c\#^2$ than that arrived at by our previous calculations; for $489.4 \times 9/8 = 540.6$, whereas our calculations based on the A major scale gave us for $c\#^2$ the value 543.75. If we assume a $c\#^2$ having 540.6 vibrations we shall find the A major scale untrue; but if we leave it at 543.75 the B major scale will be untrue. Similarly, with the note $f\#^2$: this, reckoned as the fifth of b^1, has a frequency equal to $489.4 \times 3/2$, or 734.1 : but, if it be reckoned as the major sixth of a^1, we get a frequency of $435 \times 5/3$, or 725.

Just as unsuccessful must be any attempt to obtain the interval of an octave by building up six full tones. If the frequency of the first tone is multiplied six times by $9/8$ we arrive at a frequency which is by no means double the frequency of the first tone. The result will be no more successful if we try to build up a series of four minor thirds —that is to say, if we multiply the frequency of the first tone four times by $6/5$.

Equal Temperament

These and similar inconveniences, all of which make it impossible to modulate from one key to another, make it necessary to depart from the pure acoustic ideal of the "Just Intonation" and take refuge in a compromise. At the close of the seventeenth century—mainly by the efforts of Andreas Werckmeister—the "Equal Temperament" system of tuning was introduced, dividing the interval between the fundamental note and its octave into twelve completely equal parts. If the frequency of any given note is multiplied by $\sqrt[12]{2} = 1 \cdot 05946$, the frequency of the next semitone is obtained. Thus the frequencies of the A major scale, starting from a^1 and calculated on the basis of the "well-tempered" system, are as follows :

$$a^1 \; 435$$
$$b^1 \; 435 \times 1 \cdot 05946^2 = 435 \times 1 \cdot 12246 = 488 \cdot 3$$
$$c^{\sharp 2} \; 435 \times 1 \cdot 05946^4 = 435 \times 1 \cdot 25992 = 548 \cdot 1$$
$$d^2 \; 435 \times 1 \cdot 05946^5 = 435 \times 1 \cdot 33484 = 580 \cdot 7$$
$$e^2 \; 435 \times 1 \cdot 05946^7 = 435 \times 1 \cdot 49831 = 651 \cdot 8$$
$$f^{\sharp 2} \; 435 \times 1 \cdot 05946^9 = 435 \times 1 \cdot 68171 = 731 \cdot 6$$
$$g^{\sharp 2} \; 435 \times 1 \cdot 05946^{11} = 435 \times 1 \cdot 88724 = 821 \cdot 2$$
$$a^2 \; 435 \times 1 \cdot 05946^{12} = 435 \times 2 \qquad\quad = 870$$

If we compare these frequencies with those calculated on the system of "Just Intonation" on page 27, we see at once that the octave is the same, and that the fifth and fourth vary very little, while the other intervals diverge more or less markedly. In other words: in the "Equal Temperament" system of tuning the octave is completely pure, the fourth and fifth are almost pure, while the remaining intervals are somewhat out. On the other hand, the "well-tempered" tuning makes possible any kind of modulation. Keeping to "Just Intonation," we obtained different results when calculating the frequency of $c^{\sharp 2}$ first as the third of a^1, and then as the second of b^1. But with "Equal Temperament" the same result is reached in both cases, for $435 \times 1 \cdot 05946^4$ is $548 \cdot 1$, and $488 \cdot 3 \times 1 \cdot 05946^2$ is $548 \cdot 1$. Similarly, with "Equal Temperament" the octave may be obtained from six full tones, or from four minor, or three major thirds.

PLATE I

Woodcut from Franchinus Gafurius, *Theorica Musicae* (Milan, 1492)

It shows with the help of hammers, bells, glasses filled with water, strings and pipes the mathematical relationships producing the intervals of the fifth octave, ninth, twelfth and double octave

PLATE II

1.—Drum from the Stone Age

About 3000–2500 B.C.

Found in Central Germany

2.—Bone flute from
the Stone Age

Found at Bornholm
(Denmark), about 3000–
2500 B.C. (cf. S. Muller)

3.—Player of the Lur

Drawn by Angul Hammerich

The "Equal Temperament," beginning with the Piano and the Organ[1], has gradually conquered all the instruments. Strings and voices are able—technically speaking—to maintain a true natural pitch; but only so long as no extreme modulation is demanded of them. Owing to their perpetual collaboration with the pianoforte as well as with the wind instruments, most of which are invariably tempered, singers and strings have to push their sense of just intonation into the background.

Standard of Pitch

In all our foregoing calculations we have started from the assumption that a note of 435 double vibrations per second corresponds to the pitch of a^1. This is a figure which was fixed at a conference held in Paris in 1858. The conference was made necessary by the existence of variations of pitch, not only between one country and another, but even between one choir or orchestra and another in the same locality. Since string and wind instruments sound more powerful and more brilliant the higher they are pitched, orchestras have always shown a tendency to raise their pitch. For singers this raising of the pitch was dangerous, since it imperilled the quality of their high notes. This cleavage was to be obviated by the Paris conference, and a far-reaching unification was certainly achieved by it, for as compared with the extreme variations of pitch experienced in earlier centuries a certain international uniformity does now prevail. On a lesser scale, however, the struggle for a standard pitch continues even to-day.

[1] The first great master who used the Equal Temperament tuning for his creations was J. S. Bach. In his *Das Wohltemperierte Klavier* he composed a work which passes through every key. Before the introduction of this Temperament this composition could never have been performed on any keyboard instrument.

Now that we have dealt with the phenomena of sound in general we are in a position to examine the acoustic phenomena to be observed in the various types of musical instrument. First of all we will consider the *Stringed Instruments*.

Acoustics of Stringed Instruments

The vibration of strings—as we have explained—is of the transverse kind. Since a string, if it is to sound at all, must be stretched between two points, its vibrations cannot extend beyond these points. They therefore produce not progressive but stationary waves, which are thrown back at the fixed points, the "nodes" of the sound wave. The pitch of a string is dependent on its length, thickness, and tension, and on the specific gravity of the material of which it is made. If we increase the length of the string the frequency of vibration and the pitch correspondingly decrease. For example, if we double the length of a string it will sound an octave lower; if we treble the length it will sound a twelfth lower. Similarly, the pitch rises in inverse ratio to the thickness of the string; and, finally, the frequency varies in direct ratio to the square root of the tension and in inverse ratio to the square root of the specific gravity of the material employed. Thus if c^1 is sounded by a string whose tension is equal to one pound, the tension produced by a four-pound weight will give us the note c^2, a tension of nine pounds will give us g^2, a tension of sixteen pounds c^3, and so on. Finally, if the strings are made of materials whose specific gravity stands in the ratios of $1:4:9:16$, the pitch will fall by an octave, a twelfth, and a double octave respectively. Since steel has a disproportionately high specific gravity as compared with gut, a steel string can be much thinner than a gut string producing the same note. The wrapping of a string with wire makes it at once thicker and heavier, so that its frequency and therefore its pitch is lowered.

In the majority of stringed instruments the performer can reduce the effective length of the strings either with his finger or with some special contrivance. If the performer shortens a string to 8/9 of its original length, the frequency of the newly-formed note will stand to the frequency of the original note as 1 : 9/8; the pitch, in other words, will rise by the interval of a full tone. Similarly, if the stopping of the string reduces it to 2/3 of its original length the resulting note will be a fifth higher; and if the length of the string is exactly halved the pitch will rise by an octave.

Harmonics ("Flageolet"-Notes)

A special case arises when the performer presses his finger only lightly on the string. This causes the string to vibrate in sub-sections with the consequent production of unusual sounds which are called harmonics or flageolet-notes, because of their likeness to the tone of a flute. The acoustic principle is shown in Fig. 3. If we start with the assumption that the unshortened open string vibrates in the manner shown in diagram 1 (although in reality the picture should be infinitely more complicated), then the only nodal points—i.e. the points which are unaffected by the general movement—are formed by the two fixed ends of the string. But if a finger is placed lightly on the string at its centre (diagram 2) a new nodal point is set up at this spot. The string now vibrates in two equal sections, each of which, being half the length of the whole, sounds an octave higher than the empty string. Now if a finger is placed a third of the way down the effective length—i.e. at point b^1 or b^2—again pressing lightly (as in diagram 3), the string will be made to vibrate in three equal subsections.

The resultant harmonic thus corresponds to a note with a frequency three times higher than the fundamental tone, i.e. its octave plus a fifth. In the same way harmonics can be produced of four times the frequency of the fundamental tone (diagram 4), i.e. the double octave; or five times, i.e. the double-octave plus a major third, by touching the string lightly at a quarter, or a fifth, of the way down its proper length.

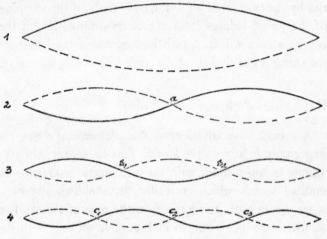

FIG. 3.—Diagrams of transverse waves

Even when the string is not made to produce harmonics it tends to vibrate in a manner which has a certain similarity to the mode of vibration that appears when such notes are produced. That is to say, the string will endeavour to produce the wave-pattern shown in Fig. 3 at 1, 2, 3 and 4, and also a whole series of other wave-patterns *simultaneously*. That it should really so vibrate is, of course, impossible, and the result is a combined wave-pattern of extreme complexity. Every sectional wave within the whole corresponds to a harmonic within the single note. If, for instance, the string endeavours to vibrate in such a manner that the patterns shown in diagrams 1, 2 and 3 of Fig. 3 are produced simultaneously, the first, second and third harmonics will be comprised in the sound emitted by the string. If, on the other hand, the total wave includes the forms of wave which occur when the string vibrates in 4, 5, 6 or 7 sub-sections, then the fourth, fifth, sixth and seventh harmonics will be present in the sound. In short, the pattern of the wave determines the constitution of the sound.

Quite a considerable influence on the formation of tone-colour is also exerted by the point from which the string is set vibrating. In stringed instruments, whether the string is bowed or plucked, an arc of vibration forms round the point of contact. Thus, if the middle point of a string is bowed or plucked the arc of vibration occurs in the middle. This means that the harmonics resulting from a nodal point in the middle must be lost. The second, fourth, sixth, eighth, and in fact all the even-numbered harmonics are absent, so that the tone produced has a hollow and nasal character. Similarly, when the string is plucked or otherwise set in vibration at a point corresponding to one-third of its length, the third, sixth, ninth, twelfth and fifteenth harmonics are lost. If, however, the string is set in vibration at a point near its fixed end the vibration will be based on innumerable subsections, giving rise to higher overtones. The sound in this case will be stronger and more expressive than a tone which is poor in harmonics. Thus, in the majority of string instruments this position is the one chosen.

Thick strings are less capable of vibrating in many subsections than thin ones. Thus the sound of thin strings is richer in harmonics and more vigorous. Even for the low notes the employment of thick strings is therefore avoided, preference being given to thin strings wound round with wire, which give a deeper note, thanks to their greater weight, and at the same time do not lose the elasticity of thin strings.

The agent employed for setting the strings in vibration also has an important influence on the constitution of the resultant sound. If the strings are agitated by a comparatively hard object, such as a metal plectrum (as in the zither), a quill (as in the harpsichord), or a thin, leather-covered hammer (as in the first pianofortes), the closely-serried higher overtones are predominant in the sound, which is now sharp and shrill, or else a metallic tinkle. This effect is especially noticeable in the case of thin metal strings, while with the less elastic gut the highest overtones die away more quickly. If, however, we pluck the string with the bare finger (as in the guitar), or strike it with a felted hammer (as in the modern pianoforte), the first harmonic emerges more strongly than the higher ones. The sound—especially when gut is used—is fuller and softer.

When a stringed instrument is played with a bow, the rosined horsehair of the bow is drawn over the strings, pulling them from their position of rest until their elasticity forces them to fly back again. But the bow immediately pulls them forward once more, and the whole process is repeated. This somewhat jerky mode of excitation is, up to a certain point, favourable to the production of the higher overtones, and endows the sound—since the first few overtones are still predominant—with a characteristic plasticity and expressiveness.

Resonance or Sympathetic Tone

In the Viola d'amore, a viola-like string instrument made in Europe since the seventeenth century (see p. 151), wires are stretched beneath the finger-board which can neither be shortened by the performer nor reached with the bow. These strings, however, begin to sound without direct intervention as soon as the notes to which they are tuned occur as overtones of any of the notes played on the strings lying above the finger-board. These steel strings continue to sound after the strings played on by the bow are silent, a fact which has a marked influence on the tone of the instrument. This phenomenon is known as sympathetic tone or *resonance*; and the strings of the Viola d'amore which are thus made to utilize this principle are accordingly called sympathetic strings or resonance-strings. The explanation of this phenomenon is simply that the vibrations induced in the outer strings by the bow are transmitted both through the air and through the fixed parts of the instrument. Directly the sound-waves meet a string of the same frequency, this will begin to sound. The phenomenon of resonance is by no means limited to strings. It may be observed in elastic objects of metal, glass or wood, or even in columns of air enclosed in tubes or globes.

Sounding Boards

If we take a tuning-fork—a U-shaped piece of steel furnished with a stem, such as is often used to obtain the standard A,—strike it against a hard object, and hold it in the air, we hear a weak but rather sustained note. If we hold the stem against a table-top after the fork has been struck, the note will not sound for so long, but will be perceptibly stronger. The vibrations of the fork are now transmitted through the stem to the table-top, and this, because of its much larger surface, sets a greater number of air-particles in motion, thus producing a far stronger note than can be emitted by the tuning-fork alone. The table-top's own note plays no appreciable part in this; both high and low notes will be impartially reinforced. Use is made in music of this phenomenon, more especially in stringed instruments. The strings by themselves would sound very weak, so they are stretched above an elastic wooden plate, or else across a thin wooden box with air-holes in its upper surface; and this materially strengthens the sound. Such sounding-plates, sounding-boards and sounding-boxes facilitate and intensify the radiation of the sound-waves produced by the strings. Theoretically speaking, the sounding-board of a stringed instrument should only reinforce the note emitted by the strings without in any way affecting its tone-colour. In actual fact, however, the shape and the material of the sounding-board have a very great influence on the tone of the instrument. When we come to consider the structure of the older violins we shall examine the question more fully. Here it suffices to say that the *size* of the sounding-board is of particular importance with regard to the tone. Every resonating body has a lower limit beyond which it does not readily respond to vibrations. The deeper the notes to be played on a stringed instrument, the larger must the sounding-board be. In the case of the violin and the 'cello this principle has received due recognition. But if we turn to the viola, which could not be held upon the shoulder if it were any larger, we find the sounding-box too small for the performance required of it. Although the viola goes a full fifth lower than the violin, the sounding-box is only about 10 per cent larger. Thus the fundamental tones in the lower range of the instrument are only incompletely reinforced, which gives the lower notes their characteristic colour— a hollow and faintly nasal quality.

PLATE III

Celtic Silver Kettle from Gundestrup (Denmark), about first century A.D.

The priest on the left is performing a sacrifice; the three men at the right are playing the Karnyx

PLATE IV

Greek vase from the middle of the fifth century, B.C.
Vienna, Museum of Fine Arts

Two muses with musical instruments. The sitting muse playing the Aulos produces
notes to enable the standing muse to tune her Lyre

Acoustics of Wind Instruments

As with the stringed instruments, so with the wind instruments, the air enclosed within the tube of the instrument vibrates in static waves. But while in the case of strings the waves are transverse, the wind instrument produces longitudinal waves. Consider the case in which the air-column in a tube with open ends is set in vibration: we see at once that an arc of vibration or "loop" will be set up

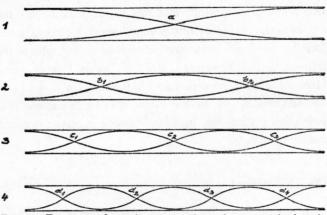

FIG. 4.—Diagrams of sound waves inside a tube open at both ends

at either end; at these points the vibrations in the tube impart their energy to the outer air, so that the end of the tube represents the point of greatest movement. But since there must be a nodal point between two loops, the simplest form of vibration is that shown in Fig. 4, diagram 1[1]. The next form of vibration, with two nodal points, is shown in diagram 2. Diagram 3 shows three nodal points, and diagram 4, four nodal points. Similarly, of course, five, six, or more nodal points may be formed.

If we now compare in Fig. 4 the distances lying between

[1] For the sake of clarity I have shown transverse instead of longitudinal waves in Figs. 4 and 5.

the adjacent loops in 1, 2, 3 and 4, we shall find that the distance in 2 is half as great as the distance in 1; in 3 it is one-third as great as in 1; and in 4 a quarter as great. The distances between the individual loops—in physics such a distance is called a "half wave-length"—stand in the ratio of $1 : \frac{1}{2} : \frac{1}{3} : \frac{1}{4}$.

In considering the diagrammatic presentation of the vibrations of strings in Fig. 3 we saw that the smaller the interval between two neighbouring loops (or between two nodal points, which amounts to the same thing), the higher is the frequency of the vibrations. We can see therefore that the (half) wave-length stands in inverse ratio to the frequency. This principle is also valid in the case of tubes. Here, if the half wave-lengths are in the ratios of $1 : \frac{1}{2} : \frac{1}{3} : \frac{1}{4}$, the frequencies are in the ratios of $1 : 2 : 3 : 4$, and the respective pitches are, fundamental tone : octave : twelfth : double octave.

Overblowing I

In our discussion of stringed instruments it was shown that the player can induce the formation of artificial nodal points in a string, and can therefore—without altering the length or tension of the string—produce in succession some notes of the series of harmonics. The same series of harmonics can be obtained in a pipe. This process, which is analogous to the production of "flageolet-notes" on the violin, is described as "overblowing." In the case of a pipe, we have only to alter the method of blowing in order to produce various overtones one after another. These overtones, however, are not produced only in succession, but, just as in a stringed instrument, also simultaneously. According to their number and their individual strength they determine the tone-colour of the pipe.

Stopped Pipes

The diagrammatic representation of vibrations in Fig. 4 has to be modified if the pipe is closed at one end, or, to use the technical term, *stopped*. A loop is still formed at the open end, but at the stopped end free vibration is impossible, so that a nodal point is formed instead. Diagrammatically, then, we have the pattern shown in diagram 1 of Fig. 5. If a second nodal point arises we have the pattern shown

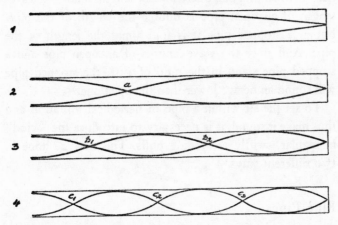

Fig. 5.—Diagrams of sound waves inside a tube closed at one end

in diagram 2; three nodal points afford the pattern shown in diagram 3; and with four nodal points we have the pattern shown in diagram 4. If the dimensions of the half wavelengths in diagrams 1, 2, 3 and 4 are compared, we see that in 2 the half-wave-length is only one-third of the half-wave-length in 1; in 3 it is only one-fifth; and in 4 only one-seventh. The ratios, then, are as $1 : \frac{1}{3} : \frac{1}{5} : \frac{1}{7}$, and the frequencies as $1 : 3 : 5 : 7$. From this we arrive at the important conclusion that in a stopped pipe only the odd-numbered overtones may be obtained and that their sound

contains only odd-numbered harmonics. A further peculiarity of the stopped pipe is that its fundamental tone, and
with it the whole series of overtones, lies an octave deeper
than in an open pipe of the same length. This is shown by
comparing the diagrams in Fig. 4/1 and 5/1. In the open
pipe (Fig. 4) the interval between two loops—that is, the
half wave-length—is fully contained by the pipe; but the
stopped pipe, on the other hand, (Fig. 5) contains only
the interval between a loop and a nodal point, i.e. *half* a
half wave-length, or a quarter wave-length. Thus the wave-
length of an open pipe is double the length of the pipe,
but in a stopped pipe it is four times the length of the
pipe. And since the wave-lengths of an open pipe and a
stopped pipe stand in the ratio of 1 : 2, the stopped pipe
will sound an octave lower than the open one.

To set the air within a pipe in periodical vibration and
thus make it sound, it is necessary to introduce the "wind"
in regular, swiftly succeeding puffs. This may be done in
two different ways.

Flue-Pipes

In flue-pipes, which include the Flutes and a great number
of organ pipes, the wind is directed against a sharp edge
contrived in the side of the pipe, so that it alternately passes
into the tube and is dispersed outside it. In its simplest
form this process may be observed in a modern Transverse
Flute. The flute-player blows through his very slightly
parted lips a compressed and flat stream of air against the
sharp edge of the mouth-hole or *embouchure*, which is
cut in the side of the instrument, close to one end. This
stream of air is split by the sharp edge; some of the wind
enters the tube, some is dispersed outside it. The air entering
the flute causes a compression of the air already present.

When the pressure inside the tube is great enough, it over-comes the pressure of the wind directed at the mouth-hole. The compressed air escapes from the tube, carrying with it air from the interior. The air within the tube is now rarefied, so that the performer's breath once more enters the interior of the Flute. This process continues uninterruptedly, pro-ducing within the pipe the periodic compression and rarefaction of the air necessary to set the air in vibration and produce musical sounds. The Recorder and the flue-pipes of an Organ also function in this manner, except that here the flattened stream of air required to make the pipe sound is not given its peculiar form by the musician's lips; its shape and direction are determined by a device which compels the wind to pass through a slit before reaching the sharp edge.

Lip-Reed Pipes

The method used to produce sound in flue-pipes is fundamentally different from that used in reed-pipes, an order which includes all wind instruments apart from the Flutes, and also the reed-pipes of the Organ. One of the simplest examples of the principle of the reed-pipe is afforded by the Trumpet. In this "lip-reed" instrument the performer presses the mouthpiece of the Trumpet to his compressed lips. The breath from his lungs produces a compression of the air in his mouth-cavity. The tongue, acting as a valve, is sharply withdrawn so as to admit the breath between the slightly parted lips, and a puff of air passes through the mouthpiece into the interior of the instrument. At once the lips, through their elasticity, return to their original position, almost sealing the mouthpiece of the Trumpet once more, until a new access of pressure forces them open again, sending a second stream of air into the mouthpiece. This process is repeated continually, and the periodic blasts of air down the tube produce the necessary compression and rarefaction of the air-column within the instrument.

The same method of production is employed in the Horn, the Trombone, the Tuba, the Cornet, etc.—in short, in all those instruments which the musician usually calls "brass instruments."

Double Cane Reed-Pipes

In the Oboes and Bassoons a similar method is adopted, but here the function of the human lips is assumed by a double reed—two laminae of thin cane (*Arundo donax*)

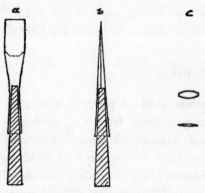

Fig. 6.—Diagram of a double cane-reed

bound together (Fig. 6*a* and 6*b*). These laminae are so adjusted that a narrow chink remains open between them.

If the performer places the double reed which protrudes from the upper end of the Oboe or Bassoon between his lips the elastic reed begins to vibrate under the pressure of his breath. The slit between the two laminae opens and closes alternately (Fig. 6*c*), allowing the air to enter the instrument in periodical puffs.

The foregoing method of sound production—by the human lips in the brass wind instruments, and by the cane-reed in the Oboe and the Bassoon—is based on the acoustic principle of the *double reed*, in which two reeds beat against each other.

Single Cane Reed-Pipes

As opposed to this, however, we have the principle of the *single reed*, as applied in the Clarinet. Here a single cane-reed—a lamina of *Arundo donax*—is affixed to a frame or ·table in such a manner that a narrow chink remains open

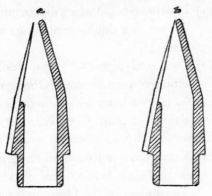

FIG. 7.—Diagram of a single cane-reed

between the reed and the frame (Fig. 7). If the performer takes the reed and the frame (sometimes called the "beak," because of its external appearance) between his lips, the elastic reed will begin to vibrate when he blows, and will thus alternately close and open the slit (Fig. 7*a* and 7*b*), so that the air, after passing through the "beak," will again enter the instrument in periodic puffs. Thus the single reed of the Clarinet performs a similar service to that of the double-reed of the Oboe.

In all the reed-pipes so far discussed, the reeds provide the means of setting the air in vibration, while the pitch of the fundamental tone depends preponderantly on the length of the tube containing the air. But in addition to such wind-instruments there are others which have no instrumental tube at all. In these, hardwood or metal reeds are used, and the pitch is determined entirely by the length, thickness and elasticity of the reed itself. There are altogether five different kinds of reed instruments:

(A) Pipes with a vibrating column of air enclosed by an instrumental tube (usually known as wind instruments).

> (1) Lip-reed pipes in which the compressed human lips act as a double reed (Brass wind instruments).
>
> (2) Cane-reed pipes with two flexible laminae acting as a double reed (Oboe and Bassoon).
>
> (3) Cane-reed pipes with a single flexible lamina acting as a beating reed (Clarinet).

(B) Instruments without a vibrating column of air.

> (1) Metal reed (or hardwood reed) pipes with a single (hard) beating reed striking a frame. (Reed-pipes of the Organ and the Regal.)
>
> (2) Instruments with a single (hard) and freely vibrating reed. This reed vibrates, moves freely *through* the opening of a frame (reeds of the harmonium, the accordion, the mouth-organ, etc.).

Human Voice

A certain similarity to the working of the reed-pipes is seen in the functioning of the human larynx. The larynx, surrounded by cartilage, and provided with numerous muscles, has as its most important component the two vocal cords or ligaments, between whose edges is a chink,

PLATE V

Greek vase, beginning of the fifth century. Vienna, Museum of Fine Arts

Flying Nike holding a Kithara. A plectrum is inserted between the strings

PLATE VI

1.—Greek vase. Fifth century B.C. Vienna, Museum of Fine Arts

A player of the Aulos; the Phorbeia is fastened across his cheeks

2.—Roman Mosaic from the Amphitheatre of Zliten (after S. Aurigemma)

A gladiatorial game accompanied by music on one straight Tuba, two Cornua
and one Hydraulis

the intramuscular or vocal glottis. If we wish to utter a sound the ligaments of the glottis are so tightened that the glottis is closed. The pressure of the air from the lungs then forces it open, and a stream of air escapes, the air-pressure on the glottis relaxes, and the glottal ligaments return to their closed position. This process is repeated, and the periodically compressed and rarefied air makes the sound. The pitch depends chiefly on the length of the glottal ligaments, and on their tension, which can be regulated at will. In children the glottal ligaments are only 3–4 lines in length; but at puberty the voice "breaks." The glottal ligaments then grow, in women, to some 6 lines and in men perhaps to 9 lines in length. As a result of this growth the female voice becomes a little deeper, and the male voice a great deal deeper. The by no means infrequent castration of boys in eighteenth-century Italy resulted in the preservation of a boy's voice regardless of age, while quite extraordinary effects were produced by the increased strength of the lungs and the enlarged capacity of the chest.

The sounds arising from the larynx would be very weak indeed if the human body were not provided with various resonating devices not unlike the sounding-boards of the stringed instruments. These are the thoracic cavity, the mouth, the nasal cavities, and the frontal sinuses. The precise function of these cavities is still debated, but it can be generally stated that when singing low down in the scale the thoracic cavity is brought into play, and we then speak of the chest-notes or chest-register of the human voice. But in the case of the high notes the head cavities operate as sound-boxes, and we speak of head-notes or the head-register. In some untrained singers the difference of colour between the chest- and the head-notes is very great, but trained singers can pass from one to the other imperceptibly.

D

Overblowing II

Let us now examine the method of producing different sounds on a wind instrument provided with a tube.

Once the performer has set the air-column within his instrument vibrating periodically—when he has, in a word, made the instrument sound—his next preoccupation is the production of notes of different pitch. This may be contrived in a variety of ways. The most natural is the method of *overblowing* already mentioned. By gradually increasing the force of the wind-stream the performer may produce within the tube not merely one nodal point, but two, three, four, and more. He obtains in this way the octave, the twelfth, the double octave, etc., of the fundamental note.

In practice every wind instrument has at its disposal only a limited number of overblown notes or harmonics. If the instrument has a wide bore—that is, if the diameter of the tube is large in comparison with its length—the deeper harmonics will be obtainable; but if on the other hand its bore is narrow, the higher overblown notes will be produced. In such a narrow-bored instrument—and the Trumpet, for example, belongs to this class—the first harmonic, the fundamental note, cannot be played at all.

The tension of the human lips can be varied within wide limits, so—if the performer is sufficiently skilful—a large number of harmonics can be obtained from the brass wind instruments, their production being favoured by the comparatively great length of the tube. The reeds, on the other hand, are much less elastic, so that in the Oboe and Clarinet —in which, moreover, the tube is comparatively short— only a few harmonics can be obtained. The same may be said of the short Flutes, on which overblowing will produce hardly more than the second and third overtones.

To produce overblown notes on cane-reed instruments, the frequency of vibration proper to the reed is modified by pressure of the lips or teeth. Overblowing may also be assisted by opening a small vent, known as the *speaker* hole, covered by a key exactly over a node of the air-column, which is caused to vibrate in sections. If the reed is protected from contact with the mouth-parts, and a speaker-hole is lacking, as in the Bagpipe and some medieval instruments, overblowing is impossible.

In respect of overblowing, the position of the Clarinet is peculiar. Acoustically, with its predominantly cylindrical bore, it behaves like a stopped organ-pipe. One result of this is that, overblowing does not produce the even-numbered harmonics. The first is followed by the third, and this by the fifth. Similarly, in the sound of the Clarinet the even-numbered overtones are only faintly audible; they emerge more strongly only with vigorous over-blowing. The high notes of the Clarinet have therefore a sharp, strident quality, which is entirely absent from the low notes of the instrument, with their rather hollow character. Lastly, the Clarinet, in its quality of stopped pipe, sounds deeper than an Oboe of about the same length.

Finger-holes

The natural tones may be produced by the performer without any special, mechanical aid. But to produce the chromatic, or even the diatonic scale on a wind instrument some special device is required. It is true that the harmonics, from the eighth upwards, lie so close together that they embrace the whole diatonic scale. But the higher harmonics can be obtained in practice only on the long, narrow Trumpet and French Horn, and on these only by skilled performers. The chromatic scale, however, is unattainable even by them. Accordingly, to bridge the great spaces lying between the deeper natural notes, finger-holes were introduced at a very early date. As long as it is closed a finger-hole bored in the wall of the tube does not affect the length of the vibrating column of air; but if open it allows the air to escape before the end of the tube is reached, its effect being then analogous to that of the performer's finger when this curtails the length of a string in a stringed instrument. The effect of the finger-holes depends on their size and position; the nearer they are to the bell of the instrument, and the smaller their diameter, the less will be the raising of pitch when they are opened. Conversely, the nearer the mouthpiece they are, and the greater their diameter, the greater will be the raising of pitch brought about by their opening.

Keys

A great improvement in the employment of finger-holes is effected by means of keys. These are covers made to fit the finger-holes, worked on the lever principle by the performer's fingers, which enable him to open or close finger-holes lying far apart, or too large to be stopped by his finger-tips alone. These keys have made it possible to bore wind instruments in an acoustically ideal manner, regardless of the exigencies of easy fingering.

Stopping of the Horn

With Horns and Trumpets the employment of finger-holes to obtain the chromatic scale is acoustically undesirable. When the finger-holes are open the sound is ragged, lacking in roundness and beauty. Another means of achieving the same end had therefore to be sought.

With the French Horn a most primitive method was employed from about the middle of the eighteenth century. The right hand was inserted into the bell of the instrument, turning the original open pipe into something like a stopped one. This method, however, had the disadvantage that not only did it deepen the note, but it also gave it a tight, compressed quality. Thus "stopping" as a means of deepening the note was not applied to other instruments except the Trumpet to a limited extent, and it gradually fell into disuse when a better method was discovered.

Slide of the Trombone

The Trombone, on the other hand, has been perfectly adapted from the beginning of its development to the production of the chromatic scale. Here a metal sleeve, which slides over the main tube, can be pulled in and out, thereby altering the length of the whole instrument. The farther it is drawn out, the deeper is the fundamental note of the instrument, and with it the whole series of harmonics.

Valves, etc.

A similar result is obtained by the various crooks, "inventions," valves and pistons of the Horns and Trumpets. Common to them all is the purpose of enlarging the effective length of the instrument by the interposition of additional lengths of tubing, thereby deepening the whole series of natural notes. The valves or pistons in general use, which represent, for the time being, the final solution of this problem, are the semitone, the full tone, and the one-and-a-half tone valve. If the semitone valve is called into play —by pressing down a piston or key—the air is compelled to make a detour through a supplementary tube just long enough to lower the whole series of natural tones by a semitone. The other valves work in precisely the same way, and if all three pistons are used in combination they will cover the interval of a fifth between the second and third harmonics. The operation of these valves is illustrated by the accompanying diagram, in which the harmonics produced by the performer's lips are indicated by letters, the interposed valves by numbers, and the notes that are actually sounded by musical notation.

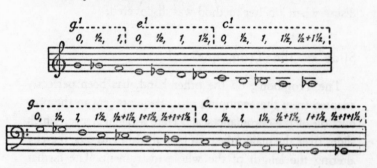

Acoustics of Rods, Bars and Tubes

In addition to strings and pipes, elastic rods, bars and tubes, vibrating transversely, are used for musical purposes.

In such instruments the frequency of the vibrations depends partly upon the material employed, partly on its size. The more elastic the material the higher the frequency; the greater its specific gravity the lower the frequency. If equal-sized bars of lead, clay, tin, brass and iron are suspended side by side the leaden bar will give the deepest note, clay the next lowest, then tin, then brass, then iron. Similarly, boxwood gives a far deeper note than pine. Further, with cylindrical bars the frequency rises with the diameter, and with prismatic bars with the thickness, while it lessens with increasing length. On the other hand, the breadth of a bar of prismatic shape has no effect on its frequency; thus if a prismatic bar whose thickness is half its breadth is laid on its edge, it will sound an octave higher than before. Tubes sound higher than solid cylinders of the same length and diameter; and their pitch rises in proportion as the walls are made thinner.

Bars may be fixed in a variety of ways. If they are supported at two points, each a quarter of their length from the end (as in the Xylophone and Glockenspiel), nodes of vibration are formed at these points, while arcs of vibration are formed at either end and in the centre. Tubes, on the contrary, are best suspended by one end (as in tubular bells), forming a node at the fixed end and an arc of vibration at the free end. This form of vibration is related to that of the stopped pipe (see Fig. 5).

With bars and tubes the overtones are inharmoniously placed (i.e. in a most complicated numerical ratio), so that the sound has more or less of noise in it. If the overtones are very close together—as in the Triangle, struck with a metal rod—it is out of the question to talk of pitch; we have simply a very light tinkling sound. But when the overtones lie well apart from each other—as in the Xylophone—the pitch is recognizable. The sound is hollow in this case, but is at the same time sharpened by the inharmonious admixture of overtones. Lastly, in the case of suspended tubes, the sound is mellower and fuller, owing to the column of air enclosed within the tube.

Acoustics of Plates

With plates also, which always vibrate transversely, the frequency increases with the thickness and the elasticity of the material employed, but is in inverse ratio to the specific gravity of the material and the diameter of the plate. The overtones produced by vibrating plates are mostly inharmonious, so that the result is either pure noise or something very like it. The pitch cannot be determined—at any rate, so far as European gongs and cymbals are concerned. In a Gong the nodes of vibration are in the edge, while the arc is in the centre. Just the opposite applies to the Cymbals; here the node is in the centre and the arcs at the edges.

Acoustics of Bells

Bells may be regarded as a variety of curved plates. Their frequencies increase in proportion as the diameter of the bell, the thickness of the sound-bow (that part of the bell against which the clapper strikes from the inside) and the mass of metal used decrease. The overtones are preponderantly inharmonious; so that the sound of a bell—although bells may be tuned—is more noisy than musical.

Acoustics of Drums

Like every other solid employed for musical ends, membranes also vibrate transversely. Their frequencies decrease as the length, width and thickness of the membrane increase. On the other hand, they increase with increasing tension. In the circular membranes most frequently used for musical purposes the overtones come very close together and are inharmonious. The sound is thus indistinct and noisy. In the case of the Kettledrum only the cauldron-shaped sounding-box—magnifying certain of the overtones—proves so favourable to the formation of a musical tone that it is possible to tune the instrument to a given pitch.

PLATE VII

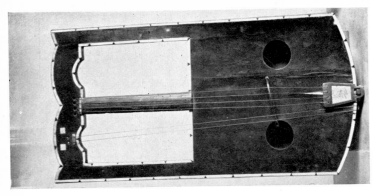

2.—Crwth. Vienna, Society of Friends of Music

1.—Roman Sarcophagus of a musician. Museum of Arles, France
(after E. Espérandieu)

Hydraulis, the case on the wall is probably meant for a Pan-pipe (Syrinx)

PLATE VIII

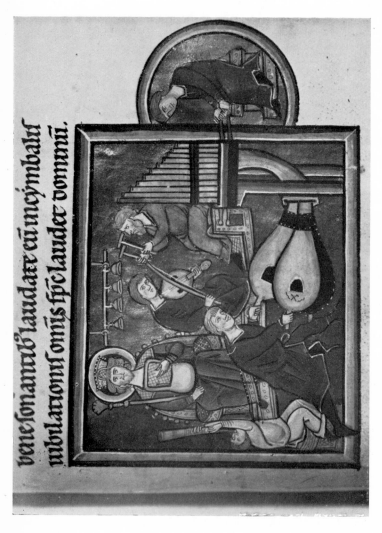

Psalter of St. Elizabeth. Thirteenth century, Cividale del Friuli, Archaeological Museum
King David, playing the Rotta, with his musicians, who are playing the Horn, the Vielle, the Chime-bells and (two men) the Organ

Electric Instruments

The development of the radio has been responsible for the invention of not a few new instruments, which, unlike the instruments hitherto discussed, do not produce the sound by means of vibrating strings or columns of air, or elastic metal or wood, etc., but by electric methods.

If two thermionic radio valves are made to produce electrical vibrations of different frequencies, the result is a vibration whose frequency amounts to the difference between the two original vibrations. This resulting vibration can be made audible by means of a loud-speaker. A variable condenser makes it possible to change the pitch of the tone produced. This principle is exploited in the Aetherophone, the Trautonium, and other instruments constructed during the last few years.

Another method has been used in the Hammond Organ, invented in America. Here discs which are faceted at the edges are rotated in the field of electro-magnets. Their various frequencies are mixed synthetically to produce an enormous variety of different sounds.

Mention should also be made of the photo-electric method, as used in the Superpiano and Rangertone. Here light rays which fall through a perforated rotating disc on a photo-sensitive valve are used for the production of acoustic vibrations. The number of holes and the speed of the rotation determine the pitch of the resulting sound.

I

PREHISTORY AND ANTIQUITY

Stone Age

The history of musical instruments may be traced back in Europe for some 25,000 years. As far back as the early Stone Age man learned how to cut teeth in a bone and produce a rasping noise by rubbing it against a rough surface. He fastened a thin, elliptically-shaped bone to a thong, and by whirling this implement, which we now call a "bull-roarer," swiftly through the air, he produced a whirring note. He bored through the foot-joints of the reindeer in order to fashion a primitive pipe with a penetrating note.

In the later Stone Age man began to use clay in the construction of musical instruments. He made clay drums shaped like a cup or an hour-glass and even provided with eyelet-holes for the lacing of the skin (Pl. II, 1). His bone flutes had now made considerable progress, and were furnished with finger-holes, so that within certain modest limits tunes could be played on them (Pl. II, 2).

No aesthetic effect, in the sense of the present day, was achieved or even desired. These, the most ancient of all European musical instruments, served for ritualistic ends. Their sound was not intended to give pleasure; on the contrary, its object was to induce fear and terror, not only in men, but also, and above all, in evil spirits. And in driving away the hostile forces, their purpose was to succour and strengthen the forces of life.

This struggle for the furtherance, preservation and propagation of life stood at the very heart of every act of ritual performed by the men of the Stone Age, as it did for all other men on the lowest rung of the cultural ladder. In this way their musical instruments became inseparably bound up with the mental processes involved. The toothed bone became the instrument of the love-spell, as it still is to-day among countless primitive peoples. The whirring of the "bull-roarer" symbolizes the voices of dead ancestors, in whose vital energies the children also must share. The Flute is an instrument of the fertility-spell. The Drum plays an important part in the cult of the dead. Confirmation of the magical functions of early instruments may be found—to take only a single example—in a rock-drawing of the Stone Age showing a flute played by a masked dancer who is shrouded in the skin of a wild beast, which turns him into a horrible and diabolic figure.

From these supernatural implications musical instruments have never been wholly freed. In spite of the ever-growing importance of the aesthetic aspects of sound that has been brought about by technical improvements in construction and manipulation, the symbolic values of the instruments have continued to carry weight, and our examination will furnish us with ever fresh examples of this, down to the very threshold of the present age.

Bronze Age

Ritual usage still occupies the foreground when we consider the most important instruments of the Bronze Age in Northern Europe, the *Lurs* (Pl. II, 3),—from the Norwegian word for a horn,—which round about 1000 B.C. were in use all over Denmark, Scandinavia and Northern Germany.

Very early in the Bronze Age men began to bind the open ends of natural horns with metal, and their next step was to fashion the whole horn in this material. Instruments shaped like the horn of an ox became plentiful, and the tusks of elephant and mammoth also were imitated. In Ireland metal horns, which have been found in graves, not only follow the curved shape of an elephant's tusk, but are also provided with a mouthpiece at the side, a relic of the days when the solid end of the ivory tusk could not be perforated, and one still retained in the ivory horns of the African savage. The form and proportions of the mammoth tusk served as the model for the peculiar S-shaped Lurs. The fact that these instruments have always been found in pairs and twisted in opposite directions may also be attributed to their origin in the tusks of the pachyderm.

The slightly conical and boldly curved Lurs, with the finely worked ornamentation at the bell end, form one of the most distinguished creations of the Bronze Age, and mark the peak of prehistoric instrument making. On these Lurs, the noble and solemn tones of which remind the listener of the French Horn and the tenor Trombone, a practised performer can produce up to the twelfth note of the harmonic series, so that, in addition to the usual triad, a series of consecutive tones becomes possible in the upper register. A further remarkable fact is that the two Lurs of every pair are tuned to the same pitch with really marvellous accuracy. One would be tempted to conclude that we have here the first evidence of the existence of part music, did not everything we know about the music of primitive peoples contradict this supposition. It is far more likely, as Behn contends, that the Lurs were blown in pairs in unison, to strengthen the tone.

Iron Age

The second Iron Age (the last two centuries B.C.) was distinguished by the presence, in every district inhabited by Celts, of the widely-spread *Karnyx*. In its original form this instrument consisted of a straight tube with an ox-horn affixed to one end so as to form a sort of bell. This bell, the characteristic curve of which was reproduced in the Roman *Lituus*, was shaped so as to resemble the open jaws of an animal; and this custom of so fashioning the bell persisted until quite recent times, being employed for certain military instruments of the early nineteenth century. The Karnyx was also made in a doubly bent form, as is shown in the reproduction of a sacrificial scene in Plate III.

The Celts also possessed a stringed instrument. Diodorus Siculus, who lived in the first century B.C., relates that their bards used a lyre-like instrument to accompany their songs, and in the fourth century A.D. we find Ammianus actually calling it *Lyra*. This must have been, in fact, an instrument not unlike the *Lyra* of the Greeks and Romans, which we shall shortly have occasion to mention, consisting of a body with an arch-like yoke fixed to it for the attachment of the strings. The Celtic name for it was *Crot* or *Cruit*, which later became the Welsh *Crwth*, and the English *Crowd*.

Greece

Of the many instruments the names of which have been handed down from the musical culture of Greece, there stand out three alone which have had a decisive influence on the history of music: the Lyra, the Kithara and the Aulos. The others, such as the stringed *Barbiton*, *Magadis*, *Pektis*, and *Psalterion*, have relatively little or no importance, and since, moreover, there is still a good deal of uncertainty as to the meaning of these names, we shall not discuss them here. This applies also to the *Salpinx*, a straight trumpet with the bell bent upwards, the use of which was purely military.

None of the three instruments most in use by the Greek musicians was indigenous to the country. The Lyra was brought by the Hellenes when they migrated into Greece from the north of the Balkan peninsula and Hungary. The Kithara came from Asia Minor *via* the islands of the Aegean. Instruments of the Aulos type were employed by Egyptians, Jews, Hittites, Elamites and Assyrians, so that Greece could hardly avoid adopting this instrument of the ancient East.

The Lyra

The *Lyra* (Pl. IV) was a lyre-shaped stringed instrument whose body consisted of a tortoise-shell with a tympanum of ox-hide. To the shell a yoke was attached; at first its arms consisted of antelope horns, but afterwards they were made of curved pieces of wood. The strings were fixed to the cross-piece of the yoke by means of fatty hide. By twisting this hide the instrument could be tuned. The number of strings, which were always of gut, never exceeded seven. The instrument was played with the bare fingers and with a plectrum, the bare left hand plucking the strings to accompany the song, and the right hand, armed with a hard plectrum, fastened with a thong, rhythmically sweeping across the strings to bridge the pauses of the song.

Kithara

The counterpart of the Lyra was found in the second lyre-like instrument of the Greeks: the *Kithara* (Pl. V). In the shape of the sound-box, the manner of attaching the strings, and the method of playing, it has much in common with the Lyra, but in other respects the two instruments are fundamentally different. While the Lyra, with its tortoise-shell body, was always light and unadorned, the Kithara had a massive and often richly ornamented wooden body. The cross-bar to which the strings were fixed had in the Kithara a handle which made it possible quickly to alter the whole pitch of the instrument, or to slacken the tension of its strings after use. The Kithara, too, did not stop at the seven strings of Homer's time, but might have as many as eleven, although this increase in the number of strings met with much resistance on the part of the tradition-minded Greeks; indeed, it is reported by Timotheus of Miletos that the authorities of conservative Sparta simply cut off four of the newly added strings of his Kithara.

The technical differences between the Lyra and the Kithara not unnaturally had some influence on the application of the two instruments. The Lyra was the instrument of the dilettante and the novice, being used only to accompany singers; the Kithara, on the other hand, was played by virtuosi, and was also employed for instrumental solos. Solo playing—known as *kitharisis*, to distinguish it from *kitharodesis*, the accompaniment of song—was practised a good deal, especially in later times. The performer used both hands and no plectrum, producing the higher notes as harmonics or "flageolet-notes."

Despite its refinement of tone, the sound of the antique Kithara must have carried to a great distance, otherwise it would have been hardly possible, at the popular competitive meetings, such as the Delphic Games, for the sound of a single Kithara to be heard by the whole audience, and even critically judged, in a gigantic open amphitheatre.

The two lyre-like instruments, the Lyra and the Kithara, were employed mainly in the accompaniment of lyrical and epic poetry. The emotional temper to which they gave expression was calm and restrained, and was aptly described as "Apollonian." In contrast to this was the passionately individual, orgiastic, "Dionysian" temper, which found its chief expression in the drama. Its instrument was the Aulos.

Aulos

The *Aulos* (Pls. IV; VI, 2), the Latin *Tibia*, was an oboe-like instrument fitted with a double reed; it was made in several sizes and was usually played in pairs. To translate "Aulos" by "Flute," as the philologists are fond of doing, is quite unwarranted. The instrument was far more like a shrill and strident Shawm, whose penetrating note has nothing whatever in common with the mild tones of the Flute. The timbre of the instrument was influenced to a great extent by the peculiar treatment of the double reed. It was not held between the performer's lips, as in the case of our modern Oboes and Bassoons, but was inserted bodily into the mouth. Thus the cavity of the mouth served as a wind-bag, enabling the performer to continue blowing uninterruptedly in the Oriental manner while inhaling air through his nose (and to save him from inflating his cheeks too far he wore a leather bandage, the *phorbeia*, round his head) (Pl. VI, 1). The shrill, strident tone of the instrument was due to the fact that the sharp note proper to the reed itself was not damped by the pressure of the performer's lips. A technical point of considerable importance is that the Aulos had not a conical bore, as have our modern Oboes, but a cylindrical one, like the Clarinet. This meant that the overblowing produced not the octave but the twelfth, and then a double octave plus a third. A small hole near the mouthpiece—the *Syrinx*—similar to the speaker-holes found in modern reed-instruments, made

PLATE IX

King David and his Musicians from a Psalter of the twelfth century.
Glasgow University Library

The Chime-bells player on the right strikes the bells marked with Re and La in order
to help the string-players to tune their instruments. King David is tuning his Harp,
two of his musicians are tuning different types of Vielle. Two others are playing on
the Double Flute and the Transverse (?) Flute. In the corners are musicians with Bells,
Psaltery and Organistrum (Hurdy-gurdy)

PLATE X

1.—Oliphant from A.D. 1198 (?) Vienna, Museum of Fine Arts

2.—Players of Pipe and Tabor. Thirteenth century. *Cantigas de Santa Maria.* Spain

overblowing possible; and with the aid of this contrivance the Aulos was able to cover no less than two and a half octaves.

To bridge the gap between the fundamental note and the first overblown note there was introduced, in the course of time, an ever-increasing number of finger-holes. At first there were only three or four; but finally there were sometimes as many as fifteen. Since so great a number could no longer be covered by the performer's fingers, the expedient was adopted of rotating rings by which the holes could be opened or closed at will, thus anticipating our modern keys. Indeed, in one way these rings were more efficient than the modern keys, for by rotating a ring in such a way that a hole was only partly covered the performer could produce intermediate tones. Further, the notes of the instrument could be wholly or partly tuned to a different pitch by affixing little cup-like tubes to the individual finger-holes, thus lengthening the path of the air before it escaped and deepening the individual notes.

It is not to be wondered at that the Aulos, in view of its high efficiency, was given an important part to play in the art of the ancient world. A single pair of these instruments—more were never employed at a time—was sufficient for the accompaniment of the Greek drama. Even real programme-music was performed upon the Aulos. In the Hellenic age there existed a composition for the Aulos which portrayed in five parts the fight of Apollo and the dragon. The subjects of this interesting composition were: the exploration of the field of combat, the challenge, the fight itself, the conquest of the dragon, and the hymn of victory.

There is still some uncertainty as to the rôle of the second Aulos, where two were played by one musician. In the earliest times the accompanying Aulos may have

E

sustained a high drone or bourdon-note in the Oriental manner, while in later times the notes of the accompaniment may have been more frequently varied. On no account, however, must we imagine the Aulos to have played polyphonic music on the harmonic basis of our modern European music; for the music of antiquity was essentially melodic, as the music of the Orient is still to-day. Even when a performer on a Lyra or a Kithara was accompanying the voice he would only decorate and play round the melody, never adding a second part or an accompaniment in chords.

Rome

As Greece fell beneath the dominion of Rome the music of the vassal state, with its other arts, was taken over by the conquerors. In accordance with their character, however, the Romans saw to it that the means at their disposal were enlarged and magnified. They constructed Lyrae and Kitharae as big as sedan-chairs, and even assembled massed orchestras of many hundred players. (Think of the single player accompanying the Greek tragedy!)

Tuba, Cornu, Lituus, Tibia utricularis

In view of the tremendous importance of the army in the Roman Empire it is not surprising to find that the various instruments were developed to meet the demands of military music, though they were, however, by no means limited to military use. First there was the *Tuba* (Pl. VI, 2), a straight, slightly conical trumpet well over a yard in length. The *Cornu* (Pl. VI, 2) was a large coiled trumpet with a very narrow bore, in some ways reminiscent of the later hunting-horn. This could be used for signalling to large bodies of troops, while the Tuba was used in the case of smaller groups. The *Lituus* was a small, straight, conical horn with an upturned bell, closely related to the Celtic Karnyx. The Emperor Nero, according to Dion Chrysostomus, "knew how to play the pipe with his mouth and the bag thrust under his arm." This passage can only refer to the bagpipe (*Tibia utricularis*) consisting of a skin bag or paunch with openings at the extremities, into which were inserted a tube to blow the air into the skin and one or more primitive pipes with single reeds of the clarinet type. The air was forced through the pipes by the pressure of the player's arm on the windbag.

Hydraulis

Tuba, Cornu and Bagpipe were used a great deal in the circus as well as in the army; and there, too, the most popular instrument of all was one traditionally ascribed to the Alexandrian physicist, Ctesibius, who was born between 300 and 250 B.C.—the *Hydraulis*, or Water-organ, a forerunner of our modern Organ (Pls VI, 2; VII, 1). Here the principle of the Bagpipe is used as the basis of an instrument furnished with a great number of flue pipes not unlike the kind used later on in the Recorder (cf. page 84). Air was pumped into a hemispherical container standing in a cylinder half filled with water. This water, acting in a similar manner to the weights used on the wind-reservoirs of later Organs, held the air under a constant pressure. From this container a tube led to cross-channels furnished with flue-pipes, which were made to sound by means of a simple but ingenious system of keys. In later instruments we even find several series of pipes in various keys, and these—like the registers of an organ—could be cut out or brought in by taps placed at the side of the instrument.

The Hydraulis had its heyday during the Roman Empire. Nero also played the organ, and Cicero proclaimed himself a great lover of organ music. Nevertheless, the instrument in its original form did not survive antiquity. The Organ which, 1,000 years after the days of Ctesibius, was brought from Byzantium to France as an unheard-of novelty, omitted the most important part of the Hydraulis, the water-compressor.

II

THE EARLY MIDDLE AGES

(TO 1300)

The turmoil caused by the migration of barbarian hordes into Europe completely annihilated the highly developed musical instruments of the ancient cultures. It is true that the finest of the stringed instruments of ancient Greece and Rome, the Kithara, led a shadowy existence for some centuries in those areas of Western Europe which were still dependent on the classical tradition; it is true that there is a slight connection between the Organ of Franconia and the Alexandrian Hydraulis; yet on the whole we can safely assert that the musical instruments of the early Middle Ages—the basis, that is to say, of the music of modern times—had no direct connection with the instruments of ancient Greece and Rome. In science and theory the influence of antiquity remained strong throughout the Middle Ages; in practice, however—and in the early Middle Ages instrumental music was entirely a practical matter—the new development was independent of classical antiquity. In short, the Middle Ages saw a new beginning as far as musical instruments were concerned.

An observation which has been made in our discussion of the instruments of antiquity applies equally well to the Middle Ages; the home of our Occidental instruments lay beyond the limits of Europe. The instruments were developed in Europe and have been brought to their present stage in this continent; but the roots of their development mainly go back to the East. We owe our modern instruments to the importations from Asia.

Instruments of the Celtic North

In one region of Europe, however, instruments of antiquity were directly inherited by the Middle Ages. The Celtic North, as we have seen, had, independently of the Greeks and Romans, lyre-like instruments in very ancient days. These lyres, which in shape are sometimes astonishingly like the Sumerian drawings of lyres, are represented in works of art from the eighth century A.D. onwards; and since national boundaries were still unknown in the early Middle Ages, we need not be surprised to find these instruments appearing at about the same time in parts of Europe far removed from the Celtic North. In the Württemberg village of Oberflacht a lyre was found in an Alemannic warrior's grave which must have dated from the fourth to the seventh century A.D. This instrument is all the more remarkable in that it is one of the extremely few stringed instruments of the early Middle Ages which have been preserved intact.

In its early mediaeval state, with tuning-pegs (which were unknown to antiquity) and five to seven strings, the *Lyre*, played as a rule with bare hands, and rarely with a plectrum, is frequently met with in the illuminated manuscripts of the time (Pl. VIII). It was known as the *chrotta* or *rotta* (old Irish *cruit* or *crot*, English *crowd*), and because of its wide distribution throughout the Germanic countries it came also to be known as the *cythara teutonica*.

Crwth

In the late Middle Ages the Lyre was pushed into the background by the appearance of other far more efficient plucked instruments. It was only in a rare variant—not plucked but played with a bow—that the instrument persisted, in Celtic Wales, even far into modern times.

In the ninth century the Fiedel or Vielle, furnished with finger-board and bow, appeared in Europe (cf. page 91) and the vogue of the new instrument was soon so great that the prehistoric Lyre fell beneath its influence. From the eleventh century we hear of stringed instruments combining the yoke of the Lyre with the neck of the finger-board instrument. These instruments, especially favoured by the Welsh bards, were notable for a flat bridge with only one foot resting on the table, while the other, as a kind of sound-post, reached through the sound hole to the back of the instrument. The *Crwth*, as it was called, had as a rule six strings, four of them running over the finger-board, the other two acting as drones, always sounding the same note (Pl. VII, 2).

Harp

Still another instrument was particularly frequent in the Celtic North: the *Harp*, a native of Syria, so beloved in Ireland that it came to figure in that country's coat of arms. Of the two most ancient European pictures of Harps, both of the ninth century, one occurs in an Irish work of art (the Reliquary of St. Mogue in Dublin), the other in a Carlovingian manuscript (the Psalter in the University Library, Utrecht), which is strongly influenced by Syrian models.

The instrument must have been brought to England very early in its career. The occurrence of the word "hearpe" in *Beowulf* (eighth century) should not, I think, be taken too seriously, for "harpa" and "hearpe" might have been used at that time for any plucked instrument. But the Harp may with certainty be traced back to the tenth century in England, and it is an eloquent fact that in a German manuscript of the twelfth or thirteenth century we find the Harp called the *cythara anglica*.

Ireland, however, was regarded as the true home of the instrument. In the fourteenth century we find an indication of this in Dante, and as late as the seventeenth century the great German musical scholar and instrumental expert, Michael Praetorius, speaks of the Irish Harp.

It is evident that this new instrument, distributed rapidly throughout the West, would have come at once into competition with the Lyre, since their uses were so similar. The outcome of this rivalry left no room for doubt. The Lyre possessed strings of equal length only; if they were too thick or too loosely strung they sounded feebly; if they were too thin or too tightly strung they were liable to break. The Lyre, therefore, had only a small, middle compass. On the other hand, the strings of the Harp were of different lengths so that the difficulty of the limited compass did not arise. Thus the music of the late Middle Ages, as it called for an ever-increasing compass, turned from the Lyre to the Harp.

The European Harp of the Middle Ages consisted of three parts (in contrast to the numerous Asiatic Harps, which were built in two parts). At the back is the sounding-board to which the strings are attached. Above is the neck, set at a sharp angle, often a little incurved, and furnished with tuning-pegs, turned by a tuning-key. In front, supporting the neck, is the pillar, which is sometimes slightly outwardly curved. The shape of the whole is heavy and squat, rather like an equilateral triangle, since the neck is little shorter than the sound-board and pillar (Pl. IX).

Horn

Among the instruments developed during antiquity in Northern Europe, independently of Greece and Rome, were included the various *Horns*. But the Lurs of Scandi-

PLATE XI

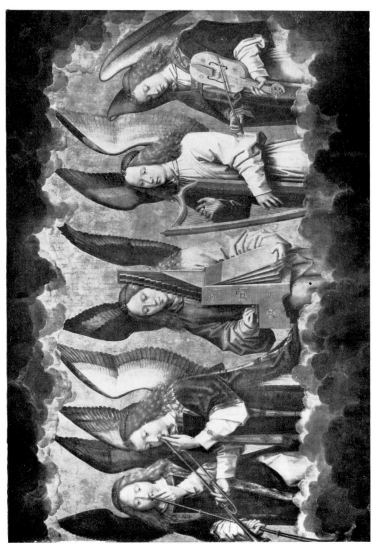

Angels making Music. By Hans Memling, about A.D. 1480. Antwerp Museum

The angels play on a straight and a folded Trumpet, on Portative, Harp and Vielle

PLATE XII

Angels making Music. By Hans Memling, about A.D. 1480. Antwerp Museum

The angels play on Psaltery, Tromba Marina, Lute, folded Trumpet and Pommer

navia and Denmark, and the finely-wrought horns of
ancient Ireland, stood in no direct relationship to the horns
of the early Middle Ages. It seems, rather, as though the
far more primitive horns that now appeared in Europe
were a throw-back to prehistoric days, if not an entirely
new beginning.

In the early Middle Ages the Horn might be either slightly
curved or straight. The curved instrument was originally
the horn of the wild ox or the bison, but before long the
practice arose of imitating the natural form in metal, a
repetition of the prehistoric procedure. Such metal horns
(Pl. VIII) were found in all sizes, from the tiny *Hifthorn*,
only a few inches long, to the Warhorn, standing as high
as a man.

Tuba

The straight horn of metal corresponded to the curved
horn in the conical shape of the tube and the lack of a bell.
This instrument, too, was sometimes made very large, so
that the performer had to support it half-way down its
length on a fork. It was usually called the *Tuba* on the
strength of its similarity to the Roman instrument of that
name.

Cornetto

In consequence of their wide bores the Horns as a rule
could sound very few harmonics besides their fundamental
note. To make these instruments suitable for anything beyond military purposes the eleventh century—the period
which revealed the creative spirit for the first time since
the beginning of the Middle Ages—adopted a device never
before seen throughout the history of the Horns and Trum-

pets; the boring of finger holes in the instrumental tube. Their number varied greatly, but six was the favourit ̀, and these gave the whole octave between the fundamental note and the first overblown harmonic. England favoured the curved horn with finger-holes; the Continent, and especially Germany, the straight form. At first natural horn was used as the material, but in later times wood prevailed. In the curved horns the tube was made of two hollowed pieces of wood glued together, over which a leather sheath was drawn to render it airtight. The instrument was called a *Cornetto*, a diminutive of the Italian *corno*, being one of the smaller horns. Similarly in Germany it was known as the *Zink*, the *Zinke* being the last and smallest branch of a stag's antlers. In England it was the Cornett.

In the social life of the period there was little place for the Horn. In its smaller form it was used by the shepherd to call his flocks and by the watchman in his tower to announce the approach of strangers. The larger form was employed for signalling purposes by the foot-soldiers in war.

Oliphant

Much more store was set on the *Oliphant*, an instrument made of an elephant's tusk, which was introduced from Byzantium in the tenth century. These valuable ivory horns, very often richly ornamented (Pl. X, 1), were part of the insignia of knighthood. The Oliphant was the horn that Roland sounded to call his friends when the Saracens surrounded him at Roncesvalles and, when defeat threatened, he strove to save his most precious possessions, his sword and his horn, from the foeman's grasp. In England, the Oliphant was also the symbol of dignity and knighthood, and he who was granted an office or a fief received from his liege-lord not a document but an Oliphant. If the instrument was made of metal instead of ivory, gold was the material used, and it is not surprising that in some representations of the Apocalypse the angels of the Day of Judgment are pictured as blowing Oliphants. Confirmation of the high value set upon it in the early Middle Ages is provided by the fact that far more specimens of the Oliphant have come down to us than of any other instrument of the time.

Organ

The Oliphant was not the only instrument that was imported from Byzantium. The Eastern Empire, heir to the classical culture, also passed on one of the most important instruments of antiquity, the *Organ*. It is true that the countries on the fringe of Europe—Italy, Spain and England—preserved from antiquity some traditions of organ construction; but the decisive stimulus to the development of the organ came with the introduction of the Byzantine instrument into Franconia during the reigns of Pepin and Charlemagne in the eighth and the beginning of the ninth century. This organ, however, was by no means the Hydraulis of antiquity, which scarcely survived the first centuries A.D. The most important feature of the Hydraulis, the cylinder half filled with water, into which air was pumped, had vanished. Instead of this complicated contrivance the organ was provided with simple bellows worked by the hands or feet, and in its altered form, as a pneumatic organ, it quickly established itself on fresh soil. As early as the end of the ninth century Franconian organ-building was so highly esteemed that Pope John VIII summoned a master from the diocese of Freising to build an organ for him in Rome.

The tenth century saw the building of one of the largest

organs of the early Middle Ages. In the year 980 A.D. an instrument was installed at Winchester which possessed no fewer than 400 pipes, 26 bellows and 2 manuals, each furnished with 20 sliders. One of those sliders alone caused 10 pipes to sound simultaneously.

In spite of such imposing dimensions, these early organs were by no means satisfactory from a musical point of view. The pipes were out of tune and too loud. There were no proper keys, but only sliders which the performer had to pull out and push back again one at a time (Pl. VIII). Thus a melody could only be rendered in the slowest tempo, and the greatest obstacles stood in the way of anything more complicated than two-part playing. It was not until the twelfth century that any substantial improvement was devised. Then by degrees proper keys were introduced, but even these were so heavy and stiff that "they had to be depressed with the full weight of a clenched fist" (Praetorius).

Portative

As a counterpart to the powerful fixed organ, often called the *Positive*, a small, portable and easily playable hand-organ was devised, the *Portative*. This was furnished with only a few pipes, of which some especially large ones acted as drones. It could be operated entirely by one man, who carried the instrument on a strap round his neck, worked the bellows with his left hand, and with his right operated the keys, which were often but small push-buttons.

The first recorded appearance of the Portative is in England during the twelfth century; but the instrument was by no means restricted to English soil. By the thirteenth century we find it distributed all over Western Europe, and soon it was to become one of the most important elements in both chamber and orchestral music.

If the Portative was dedicated exclusively to secular music, the Positive came to be used more and more by the Church. From century to century this instrument, soul-stirring through the immensity of its tone, established itself as the instrument of Christian worship. The leaders of the Church actively concerned themselves with organ-building, and no less a personage than the scholar Gerbert, later Pope Sylvester II, himself constructed an organ in Lombardy. By the close of the Middle Ages organ and church had become inseparably associated.

Glockenspiel or Chime-Bells

In its rigid inflexibility of tone the organ shows a certain relationship to another instrument, which perhaps also came to the West *via* Byzantium, the *Glockenspiel* or Chime-bells, the *Cymbala*, as the Middle Ages called it. As far back as the fourth century we find a late-Roman representation of an instrument consisting of a stand and four metal cups which were struck with a small rod. In the Middle Ages such collections of little cups—hemispherical or tulip-shaped—were very popular. These early chime-bells were tuned with a file to the diatonic major scale, hung in series from a bar, and played on with hammers wielded usually by a single performer, but sometimes by two (Pls. VIII; IX). The Christian Church, which since the sixth century had hung large, untuned bells in her towers to call the faithful to prayer, gradually came to use the Cymbala as well. In the thirteenth century the instrument was first provided with clockwork, and in the later Middle Ages it was installed in the towers of churches and city halls. Whenever the clock struck, the chimes played a little sacred tune, with the object of turning the hearer's thoughts from earthly to heavenly things in a gentle and agreeable manner.

Vielle or Fiedel

Like the Glockenspiel the *Vielle* or *Fiedel* (also called *fidula* or *lira*) may have come to Europe via the Balkan Peninsula.

Already, in a ninth century illustration—again in the celebrated Psalter of the University Library at Utrecht made at the Court of Charlemagne—we are shown a blind musician with his harp on his shoulder, who is carrying, in addition to the harp, a remarkable spade-shaped stringed instrument, played with a monstrously large bow, which, in comparison with the size of the musician, would have been about ten feet in length. Probably this is the oldest representation of any stringed instrument played with a bow in Europe; but, in view of the fact that this illustration was at first almost unique, we are not justified in concluding that the artist was depicting an instrument then widely distributed. Indeed, the marked dependence of the Utrecht Psalter on Asiatic models makes it far more probable that the painter was copying an Oriental stringed instrument (of a kind still in use in Turkestan in our days), for the monstrous bow seems to indicate that he himself was not very sure of the true nature of the instrument.

During the following centuries the Asiatic Fiedel was continually finding its way into Europe, though it soon underwent a structural transformation.

The spade-shaped body was replaced by an elliptical body with a sharply defined neck. A peg-box, lying in the same plane as the finger-board, carried the pegs standing at a right angle to the table of the instrument. The method of holding the instrument, however, was still that shown in the

Utrecht Psalter; the performer held it in front of him, supporting it on his thigh or knee.

Then, in the tenth century, there appeared in the West another and rather smaller type of Vielle. This was not held in front of the body, but supported on the shoulder; it was pear-shaped, the body being carved out of a single piece of wood, in the form of a bowl. The strings were fastened at the base of the instrument to a special board, the tail-piece of the later Violins, and were stretched over a bridge. Just as in the larger Vielle, the tuning-pegs were vertical to the top of the instrument. The circular sound-hole in the middle of the table was bridged by a small bar, running in the same direction as the strings, so that two semi-circular sound-holes were formed (Pl. IX). Precisely the same instrument is found to this day in the Near East and the Balkan Peninsula. It is evident that an instrument in widespread use among the Slavs of the Balkan Peninsula would have soon found its way into all parts of the Western world, in view of the brisk trade maintained between Byzantium and the other European countries. Even the name "Lyra," by which the instrument is frequently known among the Southern Slavs to-day, was occasionally given to the Fiedel in the early Middle Ages. But while to this very day the Fiedel has remained unchanged in its original home, in Europe it has undergone manifold transformations. First, there is the clear distinction between neck and body, which appeared after the twelfth century, as in the large Turkestan Vielle, which was held in front of the performer. At the same time, we find the instrument assuming the elliptical shape of the bigger type, while the sound-holes become narrower, approximating to the form of a letter C.

In the same twelfth century in which the small Fiedel, held on the shoulder, adopted the division of body and

neck, its model, the bigger instrument held in front of the
player, underwent a great improvement. For the first time
the body was narrowed at the waist (Pl. IX), thus enabling
the performer to move his bow freely and to play each
string independently. This was a milestone on the way
which led from the Asiatic Vielle to the Violins of the
great Italian masters. For as long as the instrument lacked
this narrow waist, the performer had no choice but to hold
his bow parallel to the table of the instrument, causing the
lower strings to sound, together with the melody, as a
perpetual, monotonous drone.

About the middle of the thirteenth century the Vielle
was already so well-known that a contemporary theoretician
made it the subject of an enquiry. Jerome of Moravia
took as his starting-point the five-stringed Vielle which
then held the field, and from his exposition we learn that
the practice of tuning in fifths or fourths, which later became
general in the case of stringed instruments, was already
applied to the Fiedel. According to him, the highest string
seems to have been tuned sometimes to d^1, and sometimes
to g^1, so that he may have been considering both the
smaller and the larger type of the instrument.

Plucked Vielle (Citole)

The increasing distribution of the Fiedel throughout
the West in the Middle Ages must not mislead us into
thinking that the adoption of so prodigious a novelty as
the bow then was could be achieved without opposition.
On the contrary, again and again throughout the whole of
the Middle Ages we meet with Vielle-like instruments which
were not played with a bow but were plucked or twanged
in the classical manner with finger or plectrum. The same
ninth century which shows for the first time, in the

PLATE XIII

Angel playing the Mandola. By Bartolommeo Vivarini. A.D. 1474.
Venice, Sta. Maria dei Frari

PLATE XIV

The Virgin and Child with two angels playing the Rebec and the Double Recorder. By Marcello Fogolino. Fifteenth century. Milan, Museo Poldi Pezzoli

Utrecht Psalter, a bowed, spade-shaped Fiedel, gives us in the Lothar Psalter the representation of a plucked Vielle of very much the same type. The larger and the smaller type, the waisted Vielle and the Vielle without a waist, were sometimes bowed and sometimes plucked. Indeed, in the late Middle Ages a special instrument was evolved from this plucked Vielle the *Citole*, *Sister* or *Cister*.

Hurdy-Gurdy

A very peculiar relative of the larger Fiedel is found in the Hurdy-gurdy, the so-called *Organistrum* or *Symphonia*, which is described as early as the tenth century by the theoretician Odo of Cluny, but not depicted until the twelfth century. The Organistrum was furnished with a wooden wheel in the interior of the instrument, turned by a crank, which pressed on the strings from below, and set them all vibrating simultaneously. The strings were shortened not with the bare fingers, but with the aid of wooden bridges or tangents, operated by a system of keys. At first these tangents appear to have shortened all three strings simultaneously (these being tuned to the intervals of a fourth and a fifth); thus there would result the typical mediaeval parallels of fifth and octave. Later, however, the lowest string at least was allowed to sound untouched by the tangent, as a drone. Any personal expression on the part of the performer was out of the question in either system; all the more so as in the early Middle Ages the Organistrum was often operated by two performers (Pl. IX), one holding the instrument on his knee and turning the handle, the other working the boxed-in wooden tangents by means of a keyboard.

The early mediaeval ideal of music was almost more perfectly realized by this instrument than by such impersonal

instruments as the Organ or the Glockenspiel. All subjectivity in expression was excluded in the case of the
Organistrum; the melody could never free itself from the
embrace of the other voices. It spoke with inflexible, super-
personal energy, and it was then held in such high regard
that it may often be seen portrayed in the hands of kings.
In the Portico della Gloria of St. Jago di Compostella, one
of the richest representations of twelfth century musical
instruments, the Organistrum is given the highest place in
the very centre of the Portico.

About the year A.D. 1000 the infiltration into Europe
of the musical instruments of the East gradually quickened
in pace. One after another, now peacefully through mer-
chants and wandering tribes, now in the train of foreign
conquerors, or as booty brought by returning Crusaders
from the Holy Land, the instruments of the highly civilized
Orient found their way into Europe. The Occident was
positively flooded with innumerable instruments, which
the Western spirit was slow only in assimilating.

Now the invaders entered Europe not only from the
North and the South-East, but from the West and the South.
The Saracens, who from the eighth to the thirteenth century
occupied Spain and parts of Southern Italy, introduced into
Europe the Arabic-Persian culture. From Spain their
instruments spread through France, and from Southern
Italy through Central and Northern Italy, into the rest of
Europe.

Lute

The most important, as well as the oldest, of the stringed
instruments introduced into Europe by the Saracens, was
the *Lute*. The very name shows its kinship to the Arabic-
Persian *Al'ud* ("The Wood"), with which the instrument

also has a close structural affinity. I am able to trace the existence of the Lute in Spain as early as 968, but for nearly three centuries to come it was only a rare visitor to Europe, and it did not reach its prime until the late Middle Ages, or the beginning of the modern era.

At first the Lute showed a certain similarity in shape to the Vielle. There was the same pear-shaped body, with a shallow bowl, and a neck growing out of the body with no definite line of demarcation. But whereas the strings of the Fiedel were fastened to a tail-piece and led over a bridge, the Lute had a string-holder which was glued directly to the table. Even more important is the position of the tuning-pegs. In the Lute, in order to counter the heavy pull of the strings, the peg-box is at right angles to the end of the neck, so that the pegs are parallel with the table of the instrument, while in the Vielle they are vertical to it. There were three to five strings, which were usually plucked with a little rod, and only rarely with the bare fingers. Here, as everywhere, the early Middle Ages avoided as far as possible any direct personal influence upon the quality of the tone.

In the thirteenth century—as had happened a century earlier in the case of the small Vielle—the division of the Lute into two distinct parts, the body and the neck, was effected. Perhaps at the same time the other most important step was taken, whereby the back of the instrument was no longer made from one piece of wood, but from a number of separate staves glued together. This meant a great gain in resonance, and with that the possibility of a different, subjective kind of playing, more in keeping with the spirit of a new age. The strings had now increased in number, and were tuned in pairs: there might be six to ten of them, with each pair tuned to the same note, or in octaves. This multiplication of the strings resulted in greater loudness—as with our present-day mandoline and piano-forte.

Guitar

Not long after the lute a second plucked instrument came to Europe from the Arabic-Persian civilization: the *Guitarra latina*, or *Guiterne*, which is to be found in Spain since the twelfth century. This instrument, from which the modern *Guitar*, one of the most important plucked instruments of our time, was directly derived, was distinguished by a slightly incurved body with a curved bowl-like back and a peg-box with tuning-pegs standing parallel to the table, as in the lute.

Psaltery

The Saracens added yet another plucked instrument. In early representations one might sometimes see King David holding an instrument resembling in outline a Harp or a Lyre, but with a sounding-board at the back of the strings. The instrument occurred also in triangular and rectangular forms, in principle very like the modern Zithers of the Alpine districts. But to this confusion of forms the Moors brought order by introducing into Europe a new kind of instrument—still distributed throughout the East under the name of *qānūn*—in the shape of a trapezoid, or of a boar's head (Pl. IX). The *Psaltery*, as the instrument has been called since its first appearance in Europe in the twelfth century, is plucked with a quill or the bare fingers. It is excellently adapted, thanks to its form, for the inclusion of a large number of strings of different length and pitch. Naturally, then, it soon drove the older forms of the instrument from the field.

Mandola

Some idea of the almost limitless capacity for absorption of the early Middle Ages is afforded by the fact that after the Harp and the Lyre, after the plucked Vielle, the Lute, the Guitar and the Psaltery had been accepted, yet another plucked instrument found its way to the West, and one that would seem to have been all the more superfluous, since in size, construction and method of playing it very closely resembled the Lute. This instrument, which can be traced back to the thirteenth century in the West, was club-shaped; the strings were taken from buttons attached to the bottom end of the body, led over a bridge, and brought to a slightly curved peg-box, which terminated in a little carved head. This was the *Guitarra morisca*, or *Mandola*, as it came to be called later on, an instrument whose nearest relative may be found to this day in the Malay Archipelago.

Rebec

Just as the Vielle was sometimes plucked instead of bowed, so there appeared a bowed equivalent of the Lute or Mandola. The Spanish thirteenth-century Cantigas de Sta. Maria, one of the richest sources for our knowledge of the musical instruments of the period, shows a narrow, club-shaped stringed instrument, supported on the knee, and having two strings. It is fitted with a peg-box which is fixed at right angles to the neck as in the Lute. This bowed Lute was the Arab *rebâb*, which later, as the *Rebec* or *Gigue*, played an important part in the development of the violin. Jerome of Moravia, in the middle of the thirteenth century, writes of this instrument, and according to him, of the two strings one was tuned in C and one in G.

Trumpet

The Saracens, in their rôle of intermediaries, by no means confined themselves to stringed instruments. To them we owe one of the most valuable wind instruments, rivalling even the Oliphant in estimation, the *Busine*, our later Trumpet, of which the first traces are found in the eleventh century in Southern Italy, in the immediate neighbourhood of Saracen Sicily. The Trumpet, which then assumed the form of a long, straight, cylindrical, or very slightly conical tube, provided with a bell, already occupied a very special place in the East, where it was reserved for priests, nobles and princes. In India monarchs would bestow it on the highest dignitaries; in Arabia it was used by the most exalted personages only, while all but the very great had to content themselves, throughout the whole of the East, with the ordinary Horn. This exclusiveness was retained by the *Busine* in Europe, where only the Court, knights, and nobles used it for signalling purposes.

Shawm

The Shawm (Italian *Ciaramella*, Old French *Chalemie*), a primitive Oboe with a conically bored wooden tube, a double reed and finger-holes, in all probability came to the West *via* Italy; at all events, the oldest known record of it comes from twelfth-century Saracen Sicily. The reed was inserted wholly into the mouth in the Eastern manner (cf. Aulos, p. 60), so that the performer was unable to control the tone-colour with his lips. Any suggestion of personal expression was avoided, and the sound of the instrument had all the power and astringent vigour demanded by the age.

Bagpipe

The same tendency to avoid personal expression explains the popularity of the Bagpipe (cf. p. 63) in the Middle Ages. The part played by the performer's mouth-cavity in the case of the Shawm is here played by a leathern bag. Although we have evidence of the occurrence of this instrument as far back as the ninth century, the Bagpipe (German *Sacphîfe*, *Dudelsack;* French *Cornemuse*) was not fully developed until the thirteenth century. It was then that the instrument was provided, in addition to the chanter, with drone-pipes; that is to say, pipes without finger-holes, which give out an uninterrupted and unvarying low note. The bagpipe was mainly a herdsman's instrument in the early Middle Ages; for that reason it was introduced into Christmas music, and well into modern times musicians have imitated the peculiar effect of the bass drones with a melody, in order to evoke the mood of Christmas.

Platerspiel

A variant of the Bagpipe was the *Platerspiel* (Bladder-pipe, Old German *Blâterpfîfe*), which can be traced back to the thirteenth century. Here, instead of the leathern bag, a bladder was used. The blowpipe and the chanter always lay in a straight line; it is most likely therefore that they were rigidly connected inside the bladder. The chanter was sometimes straight, sometimes crooked. Drones were very unusual.

Panpipes (Syrinx)

Reed instruments were by no means the only representatives of the wood-wind family during the early Middle Ages; Flutes also were not unknown.

The most simply constructed of the Flutes, but also the most complicated in respect of its performance, was the ordinary vertical Flute, in which the performer, unaided in any way, had to blow against the sharp edge of a pipe. These vertical Flutes were not furnished with finger-holes, but were made in various sizes. Bound together in series, the whole being enclosed, in the later types, in a leather case, they formed the Panpipe, or *Syrinx*, an instrument already known to the ancients (Pl. VII, 1). As the instrument mainly of the herdsman or shepherd, it often appears throughout the Middle Ages, without playing any appreciable part in the music of the times. It has survived in the Pyrenees, the Balkans, and as the chosen instrument of the "Punch" showman.

Recorder

The next stage in the development of the Flute is an instrument provided with finger-holes (the *Recorder*), in which the sound is produced in the same way as in the flue-pipes of the organ. At its upper end the instrument has a beak-like formation, which is blocked except for a narrow channel (comp. the later German names *Blockflöte* or *Schnabelflöte*, and the French *Flûte-à-bec*; in England the block in the beak is called "fipple," and the instrument accordingly "fipple-flute"). Through this slit the wind is directed in a flat stream against a sharp edge, which sets up vibrations as described in the introductory chapter (cf. p. 41).

Tabor-Pipe and Tabor

Together with the larger recorders, played with both hands, which appeared from the eleventh century onwards,

PLATE XV

Back of a French Rebec, about A.D. 1400. Vienna, Bondy
Collection

PLATE XVI

The Virgin and Child. By Giovanni Boccati. End of fifteenth century.
Perugia, Vanucci Gallery

The standing angels are playing (from left to right) the Lute, Tambourine, Cymbals,
Rebec, Bagpipe, Harp; the sitting angels play the Portative and the Dulcimer

we find in the twelfty century a small Flute called *Tabor-pipe* (French *Flûtet*, *Galoubet*, German *Schwegel*), which was played only with the left hand. This instrument had so narrow a bore that its fundamental note did not sound; thus three finger-holes only sufficed to bridge the fifth between the second and third partials. This one-handed Flute usually made its appearance in conjunction with a tambourine-like drum, the *Tabor*, played by the same performer, who generally fastened the drum to his fore-arm (Pl. X, 2), his wrist, or the little finger of his left hand, beating it with a drumstick held in the right hand. Sometimes also it was fastened to his shoulder, and then the performer used his own head as a drumstick. The combina-tion of flute and drum, which had been used by the juggler and the mountebank since the later days of the Roman Empire, has persisted in altered form down to the present time; for even to-day the drum and fife band is an accom-paniment for marching soldiers.

The Tabor was by no means the only percussion instru-ment of the early Middle Ages; several other instruments of the same class found their way into Europe with the Saracens. All of them in their Eastern home were gentle instruments, suitable for chamber-music, the thunderous quality of the percussion instruments being a development of later centuries.

Kettledrum, Tambourine, Triangle, Cymbals

The tiny *Kettledrum* (called by the French *Nacaire* from Arab *Naqqârâ*) scarcely bigger than the fist, which, in the Orient always appeared in pairs, the *Tambourine* (Old English *Timbrel*, Provençal *Temple*, French *Timbre*, German *Schellentrommel*), a small drum covered on one side with a skinhead, in whose shallow frame little bells or jingles are inserted, the *Triangle* (French *Trépie*, Italian *Treppiede*, German *Stegereyff*), a metal rod bent in the form of either a triangle or a trapezoid and played upon with a second metal rod; finally the *Cymbals* (Latin *Cymbalum*, French *Cymbale*, Italian *Cembalo*, German *Becken*), two slightly concave plates, which were softly struck together; all these had appeared in Europe before the year 1300.

Among the Oriental instruments which entered the Occident through the South and South-West of Europe there is one at least, the Recorder, which was introduced also from the East through the Slav countries. The same route was used for the entry of several other instruments which were to achieve great importance in European music.

The Asiatic *Double Shawm*, which consisted of two tubes of wood or bone bound together and provided, in all probability, with clarinet-like mouthpieces, failed to survive the early Middle Ages. Setting out from Hungary —a seventh-century Avar instrument, made of the bones of a crane, was recently found in a Hungarian burial-field—the double Shawm spread rapidly throughout the West. Thanks to its powerful, impersonal tone (the performer taking the reed right into his mouth in the Oriental manner) and its double voice, it was at first widely welcomed. But whereas the shrill double Shawm was relegated completely to the background by the new spirit which ruled the music of the Renaissance, yet another instrument coming from the East, and probably from the South-West, *via* Byzantium, proved to belong to the future. This was

Transverse Flute

the Transverse Flute, the solitary example of the various mediaeval flutes to persist uninterruptedly down to the present day. The name, of course, comes from the fact that, in distinction to other wind instruments, this flute is held transversely across the player's face. The performer blows directly—as in the Syrinx—against the sharp edge of the mouth-hole or embouchure pierced in the wall of the cylindrical tube near the stopped end. The production of the tone is not mechanical, as in the Recorder, for which reason the sound is all the more variable, being stronger, too, clearer, and more penetrating. It is probably no accident that this ancient instrument, familiar in the East long before the birth of Christ—an instrument which allows the personal element considerable free play—was not adopted in Europe until a comparatively late date, and even then had to wait before achieving popularity. It appears for the first time in Europe, in Germany, in the twelfth century; from Germany it reached other countries, and was consequently known as the *German Flute* in England, the *Flûte allemande* in France, the *Flauta alemana* in Spain.

Thus the early Middle Ages, which were peculiarly receptive to influences from the highly civilized Orient, gathered on Western soil a motley host of Oriental instruments. The immediate question, what part these instruments have played in the musical culture of Europe, is by no means easily answered. The early Middle Ages were dominated by the idea of Universality. As there were still no national boundaries, so there was only *one* science, only *one* acknowledged language—Latin—only *one* religion—the Catholic—and, similarly, only *one* art of music. The division between vocal and instrumental music which seems so natural to us to-day had not yet been made, so that the part played by instruments in the execution of the compositions which have come down to us, in musical notation, and often also with vocal text, is as a rule not definitely shown.

Nevertheless, there is good reason for assuming that so far as single-voiced music is concerned, as soon as instru-

ments co-operated the performance took place in the
Oriental manner. All the musicians played the same melody
in unison, and the melody as a rule would be sung as well.
Each player, however, would decorate and adorn the tune
in his own particular manner, according to the qualities of
his own instrument.

The powerful movement towards polyphony during
the second millennium A.D. gained complete control over
the instruments. New tasks were constantly allotted to them,
and the instruments, which to begin with had retained
their Oriental character, were gradually adapted to the needs
of the new musical practice of the West.

III

THE LATE MIDDLE AGES
(1300–1500)

While the principal achievement of the early Middle Ages relating to European musical instruments was their importation from the East, the chief preoccupation of the last two centuries of the Middle Ages was the adaptation of these instruments to Western ends. The instruments were transformed more and more radically, until their fundamental Asiatic character was no longer recognizable, while their newly-acquired European characteristics became more and more conspicuous. Moreover, a conscious process of selection was at work; certain instruments gained in estimation, while others were completely discarded, and even disappeared.

Generally speaking, the main line of development was in the direction of the free expression of the performer's personality. The exclusion of any personal idiosyncrasy on the part of the performer, which was favoured by the early Middle Ages, was now a thing of the past. The late Middle Ages laid greater stress on individuality in music, as in all other activities. Perhaps the clearest indication of this new spirit is the fact that the unvarying sound of the drones, which gave character to so many instruments of the early Middle Ages, was now relegated to the background. Instruments were now so built that they could be employed for the rendering of unaccompanied melodies.

One must not imagine, however, that because of this development instruments were used by themselves; that was a later development. The instruments of the late Middle

Ages were far too delicate and weak to stand alone. In the paintings of the fourteenth and fifteenth centuries, which are our chief sources of information concerning the instruments of the period, they appear almost invariably in groups. Yet instruments of like tone were seldom combined; indeed, the groupings were plainly so arranged as to provide the greatest wealth of contrast and variety. This becomes intelligible if we turn from the paintings to the actual scores that have come down to us. The essentially different, shrill, and apparently discordant instruments were able to differentiate the separate parts, to which the period of Landino, Dunstable and Dufay aimed to give individual characters. Effects of harmony were not sought after in that heyday of contrapuntal virtuosity, and the contrasting tones of the instruments gave full emphasis to the polyphonic life of the composition. The orchestra of the late Middle Ages was instinct with light, radiant, imponderable colours, like the paintings of the Primitives.

We must now enquire into the changes made in the individual instruments whose introduction into Europe was noted in the last chapter.

Harp

The *Harp* was one of the few instruments which crossed the line dividing the early from the late Middle Ages without undergoing a radical transformation. In the late Middle Ages there was a tendency to increase the range of the instrument, and therefore the number of the strings, but the only result of this enlargement was a slight change in the proportions of the three main members of the body of the harp. The sound-board and pillar were made much longer compared with the neck, so that strings of deeper tone could be incorporated; and thus, from the early mediaeval form, approximating to an equilateral triangle, there evolved in the course of the fifteenth century a taller, slenderer form, in which all three parts—sound-board, neck and pillar—were clearly differentiated from one another (Pl. XI).

Vielle (Fiedel)

It was otherwise with the *Vielle*. In its early mediaeval form the instrument was quite inadequate to the demands made upon it by the music of the fourteenth and fifteenth centuries, and only after a radical improvement in its construction did it succeed in regaining its supremacy over the other stringed instruments played with a bow. The smaller, shouldered type which assumed the leadership at this time had already, about 1300, replaced the primitive vaulted body by a trimly built sounding-box, consisting of a flat or slightly curved back, straight side walls (or ribs), and a table, which was usually flat. This table was pierced with sound-holes whose original plain semi-circular shape was replaced by a single slender C, or by two Cs, one superimposed upon the other (Pl. XI). The new sounding-box had the advantage of greater lightness and handiness; moreover, its resonance was infinitely superior to that of the clumsy older type. A further important improvement in the Vielle was the adoption of the incurved waist, already found in the large types held in front of the player. This waist made it possible for the musician to get at the individual strings up to a certain point, and thus to break away from the early mediaeval type of performance, with the lowest string perpetually sounding. Already initiated in the fourteenth century, this important development became the rule in the fifteenth. A third improvement related to the manner of fastening the upper ends of the strings. Generally speaking the Vielle, throughout the

Middle Ages, was furnished with five pegs, which were
perpendicular to the table (Pl. XI). In rare exceptions,
however—under the influence of the Rebec—the pegs
were arranged parallel to the table, as they are in our
modern stringed instruments. In this case the peg-box
was usually slightly recurved. The advantages of this
arrangement were the greater resistance to the pull of the
strings and the increased handiness of the pegs. Actually
the Middle Ages were still far from realizing the true value
of this improvement, and instruments with the Rebec head
were rare before the sixteenth century.

Hurdy-Gurdy

A characteristic glimpse of the artistic outlook of the age
is provided by the fate of the *Organistrum*. It is true that
this instrument was so diminished in size that keys and
wheel could be operated by a single performer. Even so
the constantly sounding drone and the rigid, unvarying
tone could not be abolished. The Hurdy-gurdy was therefore hardly regarded as a true musical instrument; it
suffered an extraordinary degree of social degradation,
sinking step by step, until it finally degenerated into the
stock-in-trade of the pedlar and the blind beggar.

Citole, Sister or Cister

Both the old Vielle without waist and the new one
with waist were also used during the late Middle Ages as
plucked instruments. On the *Citole*, *Sister* or *Cister* (Italian
Cetra or *Cetola*, French *Cithre* or *Citole*) the egg-shaped
form of body, the strings, taken over a bridge to the lower
end of the table, and the position of the pegs, all clearly
indicate that this instrument was originally nothing but a

PLATE XVII

The bellows of the old Organ in the Cathedral of Halberstadt (Germany).
Woodcut from Michael Praetorius, *Syntagma Musicum*, 1618

PLATE XVIII

A group of musicians. By Bernardino Luini. Sixteenth century. Milan, Brera

From left to right: Kettledrums, Citole, Tambourine, Triangle and Drum. The heads
of the three instruments with membranes are provided with snares.

plucked Vielle. At the same time, the qualities of a true plucked instrument are also clearly marked. The strings are arranged in pairs or "courses," as in the Lute, each pair being tuned in unison or octaves, in order to strengthen the weak tone of the instrument; for the fifteenth century, in order to give the player immediate control over the tones emitted by his instrument, favoured playing with the bare finger rather than with the quill or plectrum; and the change in the musical outlook necessitated some provision against the weakening of the tone that resulted.

Guitar

The later type of Vielle, with waisted body, in which the strings were plucked, was provided with the peg-box of the Rebec; that is to say, the pegs were parallel to the table. This instrument, which was actually very rare, was none other than the *Guitarra latina*, which from the very outset resembled the Vielle in many of its features (cf. page 80), but was now almost completely absorbed by that mighty instrument, taking over the ribs and the flat back of its body. Only the position of the pegs—which was characteristic of instruments coming to us *via* Western or Southern Europe—recalls the original construction. Since, however, the Vielle itself in the late Middle Ages sometimes adopted the head of the Rebec, this archaic feature of the *Guitarra latina* is also "modern." Such a clinging to traditional features, together with the adoption of all sorts of promising novelties, was characteristic of the remarkable transition period at the end of the Middle Ages.

Lute

Until the thirteenth century the distribution of the *Lute* was limited to Spain and France. A hundred years later the instrument must have been known in Italy and Germany, for both Dante and Boccaccio mention it, as well as Heinrich von Neuenstadt. Nevertheless, the Lute was but sparingly used, for it had a rival in its relative, the Mandola, which by virtue of its simpler construction was easier to make as well as to play. During the fifteenth century, however, the smaller, weaker and clumsier Mandola was pushed into the background by the Lute, which gradually became one of the most important instruments of the period.

Various circumstances were responsible for the success of the Lute. First, the instrument sounded most effective both in small and large ensembles, since its dry, neutral tone provided the happiest contrast to the human voice,

the wind and the bowed instruments. Then, it was favoured as a solo instrument, the clarity of its sounds fulfilling the Renaissance desire for lucidity and precision. Finally, the Lute showed a remarkable gift for adapting itself to the needs of the contemporary European music. During the fifteenth century it underwent important technical improvements. In order to enlarge its compass, the number of strings was gradually increased from five to eleven, the highest of which was designed for the clear rendering of the melody, while the others, arranged in pairs, provided the accompaniment (Frontispiece; Pls. XII; XVI). About 1480 the classical stringing of the Lute was set as shown above.

The Asiatic plectrum of the early Middle Ages was gradually abandoned, being sacrificed to the need for flexible performance. To improve the grip of the left hand

and thus obtain a pure intonation, gut nooses, the "frets," were tied round the neck, increasing in course of time from four to eight in number. Finally, as the demand for louder tone grew, the body of the instrument itself was made considerably larger, while at the same time the little sound-holes pierced here and there in the table of the older lutes were united in one large and beautifully carved "rose."

Mandola

Nothing will better illustrate the importance attained by the Lute during the course of the fifteenth century than the position of the *Mandola*. From a rival of the Lute, whose improvement it constantly obstructed in the early days, the Mandola declined during the fifteenth century into an imitator of its technically superior rival. It adopted the broad body of the Lute, the back being built up from a number of separate staves. The strings were no longer carried over a bridge to the base of the body, but, as in the Lute, were affixed to a cross-bar glued to the table (Pl. XIII). If the Mandola had not still retained its old construction, with the neck all of a piece with the body, and above all the slightly reflexed head, with a carved scroll, it might well be taken for a smaller variety of Lute. Tinctor, who in 1499 described the instruments of his time, went so far as to say: "It is quite clear that the Mandola was derived from the Lute."

Rebec

The victory of the Lute over the Mandola is the more remarkable as the Mandola was itself the victor over another instrument, which was now compelled to imitate all the modifications taken over from the Lute, even though they conflicted with its fundamental character. In the Middle Ages the player was already beginning to hold the *Rebec* (called also *Rubeba, Gigue* and *Geige*) not in front of the body but on the shoulder, in the same way as the Vielle. But in this position the straight peg-box attached to the neck at a right angle was in the way, and was superseded by the Mandola's slightly reflexed peg-box. The club-shaped Rebec thus came very closely to resemble the club-shaped Mandola, and the history of the newly created "bowed Mandola" coincided for quite a considerable period with that of its plucked original. The Rebec with its three or four strings clung as obstinately as the Mandola to the unity of neck and body, although this made any technical improvement impossible. The bowed instrument assumed the broad body of the Mandola (Pls. XIV, XV) which rendered the separate strings extremely difficult of access. Even the old sound-rose—quite unsuitable acoustically to the bowed instrument—was retained, as the model also was provided with it (Pls. XIV, XVI). Just as the characteristic of the Vielle was the embodiment of progressive elements, including the adoption of the waist, and the grafted neck, so the characteristic of the Rebec was its loyalty to tradition; it clung to its connection with the Mandola even to its own detriment. Certainly there were attempts to curtail the swelling sides and to smooth away the belly; but these were not radical enough to do much good. At the close of the Middle Ages it was at last decided to break free from the cramping influence of the Mandola, and return to the original club shape. The projecting sides were thus done away with; but the small four-stringed instrument that now remained was still too weak as to tone, and above all, because of its one-piece neck and body, it was technically too clumsy to play its part in the music of the dawning new age.

Psaltery

The *Psaltery*, like the Rebec, also followed an evolutionary by-path. Its appearance in the later Middle Ages indicates that it had made no appreciable progress throughout the centuries. It is true that the somewhat clumsy trapezoid shape had given place to the more pleasing double-winged form, as the result of the adoption of a slight waist; and in the South, the plectrum or quill, so beloved of the North (Pl. XII), was replaced by the bare finger, as better fitted to the more personal attitude to music which was part of the spirit of the Renaissance: but no real development occurred, so that we need not be surprised to find the Psaltery as such expiring with the late Middle Ages.

Dulcimer

A variant of the Psaltery was the *Dulcimer* (French *Tympanon*; Italian *Salterio tedesco*; German *Hackbrett*), which is distinguished from the Psaltery proper less by its construction than by the way in which it is played. This instrument was usually rectangular, and the strings, which were stretched horizontally over two bridges, were struck in the Slavo-German fashion with two sticks (Pl. XVI). This method of playing the Dulcimer, coming from the East, can scarcely have reached Europe before the fifteenth century; and the climax of the instrument's career was not attained until some centuries later.

Tromba Marina

At about the same time as the Dulcimer, perhaps the strangest of all stringed instruments found its way into the

West—the *Tromba Marina*, or *Marine Trumpet*. The position of its head, with pegs perpendicular to the plane of the table as in the Vielle, and still more the method of playing the instrument in harmonics, show that like the Dulcimer it was of Slavonic origin. The Tromba Marina was a truncated pyramid in shape, with either three or four sides, narrow at the base but extremely tall (from 3 to 5 or even 7 feet) (Pl. XII). The longest string was taken over a shoe-shaped bridge, one foot on which did not quite touch the table, so that when the string vibrated the free foot drummed very rapidly against the table, producing a grating sound. The method of holding the instrument was as curious as its construction. Pressing the upper end to his chest, the performer held the lower end free, and drew his bow not under his left hand, as might have been expected, but above it. Finally, the fingers of the left hand touched the strings very lightly so as to produce artificial nodes. In this way the harmonics ("flageolet-notes") were produced, which gave the instrument a similar series of overtones to that produced on a Trumpet (see p. 31). This circumstance, and perhaps too the remarkable rattling caused by the freely vibrating bridge, was responsible for the curious name, involving a comparison with the Trumpet. The Renaissance names (Italian *Tromba Marina*, French *Trompette marine*, German *Trumscheit*) all have their origin in this comparison; but in the Middle Ages the instrument was usually called by the old Greek name, *Monochord* (one-string), on account of its single long principal string. The West, particularly Germany and the Netherlands, adopted the exotic Eastern guest with enthusiasm; but its curious and unusual character prevented it from ever being completely assimilated.

Shawm and Pommer

Among the wind instruments, the reed instruments of the early Middle Ages are seen to have undergone an especially radical change. The shrill Double Shawm of the Avars, with its two pipes bound together, and the simple clarinet type of reed, has disappeared, as has also the rigid Platerspiel. The *Shawm* with the double-beating reed, the chief instrument of the group, has, on the contrary, developed appreciably. The clumsy, heavy instrument of the early Middle Ages is now made in two sizes, first, as a small, slender soprano instrument with a bell and seven finger-holes—the Shawm proper—and then as a larger contralto instrument—the *Pommer* or *Bombard* —a fifth deeper (Pl. XII). A remarkable thing about this Shawm is that the lowest hole, operated by the little finger, is duplicated, appearing both on the right and the left of the instrument, as some performers held the instrument with the left hand below the right, and some with the right hand below the left, the unused hole being stopped with wax. A similar contrivance may be found also in the Bombard, where, because of the larger size and the consequent difficulty in reaching the deepest hole, this was sometimes covered with a key protected by a little barrel. This key was fitted with a double touch-piece, one side for the right hand, the other for the left. While the Shawm and the Pommer were combined at the close of the Middle Ages with instruments of the most contrasted character, their sharp, clear tone rendered them particularly suitable for use with trumpets and percussion. They were symbolic, too, of the pastoral mood.

Bagpipe

The improvements in the Shawm automatically benefited the *Bagpipe*. In the late Middle Ages its chanter was fashioned more carefully and provided with seven finger-holes. There were still Bagpipes with one chanter only and no drones (Pl. XVI); on the other hand, after 1400 A.D. instruments were made with two drones, tuned to a pure fifth, in addition to the chanter. These drones, unlike the chanter with its double-beating reed, were usually fitted with a single-beating reed. Although the Bagpipe was still the shepherd's instrument, it was also used for dance-music and for marching-tunes; and from this it was only a further step to its military associations—which were characteristic of the Roman Empire and persist in Scotland to the present day. In the late Middle Ages even crowned heads employed pipers, who as highly valued musicians, travelled from court to court, exciting universal admiration by their playing. But the value placed on the Bagpipe as an instrument for special ends should not mislead us into thinking that it played any significant part in the musical practice of the time. On the contrary, the sharp, uniform and stridulant tone in no way corresponded to the new ideal, and above all the incessantly sounding drones prevented the use of the instrument for general musical purposes. Indeed, we have this paradoxical situation, that the older form of the instrument, without the drones, was preferred to the newer form on the rare occasions when the Bagpipe was used at all with other instruments (Pl. XVI).

Recorder

Far more popular among the wood-wind instruments of the late Middle Ages than the Bagpipe and the Shawn

PLATE XIX

Concert of angels. By Gaudenzio Ferrari. Sixteenth century. Italy, Dome of Saronno

The angels are playing (from left to right): Lute, Cymbals, Violin, a kind of Vielle, Violoncello, and Viola da braccio

PLATE XX

Angel playing the Lira da braccio. By Vittorio Carpaccio.
Sixteenth century. Venice Academy

were the gentle Flutes, now appearing in various forms. The fundamental form of Flute is the simple fipple-flute, the *Recorder*, with a reverse conical bore, tapering towards the lower end, but which looks externally like a plain wooden cylinder. Like the Shawm, it is provided with seven finger-holes, with the lowest duplicated.

Tabor-Pipe

The longer, smaller-bored *Tabor-pipe* was still mainly used, as in the early Middle Ages, with the Drum, or Tabor. This combination is especially suitable for military purposes. Drum and Pipe, later succeeded by the Fife, became the foot-soldier's instruments, and in a painting of the Battle of Sinalunga in the Palazzo Publico of Siena, the infantry are preceded by three men with Tabor-pipes and drum, and the cavalry by trumpets.

Double Recorder

Nothing more clearly illustrates the popularity of the Recorder in the late Middle Ages than the fact that it completely superseded the various double Shawms of antiquity and the early Middle Ages—whether fitted with the single or with the double reed. In the late Middle Ages also two similar wood-wind instruments were sometimes bound together, but these instruments were always two Recorders, one played with the performer's right hand, the other with his left (Pl. XIV). This, however, can hardly have been an original creation. It is far more probable that the Renaissance, in its striving toward classical antiquity, was imitating the Greek Aulos or the Roman Tibia in this form of double Flute. Indeed, this notion is so firmly rooted that even to-day the Aulos and the Tibia are usually and wrongly represented as Flutes and so called.

Portative

The commonest flute-like instrument of the time, and indeed the wind instrument most in use, was the Portative (Pls. XI, XVI). This was no accident, for quite apart from the clear, pure, mellow tone, which would have a particular appeal for Renaissance ears, it was remarkable for its technical efficiency, while thanks to its keyboard mechanism it was easy to play.

Common as are the paintings which contain representations of the Portative, it might almost be said that no two of them show exactly the same instrument. There are tremendous variations in size. There may be anything from six to thirty pipes, usually in two ranks, but sometimes in one rank, or in three. The keys may be press-buttons (Pl. XI), or lever keys in the modern sense (Pl. XVI). But the greatest differences occur in the gamut, which varies considerably in different instruments. The semitones are introduced now here, now there, and sometimes even whole tones are omitted. Since the number of pipes had to be as small as possible, in order not to make the instrument too heavy, it would seem that the maker of the Portative must have consulted the performer—if he was not one and the same person—in each individual case. It is possible, too, that the pipes were changed for the performance of different compositions.

Compared with these individual variations, the signs of the instrument's general development are slight. In the fifteenth century, which marked the Portative's prime, the drones or bourdon pipes, conspicuous for their size because they were often separated from the rest, were pushed farther and farther into the background. At the same time, Portatives were built with two rows of keys instead of one; but this at first was done only in order to save space, since the chromatic scale of the modern keyboard instruments was not found in the mediaeval Portatives.

Church Organ (Positive)

While the small, portable Portative was employed entirely for music of a secular nature—and it is significant that Raphael's St. Cecilia turns from her Portative as the strains of heavenly music fall upon her ears—the fixed, *Positive Organ* had already found a home in the Church by the end of the Middle Ages. The rapid development of this instrument since the early Middle Ages is illustrated by the data relating to the Halberstadt Cathedral organ, as placed on record in 1618 by the great composer and musicologist, Michael Praetorius. This instrument, built in 1361 and renovated in 1495, had no fewer than three hand-claviers or manuals, and one pedal-board. The introduction of the pedals was probably due to the fact that with the larger pipes a particularly great effort was required to overcome the heavy air-pressure in giving the wind access to the pipes. This effort was exerted more easily by the feet than by the hands, a fact which gave rise to the notion of contriving a keyboard for the feet.

The Halberstadt organ is the earliest instrument to which we can point with certainty as covering the chromatic scale. And since it is hardly conceivable that a large number of keys and pipes were added when the old organ was renovated, it is highly probable that the all-important acquisition of the chromatic keyboard on the part of the great organ had been made as far back as the fourteenth century. On the other hand, even far into the fifteenth century, there existed not only Portatives but also church organs with Bb, F# and C# as the only chromatic tones.

According to the testimony of Praetorius the two middle

manuals of the Halberstadt organ were designed for the
normal two-part playing. The two outer ones, the Descant
manual, in which each key sounded as many as thirty-two,
forty-three, or even fifty-six pipes, and the pedal board,
where each pedal key controlled sixteen, twenty, or twenty-
four pipes, were provided for particularly powerful effects
when, in Praetorius's words, the organ " must have given
out sound of an exceeding loudness, a very powerful
clamour."

The great number of pipes governed by the individual
keys and pedals was made possible by the use of *register-
stops*, which in a way were known even in antiquity. The
Middle Ages particularly favoured the "mixtures" in which
every note was accompanied by several fifths and octaves
based upon it, so that the fundamental note sounded fuller
and richer. It was gradually realized that the structure of the
pipes had a great effect on their tone-colour, and whole
ranks of pipes were then built, some with a wider and some
with a narrower bore, some conical, some inversely conical,
or stopped. With the fifteenth century there began the use
of the sharper, shriller reeds, in which the pitch was determined by a simple metal reed and the tone-colour by a
bell-mouth. All these various groups of pipes could be
connected with the keys by the register stops, and in view
of this, it is not surprising that the Halberstadt organ
already had a comparatively large number of pipes. The
Organ of the late Middle Ages also needed a tremendous
amount of wind. Even in the fourteenth century we find
twenty-four bellows, operated in pairs by the feet, with
one man to each pair (Pl. XVII). In this the dimensions
of the monster Organ at Winchester are almost equalled;
but in other respects even the average Organ of the late
Middle Ages surpassed that unique marvel of an earlier
century.

Transverse Flute

The *Transverse Flute*, the last representative of the flute family, which was so important in the late Middle Ages, was employed in that period above all as a military instrument. In its simple cylindrical form, with its normal six finger-holes (there was no hole for the little finger), it became, like the Tabor-pipe, associated with the drum, and was thus the regular companion of foot-soldiers. The Swiss lansquenets, who played so important a part in the military history of the times, preferred the Transverse Flute, and soon it became generally known as the *Schweizerpfeiff*, or *Swiss Pipe*, and later as the *Fife*.

Trumpet

While the Flutes were the most widely distributed wind instruments of the late Middle Ages, the *Trumpets*, on the other hand, were the most highly valued. In contemporary paintings they are shown as attributes of the Three Kings, and they are introduced at the coronation of the Virgin. Among the angels who serenade the Saviour or the Mother of God there is usually a trumpeter, although the Trumpet, as a rule, is an exclusive instrument, which avoids the company of ordinary stringed and wind instruments. In paintings of peasant weddings, fairs, or groups of itinerant musicians, the Trumpet is never seen. Another indication of the regard in which the Trumpet was held in the late Middle Ages is the fact that, like the Shawm and the Organ, it was made in two different sizes; the smaller form, which was barely as long as a man's arm, and was often made of wood, was especially popular in Italy, and its small size was clearly expressed in its name—Latin *Tubecta*, Italian *Trombetta*, the first a derivation of *Tuba*, the second of *Tromba*. The parent instrument, the *Busine*, which stood as high as a man, was forced for practical reasons to adopt another shape. The long, straight, slender tube (Pl. XI), from which a heavy banner was often suspended, although made in several sections provided with ferrules or sleeves at the joints, showed a persistent tendency to assume the curved form; and in the fifteenth century someone hit on the notion of bending the instrument. All sorts of curves were tried, until at last, at the beginning of the modern period, the flattened loop (Pls. XI, XII) was generally adopted. In its essentials this form has persisted down to the present day. Of course, these folded Trumpets were also made in sections, with the joints covered by ferrules which also served for ornamentation.

Slide Trumpet

It seems hardly probable that the trumpeters of the late Middle Ages had the technical equipment necessary for blowing diatonic melodies without any mechanical aid. Doubtless they confined themselves chiefly to easy fanfares. Occasionally, however, the possibilities of the instrument seem to have been enriched by the use of a simple contrivance which we may see depicted in contemporary paintings. The mouthpiece of the Trumpet was fixed to a long tube, which could be made to slide in and out of the main tube. The performer held the mouthpiece with his left hand, and the instrument in his right (Pls. XI, XII). By drawing out or pushing in the main tube he changed the effective length of the instrument, and with it the whole series of notes. Such forms must have persisted for a long time; at any rate, the occasional indication of a *Tromba da tirarsi*, or Slide Trumpet, in Bach's scores seems to suggest as much.

Horn

The regard enjoyed by the slender, cylindrical Trumpet had a detrimental effect on the older, conically bored *Horn*. The *Oliphant*, that most costly and aristocratic type of horn, vanished completely in the late Middle Ages. The small *Cornetto* was of no great importance, and therefore made no progress. The only type to be developed was the great resonant metal Horn used as a signalling instrument by the ordinary foot-soldiers (the mounted nobles employing the Trumpet for this purpose). This development was along similar lines to that of the Trumpet: to prevent the long, unhandy instrument from warping, the tube was curved back upon itself. Here England seems to have led the way for the rest of Europe. At all events, the oldest representation of a mediaeval circular Horn, included by Canon Francis Galpin in his valuable book, *Old English Instruments of Music*, is of English origin. It is carved on a choir-stall dating from the end of the fourteenth century in Worcester Cathedral, and represents a man blowing a horn with a funnel-shaped bell, the instrument being curled round his body. This important improvement seems to have met with prompt acceptance on the Continent, for in 1375 and 1385 the Duke of Burgundy sent to England for a number of Horns, while in the sixteenth century the circular Horn, which was also made with smaller coils, established itself throughout the rest of Europe. In France, particularly, it was received with greatest favour.

In addition to stringed and wind instruments, quite a number of percussion instruments were used in Europe during the late Middle Ages. Of these the most important were the Kettledrum and the Snare-drum.

Kettledrum

In its original form, as introduced by the Saracens, the small, cauldron-shaped *Kettledrum* had a stretched skin barely larger than the palm of the hand. It was always used in pairs fastened to a strap slung round the performer's neck or attached to his girdle (Pl. XVIII). About the middle of the fifteenth century, however, this delicate instrument, which was suitable only for chamber music, was superseded by the mighty War-drum, which spread from the East *via* Hungary and Poland, reaching first Germany and then Western Europe. This instrument consisted of a large hemispherical copper cauldron over which a calf-skin was stretched by means of screws, and with its tremendous tone it quickly swept its smaller and older cousin from the field. Wherever the Trumpet blared—at princely banquets, at tourneys, or in the field—there also the great Kettledrums would roll. Strapped on the back of a horse, a pair of them accompanied the nobles on the field of battle. Of course, there were those who opposed the all too noisy intruder. In 1511 we find Virdung writing of the "monstrous rattle-barrels (*Rumpelfessern*)," that the Devil himself must have invented them for "the suppression of all sweet melodies and the whole art of music."

Snare-Drum

As the Kettledrum accompanied the Trumpet, so the *Drum*, with its cylindrical wooden body, was the chosen companion of the Flute. The small, flat, tambourine-like Tabor was not the only form known to the late Middle Ages. There was also an instrument with a deeper cylinder, spanned at both ends with a skinhead held by thongs, and struck now with one drumstick, now with two.

PLATE XXI

Citole made by Girolamo de Virchis in 1574 for Archduke Ferdinand of Tyrol.
Vienna, Museum of Fine Arts

The head of this beautiful instrument represents the death of Lucretia

PLATE XXII

The Guitar-player. By Marcantonio Raimondi, *Ca.* 1510–15

The right foot of the player is resting on the Guitar case

Across one of the skins a gut-string, the *snare*, was stretched which caused a stridulant rattle when the instrument was played (Pl. XVIII). This Drum, which measured scarcely more than a foot in diameter, was still used in the Oriental, early mediaeval manner—as a delicate rhythmic instrument, that is, without any particular striving after loudness.

Tambourine

The *Tambourine* was originally the instrument of wandering musicians, showmen and jugglers, who inherited it from the Bacchus-cult of the Romans. This instrument was not merely struck with the hand, but was also thrown up into the air and caught again. In the late Middle Ages it was sometimes also given a part in concerted music (Pls. XVI, XVIII).

Jingle-Ring

Besides the Tambourine there was the *Jingle-ring* (*Schellenreif*), resembling it closely, but without the skin. This instrument, which was often depicted by Raphael, as well as other painters, consisted of a shallow wooden hoop with thin metal leaves, or jingles, let into the sides. It was held in one hand and struck with the other to make the jingles sound.

Triangle

The same tendency to supplement the natural tone of the percussion instrument with a rattling or jingling sound is evinced even in the *Triangle* (Pl. XVIII). This instrument, which in the fifteenth century was made in triangular

H

form, or with four corners, approximating to a trapezium, was provided with several rings carried on the lower limb, which sounded when the Triangle proper was struck. The clear-cut rhythm was thereby blurred, as in the Tambourine.

Cymbals

Like the other percussion instruments of the Middle Ages, always excepting the later great Kettledrums or War-drums, the *Cymbals* were not by any means employed to produce a shattering noise. On the contrary, the two plates were brought together vertically with no particular effort (Pl. XVI), producing a kind of ringing sound, fundamentally different from the sharp clash of the modern convention. Thus, generally speaking, one must think of all the mediaeval instruments as being delicate, weak in tone, and averse to any developments in the direction of increased loudness.

IV

THE RENAISSANCE

(*THE SIXTEENTH CENTURY*)

The year 1500 marks one of the decisive turning-points in the history of musical instruments. Types already existing were fundamentally transformed, and a whole collection of new designs appeared. It is not too much to say that a new era was opening.

As in painting the transition from the Middle Ages to the modern era meant the gradual conquest of the means of expressing the third dimension, so in music it connoted a deepening of the harmonic sense. Instruments that were capable of playing chords, such as the Lute and Harp, the Great Organ and the newly invented keyboard instruments—Clavichord, Spinet and Harpsichord—now constituted the most important means of expression. Even the instruments with only a single voice were used for the realization of harmonic effects. They were made in the most varied sizes, in order that a consort of like types might produce an effect similar to that of a keyboard or a many-stringed plucked instrument. Scarcely one of the single-voiced instruments—strings not less than wind—escaped the general tendency to form families. Even those limited to a certain range by their individuality were turned out with ruthless logic in as many as from four to seven sizes. To-day, the giant "Great Bass Flute" reaching down to F, seems just as strange to us as the tiny "Octave-bassoon" a twelfth higher than the usual parent instrument. The sixteenth century, however, needed many members of the same family to perform a whole, multivoiced piece in one tone colour, for the single voices were required not to contrast sharply with each other, but as far as possible to blend together. It is true that in compositions with more than one choir different tone-colours occurred. Within each choir, however, the same fundamental colour was preserved. Thus, for example, in a three-choired composition all four voices of the first choir might consist of flutes of various sizes, all four voices of the second choir might be singers, and finally, all four voices of the third choir, viole da gamba. The principle remained that within a single choir no musical "foreign body" should intrude.

The employment of musical instruments was also changed in another respect. The cheerful and eager generation of the fifteenth century was succeeded by a serious and dignified race of men whose strict code of propriety was laid down in Castiglione's classic *Libro del Cortegiano* (Venice, 1528). In painting, the delicate and radiant colours of the fifteenth century gave way to deeper and richer tones. In music the gentle little Flue-organ, the Portative, the thin Rebec, the feeble Mandola, the chirruping Psaltery, and the ethereal Marine Trumpet, all fell victims to this change in taste. They were utterly swept away, or, at the very least, forfeited the last shreds of their individuality. Other instruments were refashioned with an eye to increased loudness and fullness of tone, as well as extension of range.

In one not unimportant respect, however, a connection with the Middle Ages was preserved. The sixteenth century, just as much as the preceding centuries, lacked the conception of gradual dynamic change, even partly of dynamic contrast. The majority of the instruments in use were limited to their natural loudness and the performer had neither the desire nor the skill to vary the intensity of tone. We need only visualize the mediaeval Hurdy-gurdy or the Renaissance Spinet to realize that dynamic contrasts are unattainable with them. The same applies to the Recorder, which sounds the higher octave as soon as it is blown more strongly, and the Shawm and Bombard, whose reeds vibrated freely in the performer's mouth so that the influence of the lips went for nothing. *Forte* and *piano*, to say nothing of *crescendo* and *diminuendo*, were still unfamiliar conceptions at that age.

With its peculiar mixture of progressive and conservative elements this period is like the head of Janus looking simultaneously to the future and the past.

Vielle

Hardly any instrument underwent such intensive experimentation at the beginning of the new age as the *Vielle*; and the success achieved fully justified the pains. Though various weaker offspring of the instrument, such as the *Lute-Vielle* and the *Lira da braccio*, were fated to fall by the wayside, others survived, and above all one of the most important instruments of modern times: the Violin.

Viola da Gamba

The early Middle Ages, as we have seen, had a form of Vielle which was held in front of the body, and another smaller form which was supported on the shoulder. The late Middle Ages showed a decided preference for the handier, smaller form; but with the beginning of the modern age, the taste for richer and more sombre colouring brought the larger form back into favour. True, this tenor Vielle had to undergo a thorough transformation before it could become a really practical instrument. First, in order to counter the strong pull of the strings, it adopted the

backward-slanting head of the Rebec. While this reform
had occasionally been made in the small Vielle of the
fifteenth century, there is another which is entirely to the
credit of the new age; the fundamental division of the body
of the instrument into an upper portion, a strongly waisted
middle portion, and a lower portion. The shallow waisting
of the fifteenth century Fiedel was no longer sufficient.
To get at each string individually when the instrument was
held between the knees a far more pronounced waist was
necessary, and thus originated the semicircular form of
the middle "bouts" or ribs, with distinct corners, whose
clear demarcation from the upper and lower parts of the
instrument was at the same time consistent with the aesthetic
sensibilities of the Renaissance. To make playing with the
left hand easy and avoid the use of higher positions, the
Vielle, following the model of the Lute, was given six
strings, tuned in intervals of fourths and thirds. The
string frets, too, which gave the left hand a better grip,
were adopted from the Lute. Once the main features were
established, the further qualities of the new instrument
emerged one by one. The flat back of the sounding-box
sloped off at the top, making the instrument easier to hold;
the shoulders sloped towards the neck at an acute angle;
the peg-box was crowned with a human or animal head; and
the table was pierced by the old C-shaped sound-holes of the
Fiedel. Being held between the legs this new instrument was
known as the *Viola da gamba*, "*gamba*" being the Italian
word for leg. In England it was usually just called the *Viol*.

Before long a whole family of instruments was built up
on the lines of the Viola da gamba. The parent instrument,
the *Bass Viol* (Pls. XXXI, XXXII, XXXV), was now the
largest of a series which included an Alt-Tenor and a
smaller Treble. Since these were not considered enough,
yet larger types were made as the new instrument gained

in popularity, and by the end of the century we find it in as many as six different sizes, from the Small Descant, some 28 inches in length, to the Sub-Bass, whose length was as much as 7 feet.

Viola da Braccio

While the old Vielle, which was held in front of the body, was transformed into the Viola da gamba, under the influence of the Rebec and the Lute, the shouldered Vielle was also undergoing a transformation in accordance with modern ideas. Like the Viola da gamba, it was sharply divided into an upper, a centre, and a lower portion, and it also was given the Rebec peg-box, crowned with a scroll. From the Rebec, too, it inherited its four strings; and since, in view of its smaller dimensions, the bridging of a comparatively larger interval between the open strings offered no difficulties, the instrument was tuned in fifths, a system which had already been applied in some degree to the old Vielle. The slightly older sister instrument, the *Lira da braccio* (cf. p. 116), made two not very striking, but none the less acoustically and aesthetically important, contributions: the vaulting of the table or belly and the back, and the slight overhang of both back and belly over the ribs. A new feature was the *f*-shaped sound-holes, the result of combining two C's facing in opposite directions. Thus, even before the middle of the sixteenth century, there was a new stringed instrument with alto-soprano range, supported on the shoulder—the *Viola da braccio*, *braccio* being the Italian word for arm. In England the instrument was generally known as the Viola.

The Viola da braccio, too, gave rise to a family of instruments. Working upwards, we find towards the end of the century a descant instrument described by the diminutive

Violino, while smaller still, and used above all in Germany, was the *Quart-Geige* or *Violino piccolo*, only 15 to 19 inches in length. Working downwards, we find as a counterpart to the Bass-Viol, the Violoncello, which was held between the knees (Pl. XIX), and a very rarely used *Gross-Quint-Bass*. Thus was created the family of stringed instruments which was most significant for the future of music. Praetorius, the most important theoretician of the period, gives the tuning of the new family, and we find that it corresponds entirely to that of the present-day. For the Violin g-d^1-a^1-e^2; for the Viola da braccio, or Viola (German *Bratsche*), c-g-d^1-a^1; for the Violoncello C-G-d-a. The Violino piccolo was tuned a fourth higher than the Violin (i.e. in c^1-g^1-d^2-a^2) while the Gross-Quint-Bass, in addition to the four strings of the Violoncello, had a fifth, deeper string in F_1.

Lira da Braccio

In addition to these two successful forms, the great transformation of stringed instruments at the close of the fifteenth century resulted in a number of much less fortunate constructions. One of the strangest of the new instruments, the Italian *Lira da braccio* (Pls. XX, XXXI), we have already met when discussing the Violin. The attempt was made here to adapt the Vielle to the demands of the new music while retaining its essential features. The Lira da braccio scorned the peg-box of the Rebec, as well as the structural division of the instrument into three parts. It was content with a mere suggestion of a division into two parts, an upper and a lower section, which was hardly superior to the slightly waisted effect of the fifteenth century. This instrument in principle retained the five strings of the old Vielle, although each of the two thick and slackly stretched lower strings had a companion string in the upper octave

PLATE XXIII

Spinet of the sixteenth century. Vienna, Museum of Fine Arts

PLATE XXIV

Harpsichord by Domenico da Pesaro, 1546. Vienna, Society of Friends of Music

to lighten the tone. The seven-stringed instrument thus obtained emphasized its conservative character still more strongly, the two lowest strings lying alongside the finger-board as drones, in the mediaeval fashion. Even the early mediaeval name of the Vielle—Lira—was retained, with "da braccio" added simply to distinguish it from a larger variant, of which we have still to speak.

While the Lira da braccio avoided the main stream of progressive development in all essential particulars, its makers expended the most loving care on all sorts of minor details. The noble curvature of the belly and the back, as well as their slight overlap at the edges, was first seen in this instrument, and it was not long before these minor features were incorporated in the Viola da braccio, and through it in the Violin.

It must not be imagined that the Lira da braccio, which clung so persistently to the past, led a Cinderella existence in the sixteenth century. On the contrary, this high-bred if degenerate offspring of the ancient Vielle was held in the greatest esteem. In contemporary paintings we see it again and again in the hands of angels; such specimens as have come down to us exhibit a rare beauty of workman-ship, and in this connection it is of special significance that Raphael in his fresco of Parnassus in the Vatican, defying all traditional representations, makes his Apollo play the contemporary bowed Lira da braccio instead of the plucked Lyre of antiquity.

Lira da Gamba

In spite of its conservative character, the Lira da braccio did not wholly escape the general tendency of the sixteenth century towards the formation of families. Before the year 1600, at a time when the instrument had lost almost all its

importance, a Tenor type, the *Lira da gamba*, was made,
with two to four drones in addition to its nine to thirteen
strings. This instrument, doomed in advance by the archaic
arrangement of its strings, survived for a few decades only.

Lute-Vielle

The adoption by the Viola da gamba of the stringing and
the frets of the Lute had already had the advantageous
result that lute-players could play the Viol also. But while
in this case the effect of the stimulus derived from the Lute
was entirely advantageous, the reverse must be said of a
clumsy, unintelligent blending of Vielle and Lute, which
became the fashion about this time, above all in Germany.
In the works of Virdung and Agricola, who in the first
half of the sixteenth century wrote important studies on
the instruments of their time, we find representations of
stringed instruments which show the division of the body
into three parts and the reflexed Rebec peg-box with
almost exaggerated clarity; but in the same instrument we
see the central rose of the Lute, and, instead of a bridge,
there is the cross-bar of the Lute, glued to the table to take
the lower ends of the strings. Since the strings—of which,
according to Virdung, there were no fewer than nine!—
all lay in one plane, this Lute-Vielle was as good as unplay-
able. One would regard it as merely the invention of
unpractical theorists, but for the fact that this queer instrument was occasionally represented in works of art.

It must be clearly understood that the names here given
to the individual successors of the old Vielle were sometimes
of later origin. In the sixteenth century the nomenclature
of the instruments of the period was marked by complete
indifference and confusion, and the names *Fiedel*, *Vielle*,
Viola, *Violino*, *Viol*, *Lira* were used indifferently, now for

one instrument, now for another. The separate types which had sprung from the common root were still too close to one another for anyone to trouble to differentiate them sharply by giving them different names.

Hurdy-Gurdy

The *Hurdy-gurdy* with its wooden wheel lost all its importance in an age which saw such an unforeseen development of bowed stringed instruments. Praetorius calls it "the peasants' and old wives' lyre," and scorns to treat it seriously. Brueghel has a painting of a group of blind beggars who, unaware of the danger, stumble into a river; and one of them has a Hurdy-gurdy, the badge, so to speak, of their forlornness.

Rebec

Nor did the *Rebec* fare much better. During the sixteenth century its sole function was to give of its best, that other instruments might evolve. It liberated itself from its connection with the Mandola and transmitted its best features to the new stringed instruments. The peg-box, the fourfold stringing, and even, in Germany, the original name of *Geige*, were all bestowed on the two new families. To the benefactor itself, however, no one paid the least attention. It was allowed to retain its small club-shaped body, which prevented any strengthening of tone, and steadfastly held to the ancient form, with neck and body merging into one. Thus, in the sixteenth century it was regarded as a wholly atavistic form, and excluded from the musical practice of the day. As Curt Sachs has pointed out, a revealing light is shed on the contemporary valuation of the instrument in Cima da Conegliano's painting of the fight between Apollo and Marsyas, where Apollo plays on the Vielle while the satyr who soon will be defeated has a Rebec in his hand.

Tromba Marina

The *Tromba Marina*, too, was now considered super-fluous. It is noteworthy that Praetorius, who normally was satisfied with none but his own observation, had to rely for his account of this instrument on an old description by the theoretician, Glarean.

Citole, Sister, Cittern

The Citole also in the new age clung to its old unwaisted shape, derived from the mediaeval Fiedel. Since it had up to six (and in exceptional cases even twelve) courses of strings, of which the lowest consisted of two or three strings in unison or octaves, while the highest consisted sometimes of a single string, the originally narrow elliptical body expanded until it was almost circular (Pl. XXI). From the sixteenth-century descendants of the bowed Vielle the *Citole* derived its technically improved body, with flat back, table and ribs, which became shallower towards the base. The laterally inserted pegs of the Rebec were adopted, although it could not bring itself to make a total surrender of its original pegs. Accordingly, the sixteenth-century instrument exhibited the most unusual combination of pegs which were perpendicular to the table and pegs which were parallel with it. This arrangement, which made it unique among the instruments of the time, hindered its widespread adoption. Perhaps, on the other hand, it was for this very reason that the instrument was prized by the nobility, and was often decorated in an exquisite and costly manner (Pl. XXI). In this century the instrument changed its name in England from Citole to *Cittern*.

Guitar

Scarcely less rare than the Citole in the sixteenth century was the second descendant of the plucked Fiedel, the *Guitar*, or *Quinterne*, as it was sometimes called. Only in Spain, which was the true home of the instrument in Europe, was it the object of any special interest. It was in this country, too, that in the second half of the sixteenth century a fifth pair of strings was added to the original four pairs. The resistance of the Guitar to the influence of the bowed instruments was less obstinate than that of the Citole. In addition to instruments with the fifteenth century Vielle's gently-waisted body (Pl. XXII) we find others that show a sharp division of the body into three parts, in the manner of the Viola da gamba or the Viola da braccio, a feature quite pointless in a plucked instrument.

Lute

By far and away the most important of the plucked instruments of the sixteenth century was the Lute. In the music of the time it played a part analogous to that played by the piano in the nineteenth and early twentieth centuries. It was a valued co-operator in all chamber music, was never absent from the larger ensembles, and was particularly favoured as a solo instrument. A great number of original compositions and arrangements for the Lute have come down to us both in print and in manuscript. The instrument was sometimes made of the most precious materials, such as ivory, ebony, or Brazil-wood, a practice followed only in the case of instruments which were highly prized. It is significant that, while in the Middle Ages instrumentalists were often counted as roving vagabonds, who stood without the law, in France a celebrated composer for the Lute, Denis Gaultier, was accorded high official rank. He was *lieutenant-général au baillage de Clermont*, the highest official in the province after the Governor himself. And in France all makers of stringed instruments, whether plucked or bowed, are known as *luthiers* down to the present day.

The reason for the extraordinary regard enjoyed by the Lute is easily found. It was the fortunate accident that an instrument which was already highly popular in the fifteenth century brought to the new age just that quality which was desired above all, namely, the ease with which chords can be played upon it. On the Lute a melody can be performed and at the same time accompanied. It is, more-over, an ideal instrument for providing accompaniments, forming the finest background for every kind of melody.

From a technical point of view the sixteenth-century Lute hardly differed from the fifteenth-century instrument. There were still five pairs of strings, and in addition a single string for the upper voice. The seven to eight frets were general, and so was the practice of playing with the bare fingers. The Lute, however, did not escape the con-temporary craze for forming families, and it was made in five, or even seven, different sizes; though the big, clumsy instruments, whose thick, slack strings must have produced a dull, muffled tone, can have had no more real impor-tance than the impracticable miniature type. The parent instrument, the *Recht Chorist- oder Alt-Laute* as Prae-torius calls it, with the tuning of which we are already familiar (cf. page 94), was the instrument for which the overwhelming majority of compositions were intended.

Mandola

The *Mandola* or *Mandora* was almost wholly assimilated to the Lute in the sixteenth century. The division of neck and body, which was of such importance structurally, was adopted, and the body itself was built up of many staves. The Mandola was strung with four to five single or double strings, and if it had not kept its distinctive peg-box, fixed on the neck at an obtuse angle and sometimes made in a curved form, and with that its slender body, it would have been neither more nor less than a smaller Lute (Pl. XIII). The fact that it was far from enjoying the regard in which the Lute was held, but, on the contrary, in the sixteenth century, shared the fate of the Hurdy-gurdy, and became the instrument of beggars, was due to its weak tone.

Harp

With the powerful *Harp* the case was very different. Next to the Lute it was the most favoured plucked instrument of the day. Thanks to its versatility it satisfied the new requirements of the age without being forced to undergo any radical transformation. It was admirably suited for chord playing, and could be left more or less unchanged. As the strings were increased in number the neck was lengthened in proportion to the sound-board and the pillar. The slender shape of the fifteenth century thus became gradually fuller and heavier, approaching more closely—though, of course, on a larger scale—the equilateral form of the early Middle Ages. The three structural parts—neck, sound-board and pillar—were now, in accordance with Renaissance ideas, more sharply differentiated. The stringing was at first always diatonic. It was only towards the close of the century that "chromatic harps" were built with a separate string for each semitone.

Psaltery and Dulcimer

The small and delicate *Psaltery*, which was reckoned among the Shrovetide instruments, together with its relative the *Dulcimer*, which was played by striking it with little rods, sank into insignificance in the sixteenth century. Descendants of these two instruments, however, and of another relative of the Psaltery, the Monochord, were now to be called on to fulfil important tasks.

Clavichord

The *Clavichord*, although it had no real importance until the sixteenth century, is of far older origin. Ancient Greece knew a Psaltery-like, one-stringed instrument called the Monochord, employed for acoustic measurements,

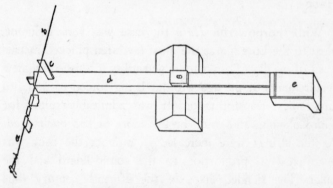

FIG. 8.—A Clavichord key

in which a movable bridge was used to shorten the string. The Middle Ages took this instrument over, and contrived a combination of several Monochords, with strings of varying tension and thickness. In the fourteenth century we find no less than nineteen Monochords combined. The crude instrument of the theoreticians was now gradually transformed into a useful instrument of music. This came about in a fashion characteristic of the times: through the adoption of important features first found in other instruments. From the Hurdy-gurdy it was learnt that strings may be shortened by the employment of tangents. From the Positive and Portative Organs the system of keys was derived which first made possible the proper development of the tangent mechanism. Thus was evolved the mechanism figured in Fig. 8. When the front part *e* of the key is depressed its back part *d* rises and the metal tangent *c* is thus impelled against the string *a–b*, which is simultaneously shortened and set in vibration. But only the section of the string marked *b* is allowed to sound, for section *a* is prevented from vibrating freely by a cloth wrapping or damper. Since the string ceases to vibrate at the point of impact with the tangent, it follows that it is quite possible to connect a single string with several keys whose tangents strike it at different points, and thus produce notes of differing pitch. The saving of space and material implicit in this principle led to the general use of this *Fretted* or *gebundenes* Clavichord, as it was called, on which up to four successive chromatic notes were played on a single string.

The debt of the Clavichord to the organ, at any rate as far as the keyboard arrangement is concerned, may be seen from a peculiarity inherited from its model. To effect a saving in the expensive material of the pipes the older organs omitted the seldom-used notes C♯, D♯, F♯ and G♯ of the lowest octave; and since space also was a consideration the keyboard was contrived in the following curious order:

D E B♭
C F G A B C

The Clavichord simply copied this curiosity of the organ:

I

known as the "short octave," although a few keys and strings more or less can hardly have mattered (Pl. XLII, 1).

As for the name of the instrument, it was originally called after the Greek model, *Monochord* (French *Manicorde*), regardless of the fact that it no longer had only a single string. Then, because the device used to shorten the strings had a certain resemblance in shape to the key of a mediaeval lock, the instrument came to be known as the *Clavichord*, i.e. Keystring (Latin *clavis* = key).

Whether the development of the Clavichord occurred wholly in the fifteenth century, or partly in the fourteenth, it is impossible to decide, in view of the complete absence of reliable evidence. In any case, it played no part in the history of music until the awakening of the harmonic sense and the consequent promotion of the keyboard instruments to the foremost rank. It attained to prominence in the sixteenth century, and the oldest dated Clavichord that has come down to us was made by the Venetian, Domenico da Pesaro, in 1543.

The Clavichord was not the only keyed stringed instrument which flourished in the sixteenth century. In addition to this gentle instrument, two other keyboard instruments were devised, employing different principles of sound production: the Spinet or Virginal and the Harpsichord or Clavicembalo.

Plucked Keyboard Instruments

Spinet and Harpsichord were both keyboard instruments in which the strings were plucked by plectra of quill or leather. On the far end of the key, in place of the tangents of the Clavichord, was fixed a small wooden rod or *jack* (Fig. 9). In its upper end was hinged a movable wooden tongue from which a plectrum of quill or leather (*a*) projected horizontally. A hog's bristle (*c*), serving as a spring, held this tongue in an upright position (phase 2). When the key was depressed the jack rose, and the plectrum plucked at the string which lay above it. After the key was released, a leaden weight (*d*) let into the bottom of the jack caused it to fall. The tongue turned aside and the plectrum slid past the string (phase 1), so that the string was not plucked a second time. Damping was contrived

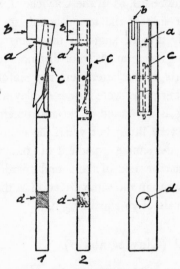

FIG. 9.—The jack of a Spinet

by means of a small patch of cloth (*b*) fixed to the upper end of the jack. The plectrum made a loop of vibration at the point of impact, whereas the tangent created a node. Thus with plucked keyboard instruments the whole string was set vibrating, not merely a part of it, as with the clavichord, and there had to be a separate string for every note. The tone of these instruments was full and loud; it could not be altered in any way by the variation of pressure on the keyboard, and thus had the disadvantage of inflexibility.

Spinet or Virginal

These plucked keyboard instruments were made in two styles. In the *Spinet* or *Virginal* (Italian, *Spinetto*, from the Latin *spina:* thorn; Middle High German, *Schachtbrett*, from *Schacht* or New High German *Schaft:* rod; French, *Eschiquier*, from a mistaken translation of *Schachtbrett*; English "virginal" is derived from the Latin *virga:* rod, or jack) the keyboard, as in the Clavichord, was contrived on the longer side of the sound-board, so that the keys were at nearly a right angle to the strings (Pl. XXIII). Since the strings were at different distances from the keys, the hinder parts of the latter were not uniform in length; so that the lower notes were harder to play than the higher ones. As long as the range of the instrument was narrow this mattered very little; but when the number of strings was increased the simple expedient of contriving the keyboard at the narrow end of the sound-board was adopted. The keys now ran in the same direction as the strings, and could all be made of an equal length.

Harpsichord (Clavicembalo)

The resultant instrument was the *Harpsichord* (Italian, *Clavicembalo*; French, *Clavecin*; German *Clavicymbel*), which was larger and louder than the Virginal (Pl. XXIV). It had, moreover, richer powers of expression, since from the Organ it borrowed the idea of the register-stop. Even in the sixteenth century harpsichords were being built which had not merely one system of strings, but two, and in exceptional cases even three or four. These corresponded to a second, third or fourth row of jacks, which with the aid of the register-stops could be engaged or cut out at will. At least one of the systems would then be tuned to an octave higher—it sounded in the 4-foot tone, as the

technical expression ran (again borrowed from the Organ)
—and thus the performer was in a position to engage
different strings alternately or simultaneously by depressing
the keys in the ordinary way, according to the position of
the stops. Towards the end of the century there were
harpsichords with two keyboards, stepped one above the
other, each of which operated one part of the stops. By
combining or contrasting the voices it was thus possible,
within certain limits, to achieve tonal and even dynamic
effects which were impossible on the Virginal.

Finally, it should be noted that the first beginnings of
both Virginal and Harpsichord are still for the most part
obscure. All that we know for certain is that under the
influence of the organ and the clavichord both instruments
were developed from the plucked psaltery, which they
completely absorbed in the course of the fourteenth and
fifteenth centuries. Germany, and above all England,
played a decisive part in this development. But it was not
until the sixteenth century that the plucked keyboard
instruments attained real significance, and their harmonic
possibilities began to be properly exploited. The oldest
dated Spinet which has survived was built in 1493 by
Alessandro Pasi in Modena. The oldest dated Harpsichord
is also of Italian manufacture. It was completed in Rome
in 1521 by Geronimo di Bologna, and is now in the Victoria
and Albert Museum, London. The same collection includes
the most valuable Spinet in existence. It is encrusted with
nearly 2,000 gems, and was built in 1577 by Annibale
Rosso of Milan. In 1867 it was bought for £1,200.

Clavicytherium

Yet a third plucked keyboard instrument may be referred to the sixteenth century—the very rare *Clavicy-*

therium or upright Harpsichord, an instrument with a vertical sound-board at right angles to the keyboard—a sort of forerunner of the upright piano. Virdung depicts it for the first time in 1511.

Wind Instruments

With the wind instruments, which in the nature of things have only single voices, and a correspondingly limited range, the formation of families played an even greater part than with the stringed instruments. This is particularly notable in the case of the instruments with double beating

Shawm and Pommer

reeds. The two sizes in which the Shawm (known in

FIG. 10.—Players of the "Gross-Bass-Pommer." Drawing by R. Effenberger

France also as the *hautbois*—the high wood) and Pommer (known in France also as the *grosbois*—or low wood)

were made at the close of the Middle Ages had increased
by the beginning of the seventeenth century to no fewer
than seven (Pl. XXVI). The larger types were now so long
that the fingers could not reach the lower finger-holes;
and thus anything up to five long-levered keys, whose
delicate mechanism was protected by a perforated wooden
barrel, were added to the instrument. These keys had two
wings, so that the performer could use the right hand or
the left at will for the lower holes. Particularly interesting
is the largest member of all, the huge *Gross-Bass-Pommer*,
nearly ten feet in length, two specimens of which are
extant. This monstrosity could be played only if the bell
was supported in church by a trestle, or in the open—as in
processions—by the shoulder of a second man (Fig. 10).

Bagpipe

The nimbus of the *Bagpipes* paled in the sixteenth century. They were no longer the instruments of princes;
they were only used by shepherds, soldiers on the march,
or dancing peasants. None of Brueghel's paintings of
popular junketings would be complete without the Bagpipe.
Nevertheless the Bagpipe also underwent the development
common to all instruments of that age. It was made in no
fewer than five different sizes, and technical improvements
were added; it might have as many as three drones, and was
sometimes even furnished with two chanters. Most important
of all, however, was the radical transformation which
occurred at the end of the century. The Irish *Uilleann Pipes*
(Elbow Pipes), or, as they are now called, *Union Pipes*,
for the first time substituted a bellows operated by the
elbow for the mouth as a source of wind, and this new
form, which in France was taken up with particular enthusiasm, was to dominate the future.

Lastly, it must be noted that from the second half of the sixteenth century there was a new immigration of Bagpipes from the East. Instruments of a Slavonic character made sporadic appearances in Germany, and in these not only the drones but also the chanters (which had an animal's horn for a bell) were cylindrical, and provided with a single beating reed of clarinet type.

To join the few reed instruments known to the Middle Ages there appeared in the sixteenth century a plenitude of new instruments. The imagination of the age was at work, delighting in its powers of invention, and seeking to discover ever new possibilities. But of all these forms only one proved to have a lasting value for the future.

Bassoon (Dulzian, Fagotto)

The *Bassoon*, at first known also as the *Dulzian*, in Germany as the *Kortholt* (short wood), and in England as the *Curtall*, may be traced back to the second half of the sixteenth century (Pl. XXVI). It consisted of a billet of wood through which two canals were bored longitudinally, their lower ends being joined. Together they thus formed a narrow conical bore, doubled back upon itself. The performer blew into the narrower end by means of an S-shaped brass tube to which the reed was attached. A small funnel—which in the "stopped" Dulzian was closed by a perforated cap, acting as a damper—represented the bell. About the end of the century the instrument was made in five sizes, from the Descant to the Double Bass but the most important of all was the Bass, the *Chorist-Fagott*, which served as a substitute for the unwieldy larger Pommers (cf. Fig. 10). Before 1600 the family as a whole was not very widely distributed.

PLATE XXVI

Musicians in a procession. By Anthonies Sallaert. Sixteenth century. Turin Gallery

Besides three Pommer players in the middle, there is one Bassoon player on the left and a Trombone player on the right

PLATE XXVII

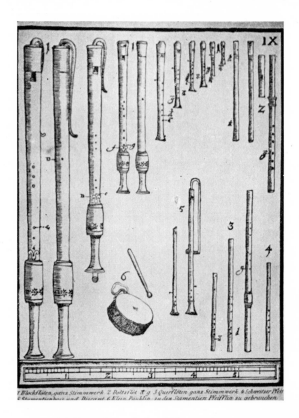

(1) Recorders of nine different sizes
(2) Four Dolzflöten
(3) Three Transverse Flutes
(4) Swiss Pipe (Fife)
(5) Two Tabor-pipes
(6) Tabor.

From M. Praetorius, *Syntagma Musicum*, 1618

Sordune

An extremely rare variant of the Bassoon was the *Sordune* (Italian *Sordone*). This consisted of a gracefully turned wooden billet containing not merely two but sometimes three parallel cylindrical bores.

Rackett

The *Rackett* (called also in Germany the *Wurstfagott;* in France the *Cervelas*) shows a grotesque exaggeration of the Bassoon principle. It consisted of a cylindrically bored tube bent nine times on itself and let into a small box $3\frac{1}{2}$ to 13 inches in height, provided with many finger-holes (Pl. XXIX, 1). In Germany and France this curious contraption enjoyed a certain vogue.

Tartölt

A variant of the Rackett is the dragon-shaped, naturalistically painted *Tartölt*. A complete set of five different sizes is in the possession of the Vienna State Collection of old musical instruments.

Krumhorn, Schreierpfeifen, Rauschpfeifen, Bassanello, Cornamusa

The sixteenth century took an especial delight in constructing wind instruments in which the double reed was embedded in a wooden wind-chamber with a narrow slit to blow through. Here we have really a development of the early mediaeval *Platerspiel*, where neither personal expression nor variation of strength was desired. Overblowing was of course impossible. Since the instruments were so limited in range there was a special impetus toward the usual formation of families.

The commonest of these was the *Krumhorn* (English also *Cromorne*; French, *Cromorne*, *Tournebout*: German, *Krummhorn*), a predominantly cylindrically bored instrument shaped like a fishhook (Pl. XXVIII). Far rarer were the *Schreierpfeifen* (Italian *Schryari*), with a conical bore which, by a strange exception, narrowed down from the mouthpiece to the bell, and the *Rauschpfeifen*, again cylindrically bored, which belonged to the first half of the sixteenth century. Related to these were the *Bassanello* and the *Cornamusa*, with the vent-holes for the wind at the side.

Recorder

The wealth of forms so conspicuous in the sixteenth century reed instruments may be contrasted with the retention by the Flutes of the traditional forms. The Flutes were too highly regarded and their method of construction was too much appreciated to admit of extensive experimentation. In the case of the *Recorder*, which was then the most important instrument of this group, the dawning of the new age is suggested only by the consistent development of a whole family. The Recorder was being made in four different sizes by the beginning of the sixteenth century, while Praetorius, a hundred years later, records as many as nine different sizes (Pl. XXVII). The larger instruments have the double-winged key instead of the usual duplicate lower finger-hole, and were blown through a brass S-tube for greater ease in performance. Whether the thumb-hole at the back of the instrument (Pl. XXVII), was a sixteenth-century innovation or not cannot be decided, since we have no mediaeval

Recorders to refer to, and the pictorial representations of the fifteenth century invariably show the front of the Flute.

Tabor-Pipe

For the one-handed *Tabor-pipe* (Pl. XXVII), the English showed a particular predilection, and one John Price is cited as one of the most brilliant virtuosi of the end of the sixteenth and the beginning of the seventeenth century. This instrument was also made in two and sometimes three sizes.

Double Recorder

The *Double Recorder* was by no means common in the sixteenth century. Praetorius, who described even the most unusual instruments, leaves no record of it. Nevertheless, the instrument, consisting of two pipes, usually lying side by side, and cut from a single block, occurred in two forms; one with the finger-holes pierced in different positions, the other with the finger-holes lying side by side. The latter type, which had the advantage of being handier in performance, since the two adjacent finger-holes could always be stopped by one finger, finally won the day.

Transverse Flute

The first attempt to bring the *Transverse Flute* into line with the requirements of musical composition was made in the sixteenth century (Pl. XXV). The extremely narrow bore of the shrill Swiss Pipe (Pl. XXVII) was gradually abandoned. The bore became wider, which made the lower octave easier to blow, and no longer limited the

instrument to the highest register. Though made in several
sizes (Pl. XXVII), it was still predominantly a military
instrument, at least in the smaller sizes.

Dolzflöte

The *Dolzflöte* recorded by Praetorius (Pl. XXVII)
seems to have been a Recorder with the embouchure at
the side, and was of no practical importance.

Portative

The *Portative* occurred only during the first decade of
the sixteenth century. It was now invariably provided
with a regular chromatic keyboard, furnished with two
ranks of keys, and producing all the notes of the chromatic
scale. Despite this progress, the instrument was rapidly
losing ground. It was too small, too gentle, too feeble in
tone; and since it was played only with one hand, it was
too unsuitable for chord playing to be of use in the new
music.

Positive Organ

Between the tiny Portative and the huge Church Organ
a medium-sized organ was constructed, now usually known
as the *Positive*. Having more than one register, and being
played with both hands, it was far better able to satisfy
the musical requirements of the age. Yet because a second
person was required to work the bellows, and because it
had neither the portability of the Portative nor the fullness
of tone and the rich possibilities of the Great Organ, the
importance of the Positive also dwindled.

Regal

While the Portative and the Positive had flue-pipes, another small Organ, which was provided with beating reed-pipes, had appeared since the close of the Middle Ages. In these pipes the actual instrumental tube was reduced to rudimentary proportions, having merely an influence on the tone-colour (Pl. XXIX, 2). The pitch depended entirely on the length, thickness and elasticity of the reed. In the second half of the sixteenth century Georg Voll of Nuremberg hit on the idea of adopting for the new instrument, called the *Regal*, since it was employed to regulate (*regolare*) the singing in churches, the form of a folio volume, and this proved very popular. The twin bellows were made to look like parts of a book; the keyboard could be taken off and folded up; for purposes of transport the folded keyboard was packed into the bellows, and the closed instrument looked for all the world like a Bible. This was peculiarly satisfying to an age with so highly developed a taste for mechanical surprises and technical wonders.

Church Organ

The great Church Organ of the new age was already a highly developed and finely organized instrument, furnished with a by no means inconsiderable number of contrasting registers, from the mighty 32′ tone (32-foot) pipes to the tiny 2′ tone and even 1′ tone pipes. The all-important characterizations, 32′ tone, 2′ tone, 1′ tone pipes, which are here used, need a little explanation. If with a register of flue-pipes the depressing of the C key causes an 8′ pipe to sound C, while the D key produces the note D, and so on, it is said that the whole register is in 8′ tone, or that it is *equal*. But if with another register the depression of the C key causes a 16′ pipe to sound C_1 (and the depression of the D key, D_1), then the whole register is in "16′ tone." In this register each key produces a note an octave deeper than in the 8′ tone register. Similarly, in the 32′ tone register the pipes sound two octaves lower than the key that operates them; with the 4′ tone, on the contrary, they sound an octave higher, with the 2′ tone two octaves higher, and with the $5\frac{1}{3}$′ tone a fifth higher, and so on.

The most important register of the Organ is the *Open Diapason*, known in Germany as the *Prinzipal*, a powerful medium-bore flue-pipe, generally in 8′ tone. In great favour were also the 8′ and 16′ "stopped" registers, closed at the top, whose pipes, being only half as long as open ones of the same pitch, saved both space and material. Their tone, however, was lacking in brilliance. There were also "half-stopped" pipes, with a narrow little tube in the upper end for the exit of the wind (e.g. *Rohrflöte*), and pipes with an inverted conical bore (e.g. *Gemshorn*), so that they tapered towards the top. Of reed-pipes there were the powerful 16′ tone *trombones*, operated by the pedal, the 8′ tone *trumpets* with inverted conical tops, the 4′ tone *shawm*, and the nasal 8′ tone *fagotto*. In addition there were various mixtures whereby fifth and octave, third, fifth and octave, twelfth and double-octave or pipes tuned to other intervals taken from the series of harmonics were made to sound together. These are only a few of the dozens of registers already known at the end of the sixteenth century and recorded by Praetorius, the richest source of our knowledge of the Organ of that day. It is interesting to note that the Protestant German countries which used the Organ as an accompaniment to choral singing paid particular attention to the development of the softer registers with flue pipes, while the Roman Catholic countries, where the Organ was more of a solo instrument, favoured the multiplication of the sharper reed registers.

Hand in hand with the increase in the number of registers went a further increase in the number of pipes included in a given register, and therefore in the range of the key-boards. As early as 1519 we have a record by Anthony Duddington of an English Organ with a range of four octaves; and Pietro Aron in his *Toscanello*, which appeared in Venice in 1523, speaks in a perfectly matter-of-course way of the range C—c^3. Germany, on the other hand, had nothing to compare with this until the close of the sixteenth century. As a rule the so-called Short Octave, which has already been mentioned in our account of the Clavichord, was used for the lower range.

While in Italy great pains were taken with the develop-ment of the manuals, the *pedal* lagged behind; and the only Italian author of the sixteenth century to mention the pedal at all—Vincenzo Galilei—speaks of it in a some-what disapproving manner. In Germany, on the other hand, the land of polyphony, the pedal was zealously employed in the sixteenth century as a means to the richer development of polyphony. In Kleber's *Tabulaturbuch*, as well as in the *Fundamentum* of Hans Buchner—two impor-tant works containing organ music of the first half of the sixteenth century—the direction *pedaliter* is expressly given.

Trumpet

As the last group of wind instruments we will take those in the playing of which the human lips act as double reeds. Since with the *Trumpet* the player can do more by mere labial technique than is possible with the other wind instruments, it may be regarded in a sense as the highest type of wind instrument.

By the beginning of the sixteenth century the small Trumpet of the late Middle Ages, which was about as long as a man's arm, had disappeared. The larger form, folded in such a way as to have three straight lengths of tube lying in parallel order and united by small pieces of tube in semi-circular or U-shape, needed no further improvement. The Middle Ages had already found the classical form, which the new age would retain; and this instrument, moreover, was unaffected by the often senseless fashion of creating families. The instrument-makers of the sixteenth century were concerned less with the improvement of tone than with the aesthetic appearance of the Trumpet. It was often made of silver, and was sometimes even gilded, while the bell might be embellished with exquisite chasing (Pl. XXIX, 1). In Nuremberg and other German cities trumpet-making reached its culmination about this time, and the traditions of the art were handed down from father to son, so that in a certain sense the German trumpet-makers were the counterpart of the classical violin-makers of Italy. At the same time the art of trumpet-playing made extraordinary progress. While compositions of the first half of the sixteenth century demand only a very modest degree of technical ability in the performer, by 1600 trumpet-playing had improved so much that "a good master may sound in the high register almost all notes of the diatonic scale and even some semitones" (Praetorius). In fact, at this time, players could without any special mechanical aid, and solely by means of an exceptionally highly developed technique of the lips and the breath, blow the highest harmonics. The high social standing of the instrument inevitably led to a highly-developed art of trumpet-playing.

PLATE XXVIII

A girl playing the Krumhorn. By Vittore Carpaccio. Sixteenth century.
Venice Academy

PLATE XXIX

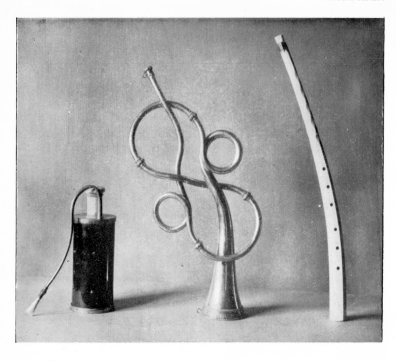

1. Rackett, silver-gilt Trumpet in fancy form by Anton Schnitzer,
Nuremberg (1598), and ivory Cornetto. Vienna, Society of Friends of Music

2. Bible-Regal and in front of it a "Regal-pipe." Berlin, Hochschule für
Musik

Trombone, Sackbut

After the disappearance of the small arm-length instrument the diminutives *Tubecta* and *Trombetta* were bestowed on the true folded Trumpet, since in the meantime a still larger variant had appeared. This was the *Trombone*, from the Italian augmentation of *Tromba*. In Germany it was known as the *Busine*, *Busune*, or *Posaune*; in Spain as the *Sacabuche* (from *sacar*, to withdraw or pull out, and *buche*, inside); in France as the *Saquebute*, and in England as the *Sackbut* (Pl. XXVI). This instrument, a relative of the Trumpet, and already known in the closing years of the Middle Ages, first attained importance in the sixteenth century. In the Slide-Trumpet we have already seen an attempt to make the Trumpet capable of diatonic playing at the lower end of the scale where the overtones lie far apart. But this form had the disadvantage that the whole instrument had to be pushed and pulled to and from the performer, to the peril of pure intonation. Another solution was now discovered. In the folded Trumpet the U-shape connecting-tube between the first two parallel tubes was not fixed fast to them, but fitted over the tubes as a movable sleeve, reaching almost to the mouthpiece. If this connecting-piece, the slide, was worked to and fro over the main tubes, the effective length of the tube as a whole was altered, and with it the whole series of natural tones. The farther away the slide was pushed, the deeper became the fundamental note, and the series of harmonics based upon it. Seven different positions of the slide made it possible to lower the fundamental note by a diminished fifth. The Trombone was thus fully chromatic from the beginning, and in later years it needed no appreciable improvement. Its tone must always have been characterized by the same nobility, power and solemnity that we admire to this day.

K

The sixteenth century at once set to work to form a
family of Trombones, and of these the Tenor, the Alto
and the Bass achieved importance.

Post-Horn

The great interest taken in the Trumpet and the Trombone now—as already in earlier times—thrust the great
Horn into the shade. The circular horn of the late Middle
Ages was very rare indeed in the sixteenth century—
unless one counts the tiny *Post-horn*, the postilion's instrument, with only two notes at the interval of an octave.
On the other hand, the small finger-hole horns of the

Cornetto, Cornett

Middle Ages, the *Cornetti* or *Zinken*, enjoyed an increased
popularity. Since the trumpeters formed a highly privileged
guild, which only with great reluctance played together
with other instrumentalists, and since the tiny treble
Trombone was more or less useless, the Trombone choir
lacked a treble voice; and this lacuna was best filled by the
Cornetto. Provided with a thumb-hole on its under side
and six finger-holes in its upper side, the instrument was
very well suited for the playing of melodies. A certain
irregularity of tone which was a feature of the finger-hole
Horns was readily overlooked, since this made it possible
to get over the difficulties of collaboration with the trumpeters.

The Cornetto was usually made of wood, more rarely
of ivory. In a straight, rounded form it was the *Cornetto
Muto* (German, *Stiller Zink* or *Gerader Zink*); in a curved,
octagonal form (Pl. XXIX, 1) it was the *Cornetto Torto*
(German, *Krummer Zink*). The curved instrument,

when fashioned from two separate pieces of wood, was provided with a black leather casing. The inevitable attempt to make a family of Cornetti resulted also in a small *Cornettino* and a large, S-shaped *Bass Cornett*.

Serpent

In Italy and France there was also a great Contra-bass Cornett, fashioned in the shape of a double S to bring the six finger-holes within the performer's reach. This bore the descriptive name of *Serpent* (Pl. LV).

Alphorn

In the mountainous regions of Europe, Trumpets and Horns, which might be either straight or coiled, were made for the benefit of herdsmen. These were built up out of long staves of wood, and in order to make them air-tight, they were closely bound with bast; the peculiar result was known as the Alphorn (Pl. XXX), a type of instrument that probably had its origin in the very distant past. They are celebrated in many folk-songs, and down to the present day they are inextricably associated with the idea of romantic Alpine impressions.

Kettledrum

Among the membranous instruments the great war *Kettledrum* (Italian *Timpano*, French *Timbale*, *Cymballe*), the faithful companion of the Trumpet, held from a social point of view the highest rank. The true home of this instrument of Eastern origin was now Germany. Duke Philip the Bold of Burgundy despatched a kettledrummer with other musicians "pour aller en Allemagne aux escoles de leur métier;" and Brantôme wrote in his *Hommes Illustres*: "Aujourd'huy les grands seigneurs d'Allemagne et généraux d'armées . . . usent de leurs cymballes quand ils marchent." Similarly, James Turner wrote in 1683: "The Germans . . . permit none under a baron to have them (i.e. Kettledrums) unless they are taken in battle from an enemy."

The construction of the Kettledrum did not change during the sixteenth century. The skin-head was held in place by a hoop, and screws helped to increase the tension. The drums were generally played by horsemen, who buckled them on the backs of their steeds.

Swiss Drum

Besides the Tabor, the companion of the Tabor-pipe (Pl. XXVII, 1), the new age also used a larger form of Drum. Instruments with two membranes, standing some 2 feet in height and 20 inches in diameter, were preferred. Their ribs were of wood, and the membranes were stretched with the aid of cords. While the Kettledrum was the knightly instrument, the double-headed Drum, since the late Middle Ages, has been the pacemaker for the infantry. It was especially favoured by the Swiss mercenaries, who fought all over Europe. Thus it came to be known as the *Swiss Drum*, the French calling it *Tambourin de Suisse* or *Tambour de lansquenet*, the Scotch a "Swesch."

Tambourine, Triangle, Cymbals

The *Tambourine*, the stock-in-trade of the mediaeval jugglers and wandering players, lost all its importance by the beginning of the new age, with the constant recession into the background of the wanderers who favoured it. The *Triangle* and the *Cymbals* also had little place in the music of the day.

Xylophone

One of the latest immigrants from the East was the *Xylophone*, known in the sixteenth century in Germany as the *Strohfidel* or *Hölzernes Gelächter*, in France as the *Claquebois* or *Patouille*; later, in Italy, as the *Timpano*. It consisted of tuned wooden rods or bars, at first cylindrical but afterwards prismatic in section. These rods rested on rolls of straw, and were struck with hammers. The instrument—which achieved a moderate distribution only in Eastern and Central Europe—hardly developed at all, since no place was found for it in serious music. The twenty-five rods which in 1528 (three years after the earliest trace of the instrument, in Holbein's *Dance of Death*) Martin Agricola attributed to the Xylophone, were not increased for a long time.

Glockenspiel

Let us conclude with an instrument whose universal rôle in the Middle Ages was later diminished to a more local one. The *Glockenspiel*, or *Chime Bells* (also German *Glögglenwerk*; Dutch *Clockspele*; French *Carillon*), was in particular favour in Flanders, Northern France and Holland during the late Middle Ages, and still more in the new age. As in Italy every city strove to outdo its neighbour's architectural masterpieces, so it was the ambition of the Northern cities to possess an unusually perfect mechanical Glockenspiel, perfect both technically and tonally. To this end the number of bells was constantly increased, and also the size of the cylinders in which the pins were fixed.

Instruments were built with more than fifty bells, with cylinders having more than ten thousand holes. Moreover, since the beginning of the sixteenth century it had become possible to play the Glockenspiel not only mechanically, but also by means of a keyboard. As larger bells and larger hammers were produced by the end of the Renaissance period a pedal board was added to the keyboard for the deeper notes. In its final form the instrument became more and more frequent in Central and Western Europe though without attaining anything like the same popularity as in its true home.

V

BAROQUE AND ROCOCO

(1600–1750)

The Seventeenth Century

When in 1618 Michael Praetorius was cataloguing the all but innumerable host of late-Renaissance musical instruments (whose numbers even the nineteenth century has hardly surpassed), the days of this gigantic instrumental array were already numbered in the North, and in the South were long past. In Italy, as a reaction to the impersonal style of the Palestrina school, there had arisen the ardent subjectivity of the Florentine dilettanti. The aesthetic ideal was no longer dignity and rigid majesty, but emotion and the genuine language of the heart. All instruments that could not sing were now relegated to the middle and lower registers, to supply the dark, uniform ground-colours which were exacted by the musical contemporaries of a Caravaggio.

The Baroque preference for extreme contrasts had a decisive influence on the sphere of musical instruments. On the one hand we note the determined efforts to provide ever deeper basses. Harpsichord and Organ extended their range downwards; bass strings were added to the Lute, and the Lute family was increased by the addition of new and bigger members. Besides, powerful wind instruments, like the Double Bassoon and the Contrabass Trombone, were now constructed. On the other hand, the highest value was set upon those instruments that were best equipped for producing a singing tone, and thus for competing with the human voice in tenderness, mellowness and emotional expressiveness. This tendency is very clearly seen in the case of the stringed instruments. The inexpressive plucked instruments yielded pride of place to the bowed instruments with their power of communicating every shade of feeling. The Violin became the queen of all the instruments, outstripping her elder sister, the sombre and heavy Viola. Her fame was borne by virtuosi throughout the length and breadth of Europe, and violin-making soared to heights barely rivalled before in any branch of instrument-making. The cooler, more reserved members of the Viola da gamba family were quickly left behind, and even in ensemble playing the leadership passed to the instruments of the Viola da braccio type. As early as the first half of the seventeenth century, there existed in Italy pure string ensembles composed of members of the Violin family, which were to form the nucleus of all later orchestras.

The same tendency towards expressiveness and tenderness had its effect on the wind instruments. The rigid double reeds enclosed in a wind-chamber, with their inability to register any dynamic shades, disappeared without leaving a trace. Only the Bassoon and the Shawm, reborn as the Oboe, survived: instruments whose reeds were unconfined, and were now held between the performer's lips in order to soften their tone. At the close of the century there were added to the wind band its two noblest singers, the darlings of the later Romantics, the Clarinet and the French Horn.

The Baroque period displayed an increased interest not only in the use of tone-colour in music, in contrasts between light and dark, high and low, thunderous threat and tender animation, but also in dynamic contrasts. The alternation of forte and piano was now widely used as an aid to expression. New, graduated dynamics, based on the principle of contrasted effects, and dependent not merely on

PLATE XXX

Alphorn, sounded on the Rhone Glacier (Switzerland) in 1937

PLATE XXXI

Allegory of Hearing. By Jan Brueghel. A.D. 1618. Madrid, Prado

The musicians in the background on the left play on a Bass-Viola da gamba, Lute and Transverse Flute. In the foreground (from left to right): Positive-Organ, Harpsichord, Bass Trombone, Kettledrum, three Viole da gamba of different sizes, Mandola, Pochette, Flute-case, Violino Piccolo, Bent Cornetto, Shawm, Lira da braccio, Violin, Bass Cornetto, Viola, Recorder, Straight Cornetto. On the right of the Lute player are different kinds of Horns. The painting on the wall at the right shows Orpheus surrounded by animals.

the actual nature of the instrument, but also on the personal control of the performer, won increasing favour, and the instrument-makers took this tendency into account.

First half of the Eighteenth Century

In the eighteenth century this was carried still further by the introduction of transitions between the rigid dynamic contrasts. Before the Mannheim school had developed its celebrated orchestral crescendo, contrivances for producing a crescendo and diminuendo were introduced into the Organ, which by its very nature seemed unfitted to them. Even to the Harpsichord, where any swelling of the tone was impossible, a device was added which facilitated the execution of dynamic transitions.

The early eighteenth century also showed an increasing tendency towards individual expression. The softer, the tenderer its tone, the more highly an instrument was cherished. The new and gentler sister of the vigorous Oboe was known as the Oboe d'amore, and a stringed instrument provided with sympathetic resonance-strings was called the Viola d'amore. Even the long-forgotten Tromba Marina was resurrected, since its harmonics appealed to the sensibilities of the tender age.

The pastoral poetry of the eighteenth century Rococo period also left its traces in our instruments. The nation which produced a Watteau and a Lancret sought for the means of expressing the new pastoral mood in music, and found it in the Hurdy-gurdy and the Bagpipe. The principle of the constantly sounding bass drone, the very thing for which these instruments had been discarded by the Renaissance, now rendered them highly suitable for the expression of pastoral sentiment.

The fundamental change in the aesthetic outlook was naturally the cause of corresponding changes in all the instruments of the high and late Renaissance. These changes we must now consider.

Viola da Gamba

As we have already seen, the subdued, silvery and slightly nasal tone of the *Viola da gamba* family told against it in the contest with Violin and Viola. After the middle of the seventeenth century the only member of the family to retain any real importance was the prototype, the Bass-Viola da gamba (tuned in D,G,c,e,a,d^1), while the higher and the lower members (Pl. XXXI), with the exception of the little *Pardessus de Viole*, a favourite in France, suffered a decline. This Bass Viol (Pls. XXXI, XXXII) still enjoyed a certain popularity during the seventeenth century. In England and Germany, and above all in France, it was cultivated by the virtuosi, who, among other things, added a seventh string at the lower end of the range, and for greater ease of playing contrived a flatter neck (Pl. XXXV). These small improvements, however, were not sufficient to preserve the instrument from decline. In the eighteenth century it became increasingly rare; and when in 1787 there occurred the death of Carl Friedrich Abel, the last of the Viol virtuosi, the Viola da gamba—in the words of Gerber, the great eighteenth-century lexicographer—was buried with him.

Viola Bastarda Lyro-Viol

A variant of the Bass Viol was the *Viola bastarda*, which had, in addition to the longitudinal sound-holes of the Viol, the rose of the plucked instruments. According to tradition, this instrument, known in England as the

Lyro-Viol, was provided by Daniel Farrant, at the beginning of the seventeenth century, with a characteristic of Oriental, and particularly of Indian stringed instruments: resonance-strings of fine wire were stretched beneath the finger-board, where they sounded sympathetically as soon as a note was produced by the bow on the strings proper which contained among its harmonics the note to which the resonance-string was tuned. This delicate ethereal accompaniment, which lent a peculiar charm to the tone of the instrument, was further heightened by the rose pierced in the table.

Though the resonance-strings of the Viola bastarda were soon discarded, they were more successfully adopted by two other related instruments.

Baryton

The *Baryton*, or *Viola di bordone* (Pl. XLV), was a seventeenth and eighteenth-century form of the Viola bastarda, tuned like the Bass Viol and built in a fantastic shape. The neck was gouged out at the back, so that not only did the resonance-strings sound in sympathy in the usual way, but they could also be plucked by the thumb of the performer's left hand. This "pizzicato" and "arco" had to be played simultaneously, which did not improve the grip of the left hand. The extreme difficulty of performance which resulted was enough to prevent any considerable distribution of the instrument.

Viola d'Amore

The alto of the Viola bastarda was the *Viola d'amore* (Pl. XXXIII), invented, according to tradition, in England in the middle of the seventeenth century. This instrument, which, like the Baryton, was frequently made with a highly fantastic contour, had five to seven strings proper (usually tuned $d, f\#, a, d^1, f\#^1, a^1, d^2$), together with an equal number of resonance-strings. The soft vibrations of the sympathetic strings gave a peculiarly affecting quality to the tone, which made the instrument a particular favourite during the eighteenth century. Vivaldi wrote a concerto for it; Bach employed it several times in his works; and even in Mozart's day there still existed a celebrated virtuoso in the person of Karl Stamitz, who died in 1801.

Violino Piccolo

The Viola da braccio family started the seventeenth century with five members. Of these the smallest, the *Quartgeige* or *Violino piccolo* was of relatively small importance (Pl. XXXI). With improved execution in the high positions of the Violin, the need for this little instrument, with its feeble tone, disappeared. In 1756 Leopold Mozart, in his *Violinschule*, rightly described the Violino piccolo as having been superseded.

Violin, Viola, Violoncello

The *Violin* (Pl. XXXIV), *Viola*, and *Violoncello* (Pl. XXXIV) were now the chief members of the family. But even these were not equally valued. For since the Viola was made a little too small for its depth (so that it could be played on the shoulder) its tone was not perfectly free; and since the Violoncello suffered from the competition of the Bass Viol, the Violin was regarded as the leader of the family.

Double-Bass

The *Gross-Quint-Bass*, Contrabass, or Double-bass, was in a sense an alien in the Viola da braccio family. Its shape underwent considerable variations. In Italy it was built more to resemble the Violin, while outside the Peninsula, especially in Germany, it assumed certain features of the Viola da gamba. There was as little uniformity in the stringing. Five strings were certainly the rule, but there were also instruments with six, more often with four, and sometimes even with three strings.

(For the tuning of the different Viole da braccio, see pages 239–40.)

Stringed-Instrument Makers

During the sixteenth century the stringed instruments had for the most part attained their final classic form. As their form met every need, the development of details could begin, while the essentials of their construction remained unaltered. The makers of the period strove to augment the tonal and aesthetic beauty of the various instruments by the selection of woods and varnishes, and by minute readjustments of the proportions, of a nature perceptible only to experts.

In consequence of an unbroken workshop tradition, and favoured by a lively demand—especially from France—certain towns of Italy and the neighbouring Tyrol succeeded in achieving supremacy in the making of stringed instruments. Although stringed instruments of every type were built by the masters of this school, their main object of endeavour was the improvement and ennoblement of the "queen of all instruments," the Violin. The first important centre of violin-making was *Brescia*; its oldest eminent master was Gasparo Bertolotti da Salò (1540–1609).

The very few examples of his work that have come down to us are still somewhat old-fashioned in detail, but they none the less show the typical shape, which was later to become the norm. Bertolotti's pupil was Giovanni Paolo Maggini (1580–1632), in whose person the Brescia school reached its zenith. Following at first in the footsteps of his master, he afterwards built his own type, notable for the height of the table vaulting. Maggini's violins are greatly treasured by contemporary collectors for the beauty of their workmanship, although their tone, with its somewhat meagre carrying-power, is not quite satisfactory.

After the middle of the seventeenth century the leadership passed from Brescia to *Cremona*. The founder of the Cremona school was Andrea Amati (1535 to after 1611), the first of the celebrated family. He left his workshop to his two sons, Antonio and Girolamo, and these were followed by Nicola, Girolamo's son, the most eminent member of the family. The violins of the Amatis have a tone of astonishing sweetness and inimitable softness. The beauty of their voice was regarded as unsurpassable in the seventeenth and eighteenth centuries, and it was not until the nineteenth century that a preference was shown for the more powerful instruments of Nicola's greatest pupil, Antonio Stradivari (1644–1737). This "master of all masters," the greatest violin-maker of all time, constructed, after decades of research, a larger, flatter type, which, although it is not inferior to the violins of the Amatis in tenderness, far exceeds them in volume and fullness of tone. The precise and careful workmanship of these violins is no less remarkable than their musical qualities: Stradivarius violins remain to this day the utterly unrivalled ideals of tonal and aesthetic perfection. The third master of the Cremona school, and again the most important member of a large family of violin-makers, was Giuseppe Guarneri (1687–1742), called *Del Gesù*, after the Eucharistic sign IHS with which he marked his violins. His instruments are less regularly built, but the tone is always particularly beautiful. The greatness of this remarkable artist—round whose life a host of legends has been woven—was not recognized until long after his death, and then by the daemonic Paganini, a congenial spirit. Under Stradivari's pupils and successors the significance of Cremona as a violin-making centre gradually declined.

The only non-Italian school which, at least for a time, was able to rival the Italian schools, was situated in the neighbouring *Tyrol*. It owed its fame to the work of the gifted Jakob Stainer (1621–81), who had a strong understanding of the taste of his age. His instruments had a highly vaulted table, and their tone was unusually sweet, tender and flute-like. During the seventeenth and eighteenth centuries they enjoyed a quite extraordinary vogue, and amateurs paid even higher prices for them than for those of Stradivari.

After these leading schools there came a whole series of French, English, American and German workshops, which were all more or less dependent on the traditions of the great Italian schools, but never equalled their models.

In addition to the members of the Violin family already described, the Baroque and Rococo periods saw a series of other instruments of related construction, but varying in size and tuning. For the most part these were short-lived and of little more than local importance.

Quinton

In France, during the first half of the eighteenth century, an instrument called the *Quinton* was made, a five-stringed Violin, tuned g, d^1, a^1, d^2, g^2.

Viola Pomposa

About the same time there appeared in Germany a tenor instrument called the *Viola pomposa*, some 30 to 32 inches in length and tuned d, g, d^1, g^1, c^2. In performance it was held neither under the chin, as the Viola and Violin, nor between the legs, as the 'Cello, but leaning against the left upper arm.

Violoncello Piccolo

Rather larger than this was the *Violoncello piccolo*, provided with five strings, tuned C, G, d, a, e^1, and held between the legs. J. S. Bach composed for this instrument, and may even have had something to do with its development.

Viola da Spalla

The *Viola da spalla* was a bass instrument of smallish size, "fastened to the breast with a strap." (Eisel, 1788).

Bassett

Almost as rare as these types was the true bass of the Viola da braccio family, known as the *Bassett*, or *Basso di camera*, which was provided with five or six strings, and in size came between the Violoncello and the Double-bass.

Pochette or Kit

In the Baroque and Rococo periods the Violin and the Viola da gamba assumed a position of such prominence that the other bowed instruments of the Renaissance—for example, the Lira da braccio (Pls. XX, XXXI) or the

PLATE XXXII

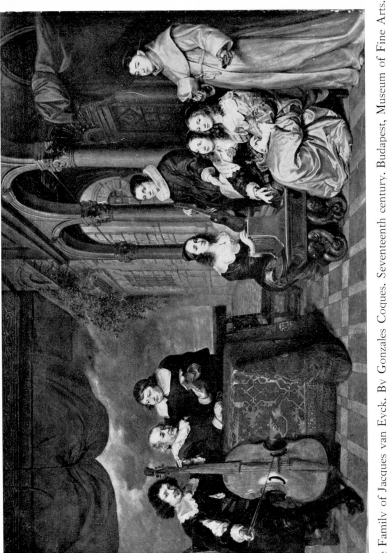

The Family of Jacques van Eyck. By Gonzales Coques. Seventeenth century. Budapest, Museum of Fine Arts. Bass Viola da gamba, Positive and Guitar

PLATE XXXIII

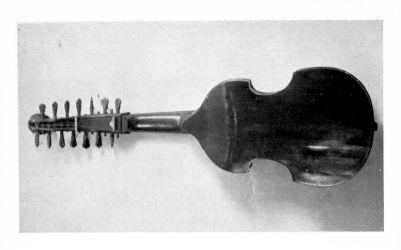

Front and back view of a *Viola d'amore*

Lute-Vielle—were thrust quite into the background. The Rebec alone—although not used in serious music—was still able to play a certain part. In a small, club-shaped form (Pls. XXXI; XXXVI, 1), and sometimes, in the eighteenth century, in the form of a miniature violin, with three to four strings, tuned to (c^1), g^1, d^2, a^2, it was used by dancing-masters to indicate the rhythm and melody of the dance for their pupils. Goethe tells us, in his *Dichtung und Wahrheit*, that as a young student in Strasbourg, he learned to dance the minuet to the strains of this little instrument. Accordingly, the Rebec was known at this time as *Tanzmeistergeige* ("Dancing-master's fiddle"), or since it was preferably carried in the pocket, as a *Pochette*. The English name, *Kit*, is possibly derived from "Kithara." It was at times made of precious materials, such as rose-wood, ivory or tortoiseshell, and decorated with gems and pearls. In the Rococo period the Pochette was sometimes built in so eccentric a fashion that the bow could be tucked away inside the instrument, and not only the bow, but even a fan or the like.

Hurdy-Gurdy

In the Rococo period—as we have recorded—the *Hurdy-gurdy* (French *Vielle*, Italian *Lira*, German *Rad-leier*) was the subject of a certain revival. Instruments were fitted with sympathetic resonance-strings, and a little organ attachment was built into the Hurdy-gurdy, where the keys not only shortened the strings, but simultaneously admitted air to the tiny pipes, while the wheel, besides acting as a bow, served also to work bellows. But much more common than these ingenious devices was the ordinary Hurdy-gurdy with three to six strings, of which two at least acted as drones (Pl. XXXVII, 2). It was the favourite instrument of the nobility which indulged in the sentimental dream of leading a pastoral life.

Tromba Marina

Yet another stringed instrument which had enjoyed the esteem of the Middle Ages was granted a temporary popularity in the seventeenth century, and more especially in the eighteenth. This was the *Tromba Marina*, which was now made in a larger and heavier form, so that it could no longer be held in the air, but had to be set on the ground (Pl. XXXVI, 2). Its body was built up of several pieces of wood, and the peg-box was similar to that of a Double-bass. In order to enhance the ethereal effect of its harmonics this instrument also was sometimes provided with sympathetic strings, which were fitted inside the body. According to J. S. Petri, the Tromba Marina was employed "in nunneries, where they had no trumpeters." However, this curious instrument, although it had come into fashion again, was very little employed in serious music. As the sentimental spirit of the period declined it disappeared anew, this time for ever.

Cittern

As with the bowed progeny of the Fiedel, so with the plucked offspring, the *Cittern*, a name which in England had during the Renaissance taken the place of the earlier Citole, the more efficient peg-box of the Violins was finally victorious in the seventeenth century, while the peculiar mixed position of the pegs used during the sixteenth century disappeared. In addition to the parent instrument (Pl. XXXIX), in which a set of nine strings of varying pitch was usual, there were several variants.

Small English Cittern

As early as 1618 Praetorius recorded: "About three years ago an Englishman came to Germany with a very small Cither, in which the lower part of the back was left half open and unglued." This little English Cittern had eight strings in four *courses* (strings tuned to the same note), being tuned in *a*, *g*, d^1, e^1. In Germany, too, towards the end of the seventeenth century, a special type of the Cittern was evolved. This was the Hamburg *Cithrinchen* with a bell-shaped outline and ten strings in five courses.

Bass Cittern

In addition to these small Citterns, the Baroque period, in its love of the extreme, and stimulated by the need for very low bass instruments capable of sounding chords, produced *Bass Citterns* (French *Archicistre*, Italian *Arcicetera*, German *Erzcister*). These were equipped with a large number of *diapasons* (bass strings not running over the finger-board) which had their own peg-box placed above the peg-box of the melody strings. In these instruments the number of strings and the tuning were subject to great variation. It should be noted that the Baroque period, which in other respects also shows a certain kinship to the Middle Ages, was reverting to the mediaeval practice in the adoption of drone strings.

Guitar and Chitarra Battente

The *Guitar* (Pls. XXXII, XXXIV) retained the set of five pairs of gut strings, tuned *A*, *d*, *g*, *b*, e^1, which was evolved in the sixteenth century, unchanged until the first half of the eighteenth century. In one point, however, it underwent a remarkable change. While the other stringed instruments were adopting the more efficient peg-box with pegs parallel to the plane of the table, the Guitar, which had adopted this arrangement from the beginning, changed over in the seventeenth century to the long obsolete arrangement in which the pegs were at right angles to the table. This change is in some degree intelligible if we consider a near relative of the instrument, which first made its appearance in the seventeenth century, though some of its features were quite surprisingly primitive for that period. This instrument, which in Italy was known as the *Chitarra battente*, and in Spain as the *Vihuela de peñola*, reveals its originally close relationship to the Fiedel more plainly than the Guitar. The *Chitarra battente* (Pl. XXXVII, 1) retained the vaulted back of the mediaeval Fiedel, which it combined with the straight ribs of the ordinary guitar. As in the Fiedel, the strings were led over the whole length of the table, to the lower edge of the body, and the pegs were at right angles to the plane of the table. A slight sloping away of the table at its lower end, and the adoption of five courses of strings, which were plucked in the mediaeval fashion with a plectrum, were the remaining features of this atavistic instrument. In Southern Italy and in Spain the *Chitarra battente* enjoyed such popularity that the Guitar could not withstand its influence, and imitated it in the position of its pegs.

Lute

The *Lute* (Pl. XXXI) of the seventeenth and eighteenth centuries lost much of the high esteem which it enjoyed during the Renaissance. In order to adapt the instrument to the requirements of the Baroque period the six main pairs of strings were supplemented by further strings in the bass; yet even these did not enable the Lute to hold its own against the deeper Archlutes, especially the Theorbo (see below). Moreover, the large number of strings, for whose tuning there were no fixed rules, gave rise to many inconveniences; so that J. Mattheson wrote in 1713 (*Neu-Eröffnetes Orchester*): "If a Lutenist reaches the age of eighty he has assuredly tuned his Lute for sixty years . . . and yet now there is trouble with the strings, now with the frets, now with the pegs, so that I have been told that in Paris it costs as much to keep a Lute as to keep a horse." Shortly after these words had been written the Lute became a thing of the past; and it speaks well for its former importance that even in its last years it found a biographer. In 1727 appeared E. G. Baron's *Untersuchung des Instruments der Lauten* (Treatise of the Lute), a work which endeavoured to plead the cause of the Lute, but was really no more than its obituary.

Archlute

The bigger types of Lutes, the great *Archlutes*, which were being made as early as the sixteenth century (though it was only in the seventeenth century that they won a position of importance), were better able to satisfy the Baroque demand for instruments capable of giving a bass accompaniment. These Archlutes, which occur in various forms, always possessed—like the Bass Citherns—in addition to the ordinary head for the finger-board strings, a second head or peg-box for the diapason strings (not stopped with the fingers) which ran beside the finger-board. The deeper strings were longer than the higher, and there was no need to stretch them as laxly as in the Lute, so that the tone of the instrument was improved. Several different types of the Archlute were employed.

Theorbo-Lute

The *Theorbo-Lute* (Pls. XXXIV, XXXIX) retained the body, neck and reverted head of the Lute, and placed the additional peg-box beside the main head; sometimes parallel with this and sometimes in the plane of the neck.

Theorbo

The (*Paduan*) *Theorbo*, unlike the Lute, had the main head only slightly reverted; the second peg-box, also slightly reverted, was joined to the first by a short connecting-piece. In the seventeenth century the strings were generally single; in the eighteenth they were usually paired.

Chitarrone

The (*Roman*) *Chitarrone* (Pl. XXXVIII, 1) reduced the size of the body, but increased the length of the bridge-piece connecting the two peg-boxes; the total length of the instrument was from 5 to 6 feet. Besides these instruments, which in the Baroque period were very frequently employed,

Angelica

the *Angelica* was of subordinate importance. This was a kind of Theorbo whose seventeen strings were diatonically tuned, as in the Harp, which made it easier for dilettante musicians to play.

Mandola

The *Mandola* (Pl. XXXI), which seems very small compared with the preceding giants of the instrumental world, was known in the seventeenth century by all sorts of diminutive names: *Pandurina, Mandurina, Mandürchen, Mandoline*, etc. It was made with the characteristic reverted or gently backward-curving head, and had at first five or six pairs of strings, which were afterwards replaced by single strings.

Mandoline

Besides this instrument, which, in order to avoid confusion, we shall continue to call the Mandola, there was in Italy a related instrument, the *Mandoline* proper. Its relation to the Mandola is like that of the Chitarra battente to the Guitar. In the Mandoline also the table slopes away at the lower end, the wire strings are carried over a bridge to the lower end of the body, and are tuned by pegs at right angles to the plane of the table. It is a stringed instrument with all the marks of great antiquity, which must have been employed for centuries past in Italian folk-music, and which only in the seventeenth century was brought to the knowledge of the rest of Europe. The great antiquity of the instrument is confirmed by the method of playing it. The strings of the Mandoline are set in vibration in the Oriental manner, by a plectrum, to which a constant vibratory movement is imparted.

The Mandoline was fitted, in various parts of Italy, with four, five or even six courses of strings. In the eighteenth century the Neapolitan Mandoline came to the fore; with its four pairs of strings, tuned as in the Violin, it was the only plucked instrument which was capable of performing music written for this highly esteemed instrument. Outside Italy the Mandoline was hardly ever met with until after the middle of the eighteenth century.

Mandolone

It is not surprising that the musicians of the period added a bass instrument to the little Mandoline. This was the *Mandolone*, which in the eighteenth century was sometimes made with seven or eight courses of paired strings.

Colascione

Italy was also the home of the *Colascione*, a Lute of Asiatic origin, with a small body, a very long neck, a reverted head and five or six courses of strings. This instrument had its period of popularity in the seventeenth century. In the eighteenth century it was discarded by serious musicians in its native Italy, though in northern countries it was still occasionally used as a bass instrument, owing to its depth of tone.

Harp

As regards the *Harp*, the principal aim of the Baroque period was to enable it to play the chromatic semitones which had long ago been produced by all the other stringed instruments. The most immediate solution was provided

Chromatic Harp

by the *Chromatic Harp*, which had a separate string for each note of the chromatic scale. Praetorius mentions an instrument so constructed, and even in the nineteenth century attempts were still being made to perfect the system, though the great number of strings required makes such Harps very cumbersome, and unlikely to survive. More successful than the Chromatic Harp was the *Hakenharfe*

PLATE XXXIV

A group of musicians. By David Ryckaert III. Seventeenth century. Vienna, Czernin Gallery

The musicians play (from left to right) on: Guitar, Violin, Recorder, Theorbo-Lute, Violoncello, Cornetto and Spinet

PLATE XXXV

La Barre and musicians of the French Court. Attributed to Robert
Tournières. *Ca.* 1705–15. London, National Gallery

Seven-stringed Bass Viola da Gamba and three Transverse Flutes, one-keyed and made
in three sections. The principal figure was formerly wrongly identified as Lully. According to Tiersot, the seated flautists are probably the brothers Piesche, and the gambist is
either Forqueray or Marais.

Hakenharfe

(Pl. XXXVIII, 2), *Hooked Harp*, *Harpe à crochets*, invented in the Tyrol, in the second half of the seventeenth century. On the neck of a diatonically tuned Harp a varying number of pivoted hooks were attached, which, being pressed against the strings, shortened them sufficiently to raise the pitch by a semitone. As a popular instrument the Hakenharfe is still in use to-day—notably in Czechoslovakia.

Pedal Harp

The difficulty arising from the fact that the harpist, in order to alter the pitch, had to cease playing with one hand, was solved by the invention (in Germany, about 1720) of the *Pedal Harp*. By a fortunate inspiration, all the hooks which served to raise the pitch of the same note in the different octaves were attached to a common mechanism, actuated not by the player's hands, but by his feet. With the help of seven pedals, which could be fixed in their depressed position, it was now possible to raise all the notes of the diatonic scale by a semitone.

Like the Renaissance, the Baroque period set its own aesthetic stamp upon the Harp. The front pillar took the form of a classical column, supporting a heavy volute which constituted the end of the neck. The Harp, which was often gilt, became more massive and imposing.

Pointed Harp

The Psaltery, which was plucked with the finger, made its appearance, in the seventeenth and eighteenth century, in a more efficient variant, known as the *Pointed Harp*

(Italian *Arpanetta*, German *Spitzharfe*). This instrument has the form of a wing, and possesses a sound-box placed between two ranks of strings. On one side of the sound-board are the high strings, which are of steel, and on the other the low strings, which are of brass. The player stands the Pointed Harp on the table, or rests it on his knees. With one hand he plays the melody on the front of the instrument; with the other he plays the accompaniment on the farther side.

Dulcimer

The *Dulcimer* (German *Hackbrett*) (Pl. XXXVI, 1), in which the strings were struck with mallets, was not rarely encountered in the Baroque period. Although in this instrument each course consisted of two, three, four or even more strings, an ingenious arrangement made it possible to include strings yielding all the chromatic tones within a comparatively small space. At the beginning of the eighteenth century the Dulcimer was improved by Pantaleon Hebenstreit, who built a larger and more sonorous instrument, with strings of gut and wire, which covered from four to five octaves. This was known as the *Pantaleon*. Even Hebenstreit's improvement could not raise the instrument to a position of real significance. Apart from other defects, the prolonged reverberation of the strings made the execution of rapid passages impossible; and in the comparatively lightly-built instrument it was difficult to keep such a very large number of strings (and there might be up to 100) correctly tuned.

Zither

A relative of the Psaltery and the Dulcimer is the *Zither*, the interpreter of folk-music. This instrument, whose ancestors may be found in Asia Minor, occurs in the Alpine regions of Central Europe (German *Scheitholz*), and also in Scandinavia (Swedish *Hummel*, Norwegian *Langleih*, Danish *Humle*) and Holland (*Hommel*). It consists of a straight and narrow, or sometimes curved, body; of the strings some (the "violin" strings) run over frets, while others are diapason strings, which are not stopped. They are plucked with the thumb and fingers of the right hand, or with a plectrum. During the Baroque and Rococo periods this popular instrument was gradually enlarged and equipped with an ever-increasing number of strings. As it became more efficient, it was naturally more highly esteemed, and in the Alpine regions of Central Europe music and dancing are unthinkable without the Zither.

Of the Psaltery-like instruments, those that enjoyed the highest esteem in the seventeenth century, and the first half of the eighteenth, were provided with a keyboard.

Clavichord

The *Clavichord* (Pl. XLII, 1) was essentially an instrument for the private house. It was the solo instrument for small rooms; and it was also the instrument which gave the performer the most immediate control over the tone. Even the *vibrato*, which was otherwise restricted to the bowed instruments, could be produced by a quiver of the fingers resting on the keys. The Clavichord was therefore the instrument which was most in accordance with the subjective temper of the age. It was the favourite instrument of the emotional Philipp Emanuel Bach, and Schubart said of it: "He whose heart is often fain to find relief in tender sentiment will choose the Clavichord."

Technically, the instrument underwent a trifling yet characteristic transformation towards the end of the seventeenth century. Since in view of the continually increasing compass of the instrument it was desirable that the chromatic semitones should be available even in the lowest octave, and since, on the other hand, the performer was unwilling to relinquish the familiar device of the "short octave," the F♯ and G♯ keys in the lowest octave were "broken," as in the Organ. Their upper (longer) halves now gave F♯ and G♯, their lower (shorter) halves D and E as before. Not until the eighteenth century was this curious expedient of the "short" and "broken" octave discarded and finally abandoned.

In the Rococo period the Clavichord underwent a second and much more important transformation. Since the system of the fretted (*gebunden*) Clavichord made it in many cases impossible to play simultaneously notes lying close together, and since the new developments of harmony called for the removal of this restriction, in the early years of the eighteenth century "fret-free" (*Bund-frei*) Clavichords were constructed, in which every key had its own course of strings. Many performers, however, continued to prefer the small, light and more easily tuned older instrument, so that the new improvement was not universally adopted.

Harpsichord

The *Harpsichord* (Pl. XXXI) offers the strongest contrast to the Clavichord. Its more brilliant and powerful tone made it the instrument for large music-rooms and the theatre. It was the most important instrument for the execution of the figured bass, and was indispensable for the performance of orchestral music. The composer of the Baroque period conducted his work from the Harpsichord.

It is true that the tone of the instrument is not flexible

and capable of modulation, like that of the Clavichord. The direct transmission of emotion through the keys to the strings is impossible in the Harpsichord; on the other hand, thanks to its high technical development, it is capable of producing a number of dynamic and tonal contrasts. The Harpsichord of the Baroque period has a robuster tone than the instrument of the Renaissance; it has a greater compass, and sometimes also a greater number of stops or registers. Besides the 4' it has one or two 8' stops, and sometimes even a 16', and a Lute pedal (which presses felt or leather dampers against the strings, so that the tone is muted and like that of a Lute). These stops can be employed singly, or combined at will. Moreover, with the two-manual instrument one keyboard can operate the high stops, and the other the low; one can produce loud notes and the other soft. The musician, therefore, by playing alternately on the two manuals, or by playing with one hand on the upper manual and the other on the lower, or by coupling the two keyboards so that all the registers sound together, has a whole range of dynamic gradations at his command.

Spinet and Virginal

The *Spinet* (Pl. XXXIV) may be likened to a small, compact and delicate Harpsichord. It had, as an almost invariable rule, only one register in 4' or 8' tone, and one manual. As compared with the Harpsichord it had the advantage of being cheaper to produce and more easily moved about. At the same time, it was louder than the Clavichord, so that it could be employed not only as a solo instrument, but also in chamber music. It was therefore hardly less popular than the other two keyboard instruments of the period.

Until late in the seventeenth century the terms "Virginal" and "Spinet" were used without discrimination in different countries. Then both were employed in England to denote different types of instrument, the *Virginal* having a transversely oblong rectangular case (Pl. XL), and the *Spinet*, as then made in England, being approximately triangular, or wing-shaped, owing to the case being extended on the right of the keyboard, to accommodate the bass strings (Pl. XLI).

Wind Instruments. Oboe

Among the wind instruments of the Baroque period the *Oboe* played an especially important part. It came into being during the seventeenth century—above all, in France —as an improvement of the Shawm (Pl. XXXI). While the Shawm was a crudely made instrument with a wide conical bore, the Oboe is much more carefully constructed, and its bore is narrower. It has not the shrill, bleating tone of the older instrument; it is softer and more delicate. Above all, the old cup-shaped connection between the mouthpiece and the instrument (Pl. XXXI) has been discarded, so that the reed is not taken right into the mouth, but is held between the lips. The player is therefore able to exert a certain control over the strength and quality of the tone, and overblowing becomes possible. The oldest Oboe was provided with only six finger-holes, of which two, producing semitones, were doubled; it also had three keys. Of these one was characteristically provided with a "swallow-tail" lever, while the others were situated opposite each other, so as to be used by either the right or the left hand, for it was as yet a matter of choice which of the player's hands would be the lower.

The new instrument quickly became popular. In 1659

Cambert prescribed its use in his opera, *Pomone*, and before long it was the favourite wind instrument of the Baroque period. It was played in conjunction with the Violin, or as a solo instrument, and hardly any other wind instrument was more frequently employed.

Oboe d'Amore

A typical creation of this age of "sensibility" was the *Oboe d'amore* (French *Hautbois d'amour*, German *Liebesoboe*), which appeared during the first half of the eighteenth century. It was somewhat larger than the Oboe, and a third lower. But above all, it had a pear-shaped bell, instead of the ordinary funnel-shape, and this gave the instrument a softer and mellower tone. In 1722 this instrument was employed by Telemann. In the following year J. S. Bach prescribed its use for the first time, and thenceforth the Oboe d'amore was among the favourite instruments of the Leipzig master, who was led to employ it frequently on account of its mellow and intimate tone.

Alto Oboe, Oboe da Caccia

As the Oboe originated in the Shawm, so in the seventeenth century the Alto Bombard, by a process of refinement, became the *Alto Oboe* (Pl. XLII, 2). The age of "sensibility" gave it the pear-shaped bell of the Oboe d'amore. The result was an instrument with a warm full tone, which was known by the not very suitable name of the *Oboe da caccia* (Huntsman's Oboe) (Pl. XLII, 2). According to Zedler's *Universal Lexikon* (1735) it was actually employed in the chase. But this use of the instrument cannot have been very frequent, for its tone was peaceful and anything but loud; indeed, Bach employed it for especially tender passages.

English Horn

As in the Oboe da caccia, which was 30 inches in length, the finger-holes lay at a considerable distance apart, the device was adopted, before the middle of the eighteenth century, of curving the instrument like a sickle (Pl. XLII, 2), or making it in two parts, joined together at an obtuse angle. A leather case was fitted over the parts to make the joint airtight. This new form also was given a pear-shaped or spherical bell. Perhaps because the deeper-toned Oboes were particularly valued in England—Henry Purcell, in 1690, prescribed the use of a "tenor hoboy" in his *Diocletian*—it became the custom to describe this new form as the *English Horn*. (It was doubtless called a "horn" with reference to its curved form.)

Bassoon

The natural bass of the Oboe family is the *Fagotto* or Bassoon, the immediate successor of the parent instrument of the family, the *Curtall Fagott*. In the seventeenth century the instrument consisted of two tubes, which were inserted in a small block of wood, the "butt." This was fitted with three keys, to which a fourth was added in the first half of the eighteenth century. The range of the instrument was then almost three octaves (B_1-g^1).

Together with the Oboe, in 1659 the Bassoon found its way into the operatic orchestra on the production of Cambert's *Pomone*. As the bass of the wood-wind, and also for reinforcing the bass strings, the instrument achieved a position of increasing importance. Among the first masters

PLATE XXXVI

2.—A player of the Tromba Marina. From Bonanni,
Gabinetto Armonico, 1722

1.—Two musicians playing on Pochette and Dulcimer.
By F. P. von der Schlichten. Seventeenth century

PLATE XXXVII

1.—Front and back view of a Chitarra Battente. Berlin, Hochschule für Musik

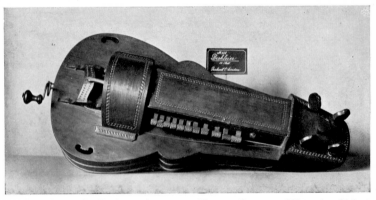

2.—Hurdy-gurdy. Eighteenth century. Vienna, Society of Friends of Music

to employ the Bassoon as a solo instrument was Handel, who in 1738, in his *Saul*, prescribed two bassoons, in order to symbolize the appearance of Samuel's ghost by their dull, hollow sound.

Contrabassoon or Double Bassoon

In its preference for sombre tones, the Baroque period created a Double Bassoon (Pl. XLIII, 1), an octave below the ordinary Bassoon. This was first made in 1620 by Hans Schreiber, in Berlin. Since on account of its great size it was troublesome to make, and since its intonation was not true, as the finger-holes were necessarily too small in proportion to the bore of the instrument, it did not attain to any great importance in practical music.

Musette

The great interest felt in France in the Oboe was extended to the Bagpipe. About the year 1610 a new kind of Bagpipe was evolved in France. The chanter was a gently-sounding Oboe, but with a narrow, cylindrical bore; while the drone was a kind of Rackett (cf. p. 133) about $6\frac{1}{2}$ inches in height, in which the bore ran up and down twelve times or more. The length and therefore the pitch of this drone could be altered. About the middle of the seventeenth century the famous maker of Flutes and Oboes, M. Hotteterre (who was also a virtuoso), added a second small, straight chanter for the highest notes. The instrument had now, although it was not overblown, a range of about two octaves (f^1–d^3). Since the supply of wind was reinforced by the use of a bellows which was compressed under the left arm, the *Musette*—as the instrument was called in France—had considerable possibilities. Lully did not hesitate to employ it in the operatic orchestra. And when the Rococo passion for pastoral poetry was at its height, the Musette became a fashionable instrument. Anyone who will examine the paintings of Lancret or Watteau will realize the part played by this instrument in the entertainment of the *noblesse*. As in the Middle Ages, the Bagpipes again became the favourite instruments of the aristocracy, and they were often decorated with tasteful magnificence.

Clarinet

The great wave of refinement, having dealt with the double-reed instruments, now reached the single-reed instruments. The origin of the *Clarinet* is controversial, but the following seems to be the most likely theory. In Western Europe a primitive Shawm or *Chalumeau* had been known from the earliest times: an instrument with cylindrical bore and a clarinet mouthpiece. The same instrument occurred in Germany, and also in Italy (*Zampogna*). In Central Europe someone hit upon the notion of adding the Chalumeau, with its single reed, to the number of serious musical instruments, as a rival to the double-reed pipe, the Shawm, which the French had improved. The transformation was mainly the work of the Nuremberg family of instrument-makers, the Denners. About 1690 Johann Christoph Denner provided his carefully elaborated instruments with two keys. His son, J. Denner, added the little hole near the "beak" which facilitated overblowing (it gave the note b^{b1}), and a third key. The new instrument was still called the Chalumeau, but also, on account of a certain tonal affinity with the highest register of the Trumpets, the *Clarino*, or more often still, the little Clarino, *Clarinetto*. It seems to have been employed first in Germany, especially in Hamburg. In 1711 Reinhard Keiser prescribed it in his *Croesus*; in 1713 Mattheson mentioned it. By 1720 it had reached Antwerp, where it was employed in a piece of Church music. But the triumphant progress of the Clarinet did not begin until the middle of the century was passed.

Recorder or Flûte-à-Bec

From the technical point of view, the *Recorder* or *Flûte-à-bec* (Pls. XXXI, XXXIV) did not undergo any essential alteration in the seventeenth and eighteenth centuries. After the middle of the seventeenth century the unpractical double finger-hole (the lowest hole) of the smaller forms was replaced by a single movable hole, the lower part of the tube being made to rotate, so that the performer could shift the little finger-hole to the position convenient to him. Moreover, at the beginning of the seventeenth century, the instrument was provided with four new keys for the lowest notes in the bass and contrabass forms. Two of these keys, strangely enough, were sometimes operated by means of pedals.

While the technical changes were inconsiderable, the aesthetic transformation of the instrument was more conspicuous. Until 1650 or thereabouts the instrument had the shape of a smooth, uncomplicated staff, as befitted the quiet, simple taste of the Renaissance (Pl. XLIII, 2). But after 1650 it assumed a shape which was obviously determined by Baroque canons of form (Pl. XLIII, 2). The tube left the lathe with expansions at either end, so that its form was made more imposing by a gracefully curved profile.

The fact that the Recorder did not undergo any further technical development may be attributed to the circumstance that it gradually went out of favour. It is true that of the eight sizes which Praetorius mentioned in 1618, three were still in use a century later: a Discant, with range f^1–f^3, an Alto, with range c^1–c^3, and a Bass, with range f–f^2. Nevertheless, Mattheson was not alone in considering—as he wrote in 1713—that one "could easily become weary and out of conceit" with the Recorder "on account of its gentle andsubdued character"; for the soft, equable tone of the Recorder could not satisfy the growing demand for subjective expression, for dynamic and tonal contrasts. Little by little it was ousted from its position, during the first half of the eighteenth century, by the Transverse Flute.

Flageolet

A variant of the Recorder is the (French) *Flageolet*, which owed its employment to the Baroque delight in extremely high notes. This instrument, which is said to have been invented by Juvigny, in Paris, at the close of the sixteenth century, was remarkable for the unusual position of its finger-holes, four being situated in the front and two at the back of the pipe. The compass of the instrument was g^2–a^4; and as a rule its parts were written one-twelfth lower than the actual tones. Under the name of *Flauto piccolo* Handel employed the instrument in *Rinaldo* and in *Acis and Galatea*; Bach also introduced it in his sacred cantatas Nos. 96 and 103.

Tabor-Pipe or One-Handed Flute

The Tabor-Pipe, which was played not only in conjunction with the Drum, but also, in the Basque Provinces of France, with a sort of Dulcimer, the *Tambourin du Béarn*, was given a younger brother in the seventeenth century, to satisfy the contemporary taste for very high registers. However, the instrument was no longer of any importance. In the eighteenth century it disappeared outside France and even more rapidly than the Recorder. Only in England did it continue for a time to lead a modest existence as a refugee.

Double Recorder

In the Baroque period both tubes of the *Double Recorder* were bored out of the same billet of wood, and the finger-holes were close together, so that each pair could be closed with a single finger. Since the width of the holes, the bore of the tubes, and the position of the flute in the block were different in each of the two instruments, it was possible to obtain an interval of a third between each pair of finger-holes. The Double Recorder was valued both in England and Switzerland. At the beginning of the eighteenth century an Englishman, Banister, was one of its most admired virtuosi; while Christian Schlegel of Basle was one of the best makers. Nevertheless, the Double Recorder was never of any general importance.

Transverse Flute

The increasing dissatisfaction with the Recorder made it necessary to look for a suitable substitute. This was found in the *Transverse Flute*, in which the act of blowing is less mechanized, and which therefore offers the possibilities of greater dynamic and tonal variety, as well as the easier production of harmonics by overblowing. Of course, the simple Flute of the Renaissance was far from adequate, and extensive modifications were necessary before it could play its part in serious music. Once more, it was in France that the transformation was effected (Pl. XXXV). In the second half of the seventeenth century the parent instrument—the Alt-Tenor of the Renaissance period—was divided into three parts: the head-joint, with the embouchure, the body, and the foot- or tail-joint. The head-joint was still cylindrical in its bore, while in the body and the tail-joint the bore was conical, the smallest diameter being at the open end, a device which enhanced the purity of the overblown harmonics. In addition to the six finger-holes there was a key for the little finger which gave D♯. In the first half of the eighteenth century the body was again divided in order to facilitate the correction of defects of intonation. After 1720 the foot- or tail-joint was also divided, and two further keys were added.

In 1677 Lully introduced the improved Transverse Flute in the orchestra of the opera. In 1713 Mattheson described it as "an instrument worthy of high esteem," and it says much for the increasing reputation of the Flute that a king, Frederick the Great of Prussia, was one of its most enthusiastic amateurs.

Church Organ

The *Church Organ* of the first half of the seventeenth century had reached a high standard of technical efficiency, and possessed a very definite musical individuality. Its technical perfection was due mainly to two achievements of the Renaissance period, the results of which became plainly apparent in the Organ of the seventeenth century. The first of these achievements related to the bellows. While in the older bellows there were many folds of leather, about the middle of the sixteenth century a new kind of bellows was introduced, which was made of wood, and contained only a single fold. The simpler and stronger construction of these bellows made it possible to provide for a more regular supply of wind, and consequently a more equable tone. Of course, the wind still reached the interior of the organ in puffs. This defect was first remedied when the air drawn into the bellows was stored in a reservoir, and only then conveyed to the pipes. Canon Galpin first noted such a reservoir in an English organ built in 1629.

Wind Gauge

A further step in advance was the invention of the *wind gauge*, by the German Christian Förner in 1667. This is a manometer-like device which makes it possible to measure the pressure of the air inside the bellows. A second important improvement in Organ construction was the ever-increasing employment of the more reliable slider sound-board as against the all too sensitive spring sound-board. As the slider sound-board and the spring sound-board are two of the fundamental components of the Organ, their function must now be explained.

Slider Sound-board and Spring Sound-board

The air pumped by the bellows passes through conduits into the undivided *wind-chest*, and from this to the *sound-board*, which contains a number of separate channels, the *grooves*. In the older form of the *spring sound-board* a special valve was fitted in the grooves for each individual pipe, whose function was to admit or interrupt the wind; but this arrangement was complicated and costly. In the newer form of the *slider sound-board*, in which each groove underlies all the pipes appertaining to a given key, the *sliders* (small boards working across the grooves and pierced with holes) admit the wind to the pipes or cut it

off. If a stop or register is to be cut out the solid portions
of the sliders close the pipes. When the register in question
is included again the slider is pulled out until the holes are
situated under the feet of the pipes, so that the wind can
enter the pipes unhindered when the key is depressed.
This arrangement is less expensive and less likely to break
down than the old form of spring sound-board, and during
the Baroque period it was universally adopted.

Organ of the late Renaissance

As regards its musical capabilities, until the first decade
of the seventeenth century the Organ was adapted above
all things to polyphonic music. Its individual registers were
clearly distinguishable one from another. They did not
merge or melt into one another. Dynamic contrasts could
be achieved only within certain restricted limits. The Organ
of the early seventeenth century could speak neither in
tones of thunder nor in ethereal whispers, and any sort of
crescendo or decrescendo was quite impossible. The tone
of the Organ was transparently clear and unromantic, in
accordance with the preference of the late Renaissance for
an unemotional and classical art.

Organ of the Baroque Period

During the seventeenth century and the first half of the
eighteenth this type of Organ was modified in the direction
of subjective expression and a more flexible and variable
tone. Some important stages in this process of development,
which even the Thirty Years War in Germany and the
wars of the Commonwealth in England were unable to
check, are here recorded.

PLATE XXXVIII

2.—Hooked Harp (Hakenharfe). Vienna, Society of Friends of Music

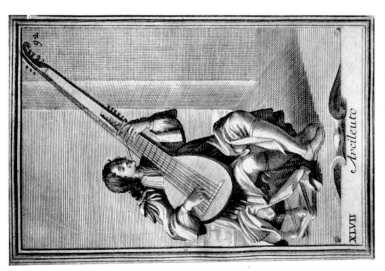

1.—A Chitarrone player. From Bonanni, *Gambinetto Armonico*, 1722

PLATE XXXIX

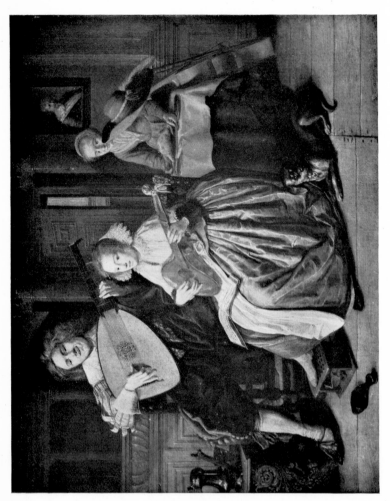

Musical Pastime. By Jan M. Molenaers. Seventeenth century. London, National Gallery

The man plays a Theorbo-lute, the woman a Cittern

Tremolo

Shortly after the year 1600 a breach was made in the traditional rigidity of the Organ's tone by the introduction of the tremolo. This is a device operating in the wind-channel, which gives the notes a tremulous, plaintive tone.

String Registers

The great interest taken in the stringed instruments during the seventeenth century led to the introduction of string registers. The colour of the narrow flue-pipes is denoted by such descriptive names as *Viola da gamba* or *Violin*. Indeed, the Organ even paid its tribute to the Baroque enthusiasm for the beauty of the human

Vox Humana

voice, inasmuch as it introduced the *Vox humana*, a reed-pipe which attempts to copy the tones of the human larynx. The Italians, who had always aimed at harmonious and colouristic effects in organ music, now took the initiative in the art of organ-building, by devising registers which were no longer clearly contrasted with one another, but became harmoniously interfused. The other musical countries of Europe followed their example to an ever-increasing extent, the more so as in the Baroque period the rôle of the Organ was by no means restricted to that of a solo instrument, but was equally important as an accompaniment to the voice and to orchestral music.

Couplers and Transmissions

Now, moreover, the employment of *couplers*, devices

for connecting the individual keyboards, together with the pipes controlled by them, became more general. Sometimes, also, by the help of *transmissions*, the pipes controlled by one manual could be brought into play by another. The combination of stops obtained by such means led to the increasing production of new tonal values, which did not very greatly differ from one another. The rigidity of tone which had characterized the Organ at the beginning of the seventeenth century was to a great extent overcome a century later by the wealth of these interpenetrating nuances. Moreover, devices were introduced which made it possible to produce a dynamic crescendo and diminuendo. As early as the seventeenth century individual

Swell

registers were enclosed in an echo-chamber, in which their tones were effectively damped, in order to produce the greatly appreciated echo effects. In 1712 Abraham Jordan, in London, devised a pedal attachment by which the front wall of the echo-chamber could be opened or closed while the organ was playing, so that a crescendo or diminuendo effect could be obtained.

But in the first half of the eighteenth century not only were the tonal and dynamic contrasts of the Organ softened, but also—which was equally important—the harmonic and tonal contrasts.

Equal Temperament

Shortly before 1700 Andreas Werckmeister declared that the introduction of equal temperament (cf. p. 27) was the urgent need of the day, and in the following decades this requirement was more and more generally observed in the construction of Organs. There was nothing to prevent the employment of any key and of any desired modulations on the "well-tempered" Organs of the day. The sensitive subjectivism of the day had effected a complete conquest of an instrument which had seemed wholly refractory.

Positive Organ

The more imposing were the dimensions of the great Organs erected in churches, the more marked was the difference of the smaller type of fixed *Positive Organ*, designed for use in chapel or music-room, or in ordinary living-rooms. These fixed organs, which were employed in accompaniment rather than as solo instruments, were generally built with only one manual, and without a pedal-board. The pipes were usually flue pipes in 4' and 2', or sometimes even in 1' tone. Positive Organs with registers of reed-pipes were accounted a rarity. This instrument, with its tender, gentle tone, was extremely popular in the Baroque period (Pls. XXXI, XXXII).

Portative Organ

Still smaller were the moveable Portative Organs, which were employed principally in processions. Nevertheless, they were generally provided with several registers, and were incomparably heavier and more elaborate than the Portative of the late Middle Ages and the beginning of the modern period, which was played by a single person. Two or more persons were needed to serve this larger Portative.

Regal

The Regal, which was usually constructed with only a single 8′ register of reed-pipes, was employed in the seventeenth century chiefly as an instrument for the execution of the thorough-bass. It was peculiarly fitted to accompany a choir of Trombones, on account of its powerful, snarling tone. As early as 1609 the instrument was put to this classic use in Monteverdi's *Orfeo*. But the sentimental eighteenth century took exception to the rigid, harsh and unaccommodating tone of the instrument, which Mattheson described, with characteristic bluntness, as "extremely loathsome." It did not survive beyond the middle of the century.

Trumpet

During the seventeenth century and the first half of the eighteenth, the art of the trumpeter remained on the same high level as that of which Praetorius spoke. Trumpet parts which go up to c^3, d^3, and e^3 occur in the compositions of the period, and Altenburg, who in 1795 wrote the history of the Trumpet, declared that even the g^3, which is the 24th harmonic, could be played. A trumpeter sufficiently expert to play such notes could produce not only tones and semitones, but even smaller intervals, merely with the help of his lips. However, the trumpeters of those days appear to have set certain limits to their competence, which resulted in a division of labour. The performer who played the highest parts, the "clarino-player," employed a rather shallower mouthpiece, which facilitated the production of the higher notes, and rarely descended into the lower register. The parts below the highest were taken by the "principal" trumpeter, who used a rather deeper mouthpiece, which was well adapted for the production of the lower notes, and only by exception ventured into the higher register. The extraordinary performances of the trumpeters, and above all of the "clarino player," made any special technical improvements of the instrument superfluous.

Although the players of the Baroque period preferred the Trumpet in D, gradually there arose a need for instruments built in other keys, so that Trumpets in B♭, C, D♭, E♭, etc., were sometimes made.

During the seventeenth century, and the first half of the eighteenth, the Trumpet maintained its inherited pride of place. It was employed always for special effects, on solemn and stately occasions, and on days of festival. When it appeared, as a matter of course it played the leading part. A *clarino* part written as an accompaniment was hardly conceivable.

Tromba da Tirarsi

The *Tromba da tirarsi* or Slide Trumpet and the *Corno da tirarsi* (Slide Horn) were sometimes prescribed in Bach's scores. The master was fond of employing them in the accompaniment of chorales when tones and semitones were to be played in the deeper octave (c^1-c^2), where the overblown harmonics lie far apart. In the early Slide Trumpet the mouthpiece was attached to a tube which the player could push into the body of the trumpet (Pls. XI, XII). With the help of this device, which was known in the late Middle Ages (cf. p. 106), every overblown note could be lowered by a semitone, a whole tone, or a tone and a half, so that it was possible to play the chromatic scale even in the octave c^1-c^2. What the precise difference was between the *Tromba da tirarsi* and the *Corno da tirarsi* is not certain. Very possibly they were identical.

Trombone

As with the Trumpet, so in the case of the *Trombone* family the Baroque period found it unnecessary to make any essential changes. At the beginning of the seventeenth century, to meet the need of the period for dark tone-colour, a Contrabass was added to the family, which was made with a slide in the bell-pipe. Its invention—according to Praetorius—is due to Hans Schreiber, a Berlin town musician. Neither the mighty Contrabass nor the little Discant survived in the general practice of that time. In the popular reinforcement of vocal choirs by means of Trombones, the Alto Trombone went with the contralto voice, the Tenor Trombone with the tenor voice, and the Bass Trombone (Pl. XXXI) with the bass voice, while the Discant devolved upon the Cornetto or the Slide Trumpet. Both the Discant and the Contrabass Trombones were generally superfluous.

French Horn

At the close of the seventeenth century the French, who had already developed the Oboe and the Transverse Flute, gave special attention to the coiled Huntsman's Horn (Pl. XXXI), which in the sixteenth century had been little regarded. They gave the instrument a slender, cylindrical, trumpet-like body, a funnel-shaped mouthpiece, and a wide bell. The new instrument (Pl. XLIV), the *Waldhorn* or *French Horn*, which was capable of sounding not only 8 to 9 overtones, as formerly, but as many as 18 to 20, was warm and tender in the *piano* passages, while the *forte* had a brilliant and pealing quality. It was soon widely distributed, both in France and in other countries. Before the seventeenth century was over it reached England (a French Horn by Bull, London, bears the date 1699), and was introduced into Germany by the Bohemian Count Sporck. In 1705 Reinhard Keiser employed it in Hamburg (in *Octavia*), in 1715 Alessandro Scarlatti used it in Naples (in *Tigrane*), and in the year 1717 Handel in London introduced it into his *Water Music*. The harmonic series of the Horn is the same as that of the Trumpet. Instruments in D and F are most frequent, but there are also Horns in C, E♭, E, G and A, and high and low B♭.

Cornett

The *Zink*, or *Cornett*, which in the seventeenth century and the first half of the eighteenth retained its Renaissance form unaltered (Pls. XXXI, XXXIV), was a favourite instrument of the Baroque period. Mersenne, writing in 1636, compared its sound to "un rayon de soleil qui paroist dans l'ombre"—a ray of sunshine piercing the darkness—and in the first half of the eighteenth century Roger North spoke of it in the most laudatory terms which the "age of sensibility" could frame: "Nothing," he said, "imitates so well an excellent voice." It has already been mentioned that the Cornett was frequently used as the treble of the Trombone choir, and as a reinforcement of the human voice.

Serpent

The *Serpent*, which, like the Cornett, underwent no technical transformation, was an especial favourite in France. ("Est hoc instrumentum valde usitatum in Gallia," wrote Athanasius Kircher in 1650). By overblowing, and with the help of six finger-holes, a range of $2\frac{1}{2}$ octaves and more could be covered by the Serpent, and Mersenne asserts that the instrument could equal the power of twenty of the loudest singers, and yet could be employed in the softest chamber-music. Handel, who first made the acquaintance of the Serpent in England, employed it in his *Water Music* (1717) and his *Firework Music* (1749).

Kettledrum

The *Kettledrum*, which in the first half of the seventeenth century was still predominantly the instrument of the German princes, began to make its way into the non-German countries, where composers gradually recognized is value for serious music. Lully was using the Kettledrum in France by 1670, and it often appears in the scores of Bach and Handel. In such music the Kettledrum was always employed in pairs, which were tuned to an interval of a fourth or a fifth. The larger instrument has usually a range of F-*c*, and the smaller of Bb–*f*. One Kettledrum is tuned in the tonic and the other in the dominant, and since the tuning-screws do not admit of a rapid change of pitch, this is usually left unaltered during the performance of a piece of music. Handel, in his *Firework Music* (1749), was one of the first composers to use three Kettledrums.

The social status of the Kettledrum, as the companion of the Trumpet, was still high during the Baroque period. Silver Kettledrums were not unknown, and they were sometimes hung with costly embroideries. Of course, it must not be overlooked that since the second half of the seventeenth century, quite apart from the use of the Kettledrum in serious music, there had always been performers who handled the instrument in a sportive and humorous manner. Such players accompanied their performance by acrobatic contortions of their hands and body; and in France and Germany we find that negro performers of the Kettledrum were all the rage. Here we seem to see a

PLATE XL

A lady at the Virginal. By Jan Vermeer. Seventeenth century. London,
National Gallery

At the side is a Bass Viola da Gamba

PLATE XLI

English Spinet, signed "Johannes Player Fecit". *Ca.* 1680. London, Victoria and Albert Museum

revival of the mediaeval connection between the musician and the acrobat or juggler.

Drum

The *Drum* of the seventeenth century resembles that of the Renaissance. Not until the eighteenth century were the dimensions of the instrument somewhat reduced. At the same time the wooden body was gradually replaced by a more durable brass shell; though this innovation did not become general until the middle of the century. Nor was the Drum immediately able to break away from its purely military employment and obtain a firm footing in serious music.

Tambourine

The *Tambourine*, regarded as a gypsies' instrument, was of no importance in the Baroque period.

Triangle

The *Triangle*, which Mersenne described as the attribute of the beggar, was in no better case.

Cymbals

Cymbals were introduced into opera in 1680 by Strungk of Dresden, and in 1703 and 1705 by Reinhard Keiser of Hamburg, who was an enthusiast for all innovations. At first, however, they were very rarely employed, their use being restricted to the evocation of exotic effects.

N

Castanets

The *Castanets* (Spanish *Castañeta*, from *castaña* = chestnut) bear a certain relationship to the Cymbals. They are pairs of small shell-shaped clappers, made of hard wood, or sometimes ivory, connected by a loop at the upper end. The player's thumb holds one half of the instrument, while the fingers strike the other half against it in short, dry, subtly rhythmical beats. The instrument is of Oriental origin, and extremely ancient. At a very early period it made its way into Spain and the culturally related regions of Southern Italy. Before long the Iberian peninsula had promoted the Castanets to the rank of the national instrument of the dance. Together with the Spanish dances it found its way into all parts of Europe. In the seventeenth century Richelieu, Castanets in hand, danced the saraband before Anne of Austria, and a century later a German dancing-master (Tauber's *Rechtschaffener Tanzmeister*, 1717) made the Castanets the subject of an exhaustive analysis.

The *Bones* of the nineteenth-century negro minstrels made from lengths of the rib-bones of oxen, are analogous in function to the Castanets.

Carillon, Metal Plates

The native Javanese instrument, which consists of tuned metal plates (*Saron, Gambang gansa*), led the Dutch, in the second half of the seventeenth century, to construct a musical instrument which Brossard (1703) describes as follows: "An instrument that consists of a row of metal plates arranged like a keyboard. These plates are struck with two little rods which have a ball at one end; a tone is produced thereby which resembles that of the Glockenspiel, which has led to people calling this instrument the Glockenspiel (*carillon*)." As a matter of fact, the "Carillon" in Handel's *Saul* was such a set of tuned metal plates (the Dutch name for the instrument is *Staalspel*). The Carillon has sometimes been provided with a keyboard, and even with a pedal.

Glockenspiel

The Dutch *Glockenspiel*, consisting of real bells, reached its culmination in the seventeenth century. Franz and Pieter Hemon of Zutphen were the great masters of this instrument. No technical improvements have been made since the best achievements of the sixteenth century, except that the iron cylinders have been replaced by copper, which is easier to work, and better able to withstand the inclemencies of weather and climate.

Xylophone

It was probably in Holland, the land of the Carillon and the Glockenspiel, that the notion was first conceived of providing the *Xylophone* with a keyboard. However, the weak and inexpressive tone of the instrument by no means justifies the expense of this technical improvement, so that the innovation has never been regarded as of practical importance.

On the whole, it may be said that the Baroque and Rococo periods, in their striving after subjective emotional expression, treated the so-called instruments of percussion—whether their sonorous elements consisted of wood, or metal, or parchment—with a certain aloofness, to be explained by the inflexible character of their tone.

THE CLASSICAL PERIOD

(1750–1810)

Compared with the wealth of instruments at the musician's command in earlier centuries, the Classical period[1] had at its disposal an orchestra of only modest dimensions. The increasing subjectivity of the last two centuries had resulted in a process of strict selection, and the composers of the period 1750–1810 had to make less than a dozen types of instrument suffice for the great majority of their works. This was in accordance with the sense of economy and the striving for lucidity and precision which characterized the Classical period.

But this handful of instruments was far more carefully treated than in earlier periods. The old carelessness in the apportioning of parts was a thing of the past. In the Baroque period the musicians themselves were allowed to decide which instruments they would use for the execution of the thorough-bass. J. S. Bach disdained to give any indications as to what keyboard instrument the Preludes and Fugues of *Das wohltemperierte Klavier* were intended for, and in his Concertos the same master unhesitatingly transferred passages of the purest string music to the Harpsichord.

[1] The conception of the Classical period is not uniformly defined. There are historians who understand by the term only the period between 1780 and 1790, while others extend it to include the entire careers of Haydn, Mozart and Beethoven. Here we take a middle view; reckoning the Classical period from the beginning of Haydn's career as composer to the completion of the greater part of Beethoven's Symphonies. This delimitation, which would include the "later Beethoven" in the Romantic period, is in closer accordance with the view generally prevailing.

The classical composers, on the other hand, regarded each instrument as an individual entity, and in their compositions they endeavoured to bring out its peculiar qualities as clearly as possible. It would not be easy to transfer a string quartet of Haydn's, a Horn concerto of Mozart's, or a Pianoforte sonata of Beethoven's, to another instrument. In such music each instrument has its own individual emotional content, which it expresses in a language that no other instrument can master. During the second half of the eighteenth century, the striving after tonal colour increasingly engaged the composers' interest and naturally stimulated the technical development of musical instruments. The tremendous improvement in the construction of instruments which occurred during the nineteenth century—one of the greatest developments which the art has ever known—had its beginnings in the Classical period.

The conscious economy of means must not be confused with puritanical austerity. The orchestra of the Classical period usually restricted itself to Strings, Oboes and Horns, to which Flutes, Clarinets, Bassoons, Trumpets and Kettledrums were gradually added. But in order to obtain special results other instruments were unhesitatingly included, and their effectiveness was enhanced by the very economy with which they were employed. In the course of this chapter numerous examples of this practice will be given. It will be seen that the marvellous instrumentation of the Romantic composers was already foreshadowed in the Classical period.

Violin, Viola, Violoncello, Double-Bass

The steady disappearance of musical instruments after the middle of the eighteenth century is particularly evident in the case of the strings. Of the many types which have been mentioned in the preceding chapters the only ones to attain importance were the members of the Viola da braccio family—the Violin, the Viola and the Violoncello, with the Double-bass, which stood midway between the Viola da gamba and the Viola da braccio. They formed the basis of the orchestra for secular and ecclesiastical purposes, and they played an essential part in chamber music, and as solo instruments in concertos. Even the ponderous Double-bass (which was generally tuned, since the end of the eighteenth century, in E_1, A_1, D, G) was not excluded as a solo instrument. Haydn wrote a concerto with orchestral accompaniment for this instrument, but unfortunately this work has not been preserved.

As regards their construction, these standard instruments underwent no alteration during the Classical period. The structural transformations and improvements made in the Renaissance and the Baroque period sufficiently met the musical requirements of the age. Moreover, in the second half of the eighteenth century the experts were too busily employed in exploiting the hitherto neglected musical possibilities of the instruments to take any special interest in structural modifications. The extension of the fingering of the left hand to higher and higher registers enlarged the upward range of the stringed instruments to a degree which the most skilful instrument-maker could never have rivalled by constructive alterations. This process was most strikingly evident in the case of the Violoncello. In 1770 Jean Louis Dupont, in his *Essai sur le doigter du violoncello*, placed the technique of the instrument on a new basis, and introduced the use of the thumb in playing the higher notes. Voltaire complimented him by declaring: "Monsieur, vous savez faire d'un bœuf un rossignol."

Viola da Gamba

Of the instruments of the Viola da gamba family, only the parent instrument, the Bass, retained something of its old importance during the Classical period. After the middle of the eighteenth century it still competed to some extent with the Violoncello as a solo instrument. The ever-increasing demands for volume of sound and robustness of tone resulted in its final disappearance.

Baryton

The *Baryton* achieved a certain importance during the second half of the eighteenth century, thanks to the music-loving Prince Esterházy, who was himself a performer on this instrument. At the Prince's court the violinist Luigi Tommasini, and above all Josef Haydn, wrote duets and trios, and other pieces of chamber-music, in which the Baryton played a decisive part (Pl. XLV). Although it was not widely distributed, this instrument held its own with great tenacity. When the nineteenth century was well advanced, S. L. Friedel, of Berlin, was able to make his reputation as a Baryton player.

Hurdy-Gurdy

The reputation which the *Hurdy-gurdy* enjoyed during the Rococo period survived into the second half of the eighteenth century. No lesser composers than Mozart and Haydn wrote music for this instrument, although Haydn's *Lira organizzata* was, of course, not the simple Hurdy-gurdy with strings alone, but the more ingenious variant with an enclosed organ attachment. Haydn's patron was the King of Naples, who delighted in playing the instrument himself. The numerous nocturnes and concertos which the master composed for the Hurdy-gurdy so gratified the sovereign that he tried to induce the composer to settle down in Naples. Haydn very nearly accepted the invitation, instead of responding to Salomon's request that he should go to London. Had he done so the history of music might well have followed a substantially different course.

The number of plucked or twanged stringed instruments was as greatly diminished as that of the bowed instruments. The leading instrument of the Renaissance and the Baroque period, the Lute, with its greater variants, the Archlute, Theorbo and Chitarrone, almost disappeared. The fashion-

Guitar

able instrument of the day was the *Guitar*, which, spreading into the rest of Europe from Spain and Italy, played an important part in France, England and Germany. In place of the inconvenient double strings it now had single strings, increased in number from five to six, and tuned to E, A, d, g, b, e^1. In point of tone the new instrument was even less satisfactory than the Lute, but it was easily tuned, and with the help of the fixed metallic frets on the finger-board it was easily played in tune. J. A. Otto, one of the leading German guitar-makers of the day, justly wrote of this instrument: "The Guitar very quickly won general favour, since for anyone who loves singing and can sing it provides the pleasantest and easiest accompaniment, and moreover it is readily carried about. Everywhere one saw Guitars in the hands of the most respected ladies and gentlemen." To this one may add that one of the advantages of the instrument was its simplicity and cheapness, so that it was not merely the instrument of aristocratic

PLATE XLII

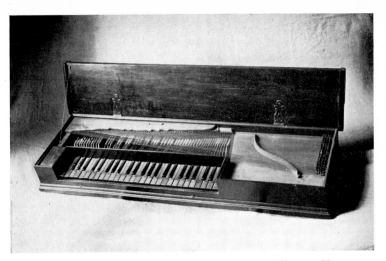

1.—Fretted Clavichord with "short" lowest octave. Vienna, University
Institute of Musicology

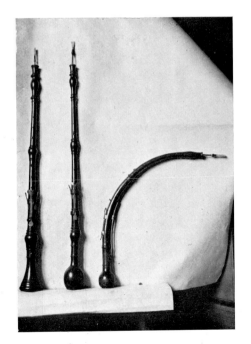

2.—Alto Oboe, Oboe da Caccia, English Horn.
Vienna, Society of Friends of Music

PLATE XLIII

 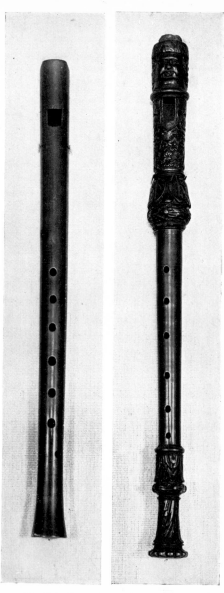

1.—Double Bassoon by Anciuti, Milan (1732). Salzburg, Museum Carolino Augusteum

2.—(*Left*) A Recorder of the Renaissance and (*Right*) a Recorder of the Baroque period. Vienna, Museum of Fine Arts

amateurs, but a genuinely popular instrument. It even became the practice to convert the valuable old Lutes—often in a most barbarous and primitive fashion—into Guitars.

Lyre-Guitar

A typical product of the French Empire period was the *Lyre-Guitar*, made in the form of an ancient Lyre, in which we see an expression of the contemporary effort to resuscitate the forms of classical antiquity. Simon Molitor (1766–1848), the Viennese composer and guitarist, wrote of this instrument in 1806: "The new Lyre (Guitar), which only a few years ago appeared in France, the ordinary Guitar being made to imitate the ancient Lyre, is a welcome sight to lovers of the beautiful forms of antiquity. Its tone —though stronger than that of the Guitar, on account of the larger body—is nevertheless dull and as though held back within the instrument." Moreover, since the two laterally-placed arms of the Lyre-guitar incommoded the player, it was never of any practical importance. This fashionable instrument, which owed its ephemeral success mainly to its adoption by the fair sex, barely survived the first quarter of the nineteenth century. An elaborate variety of this instrument was known in England as the *Apollo Lyre*.

Cittern

Among the many members of the *Cittern* family, whose strings, in the Classical period, varied from 6 to 14, was a pear- or bell-shaped instrument which, borrowing its name from the fashionable instrument of the day, was known as the *English Guitar*. In some later examples of this English Guitar the strings

English Guitar

were not tuned with pegs, but were attached to little metal hooks, which could be tightened by means of screws. Tuning was effected with a spanner of the watch-key type. In order to spare the fingers of the fair musician, Christian Klauss, a German living in London, conceived the notion, in 1783, of building a *Keyed English Guitar*, in which the strings were struck by means of hammers and keys, as in a piano. But in spite of all these improvements, by the first decade of the nineteenth century the Cittern had been thrust into the background by the Guitar.

Neapolitan Mandoline

During the Classical period the small Neapolitan *Mandoline*, with its four double strings tuned as in the Violin, became extremely popular. In the various music-loving countries of Europe it was now employed, with Guitar accompaniment, as a popular substitute for the Violin. It was even admitted on occasion to the ranks of the serious musical instruments. In 1764 Arne employed it in his *Almena*, and Grétry in 1778, in *L'Amant jaloux*. Mozart immortalized it by his *Serenade* in *Don Giovanni*, and Beethoven composed a sonatina and an adagio for Mandoline and Harpsichord.

Harp

As an instrument requiring a superior degree of virtuosity in the performer, the large and comparatively loud *Harp* was greatly valued in the Classical period. The French paid special attention to this instrument; and it was in France that the final steps were taken toward the technical perfecting of the Harp, which gave it a place among the instruments of the modern orchestra. By 1782 Georges Cousineau, in Paris, was experimenting with a view to transforming the simple pedal Harp into a double-action pedal Harp. Before long the problem was tackled by the celebrated maker of pianos, Sebastian Erard, who in 1801 applied for a patent in connection with a new type of Harp. But this type did not yet satisfy him, and he worked incessantly on fresh improvements, until at last, by the second decade of the nineteenth century, he succeeded in building an instrument which satisfied the highest requirements. This improved Harp was destined to play an important part in the future.

Aeolian Harp

The *Aeolian Harp* owed its popularity to the "sensibility" of the eighteenth century and the romantic movement of the nineteenth. The construction of the instrument is of the simplest. It consists of an ordinary rectangular box, over the top of which are stretched a variable number of strings, of different thicknesses, but all tuned to the same note. The instrument is placed where the wind blows upon it, and sometimes a special device is employed to ensure that the wind strikes the strings at the right place. The strings begin at first to sound in unison, but if the wind rises the overtones are brought out, producing harmonies of a strangely ethereal nature.

The history of the Aeolian Harp goes back into the remote past; the fascinating sound of strings vibrating in the wind attracted the attention of the ancients. It was recorded of King David's Harp that it began to sound when at midnight the north wind passed through its strings. Saint Dunstan (d. 988) was regarded as a magician because he made a Harp which played of itself when he placed it in a draught. Father Athanasius Kircher (1602–1680) was the first to build Aeolian Harps of the modern type, and the poet Alexander Pope introduced them into England in the first half of the eighteenth century. Since then the Aeolian Harp has played an increasing part in poetical literature, its gently, complaining, mysteriously ethereal strains having been often celebrated by the romantic poets.

Zither

While the Aeolian Harp is an almost supernaturally ethereal instrument, the *Zither* with fretted finger-board is an interpreter of dance music in the Austrian and Bavarian Alps, and the most popular of instruments for providing the accompaniment to folk-songs. In the Classical period the Zither exchanged its simple rectangular structure for a more sonorous curved form. Two different types now

Salzburg and Mittenwald Zithers

make their appearance: the "Salzburg" type, which is curved only on the bass side, and the "Mittenwald" type, in which both sides are curved. The use of the Zither is confined almost exclusively to the simple mountain folk, for whom it is an indispensable instrument.

Dulcimer (Pantaleon)

Like the Aeolian Harp and the Zither, the *Dulcimer* has never played any part in serious music. The complicated *Pantaleon* held its own until the '80's of the eighteenth century as the instrument of itinerant virtuosi, while the simple and basic form of the instrument survived even into the nineteenth century. But the great composers of the age paid hardly any attention to such instruments.

In the category of keyboard instruments, the types of the Baroque period all survived. Moreover, a new instrument made its appearance, the Fortepiano or Pianoforte, which steadily gained in significance, and became before the end of the period one of the most important of all musical instruments.

Clavichord

Both types of *Clavichord*, the older and the more recent, occurred in the Classical period. The little fretted (*gebunden*) Clavichord, which was so easily tuned (since one pair of strings always served to produce several notes), so inexpensive to make, and so readily moved about, was produced in its unaltered form until far into the second half of the eighteenth century. The "fret-free" (*bundfrei*) Clavichord, however, was more widely distributed, and it was now increased in size, in order to satisfy the demand for greater volume of tone.

Spinet

For the same reason large triangular *Spinets* were built which had almost the appearance of small Harpsichords and attempted to rival them in strength of tone (Pl. XLI). Some English writers apply the term "Spinet" to this form alone.

Harpsichord (Cembalo)

In the *Harpsichord* a pedal was introduced, which made

it possible to change the stops with the foot, instead of by hand, as was usual, so that the performance was not interrupted. In England, moreover, the Harpsichord was provided with a device which was intended to take the wind out of the sails of the newly invented Pianoforte. Above the strings was fixed a system of shutters (borrowed from the Organ) which was operated by a second pedal (Pl. XLVI). If this was open while the instrument was being played the tone was *forte*; if closed, the tone was *piano*. But this was not all; the new device made it possible to achieve the dynamic transitions which had become so popular all over Europe since the rise of the Mannheim school. If the shutters were slowly opened while the instrument was being played a crescendo was obtained; if they were slowly closed, a decrescendo.

The great composers of the time made abundant use of all these different types of Clavier. C. P. Emanuel Bach, composing about the middle of the century, wrote his pioneer works for the Clavichord. Josef Haydn's Clavichord is preserved by the Royal College of Music (London), and his fine English Harpsichord by the Viennese *Gesellschaft der Musikfreunde* (Pl. XLVI), and we know that the master was fond of conducting his compositions at the Harpsichord. Mozart made use of the Clavichord when he was working on the *Magic Flute* and the *Requiem*. But for Haydn, as for Mozart, the real keyboard instrument for which he wrote his sonatas and concertos was the Pianoforte.

Pianoforte

In a certain sense the *Pianoforte*, which was to oust the old keyboard instruments, incorporates the qualities of the latter. It combines the clear, limpid tone of the Harpsichord with the flexibility of the Clavichord. In the new instrument, of course, none of those qualities was so sharply defined as in its predecessors, as it was the characteristic of the Classical period to preserve moderation and avoid extremes. As regards the construction of the Piano, it will be seen that the new instrument benefited fully by the technical advances made in its predecessors, and only too soon eclipsed the latter.

The origin of the Pianoforte dates far back into the period with which we dealt in the last chapter; but as it had not then come into general use, the description of its first beginnings has been reserved for this chapter. The invention of the *Hammerclavier*—as the new instrument was sometimes called, since its strings were set in vibration by the blows of hammers—was already in the air at the beginning of the eighteenth century. How otherwise can we explain the fact that it was made about the same time in three different countries—in France, Germany and Italy? In 1716 the French clavichord-maker Marius exhibited models of a *Clavecin à maillets*—a Hammer Harpsichord —while between 1717 and 1721 the German writer on musical subjects, G. Schröter, constructed a hammer action which by his own admission was suggested by the mallets of the Pantaleon. But earlier still, in 1709 Bartolommeo Cristofori, a Florentine builder of Harpsichords, had built a Hammerclavier whose mechanism was so ingenious

Cristofori's Pianoforte

that one is tempted to regard it as the result of prolonged research. In 1711 Scipione Maffei discussed the invention exhaustively in the *Giornale dei letterati d'Italia*; moreover, two of Cristofori's instruments have survived to this day. One of these, built in 1720, and now in the Metropolitan Museum, New York, does not, unfortunately, con-

tain the action in its original form. The other, dating from
1726, which is in the Leipzig Collection of musical instruments, is substantially unaltered, so that its mechanism
may be taken as the pattern of Cristofori's invention.
Fig. 11 shows it in diagrammatic form. When the player
depresses the forward portion of the key *k* the hinder portion, and with it the *linguetta mobile,* as Cristofori called it
(the "hopper" *ho*), moves upwards. This actuates an under-
hammer *u,* which in turn throws the hammer *ha* against

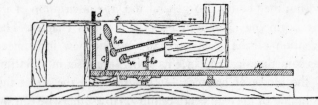

Fig. 11.—Cristofori's action, used in a Hammerclavier in the Leipzig
University Museum

the string *s.* This device ensures that the hammer falls
back immediately after the blow, whether the key is
released or held down, so that the string is free to vibrate.
The recoiling hammer is caught by the spring *c.* A damper,
d, affixed to the hinder end of the key, springs upwards
and frees the string directly the key is depressed. It falls
back against the string when the key is released.

Silbermann and J. S. Bach

The next chapter in the history of the Pianoforte was
enacted not on Italian but on German soil. The organ-
builder Gottfried Silbermann won such a reputation as a
maker of Harpsichords that he was actually credited with the
invention of the new instrument. Silbermann showed his
Hammerclavier, which was based on Cristofori's invention,
to J. S. Bach, who praised its tone but complained that

PLATE XLIV

French-horn Player. By an unknown master. About 1730

(By kind permission of the owner, Mr, David Minlore, London)

PLATE XLV

Haydn's Square Piano by Schanz, Vienna, late eighteenth century, and his Baryton, by Stadlmann, Vienna, 1732. In the background his bust (without wig). Vienna, Society of Friends of Music

too much strength was needed for the depression of the keys, and that the volume of sound was insufficient. Silbermann continued to work at the instrument, improving it until Bach was able to praise it unreservedly. But the time was not yet ripe for the Hammerclavier. The Cantor of the St. Thomas school was too steeped in the traditions of the old keyboard instruments to acquire a Pianoforte for his own use, or write music for it.

The Hammerclaviers built by Cristofori and Silbermann were often imitated in Germany and England, and were further developed. The English, in particular, showed a great predilection for the hammer action, and devised many improvements. In the second half of the eighteenth century a special type of mechanism was evolved, which is known as the "English action" (Pl. XLVII, 1).

English Action

Here the hammer is attached to a shaft which is independent of the key. At the end of the key is the hopper, which drives the hammer against the strings, moving out of the way directly the note is sounded, so that the hammer can immediately fall back into the resting position. In contrast to this device is the "German action," invented about the middle of the eighteenth century, and known also as the "Viennese action," since Vienna became the principal centre of German pianoforte-manufacture.

German or Viennese Action

Here the hammer is attached directly to the inner end of the key (Pl. XLVII, 1). When this rises the hammer, whose shaft is held by an "escapement" just beyond the key strikes against the string. After the hammer has struck its blow the escapement releases the shaft, so that the lever falls back into the resting position.

J. A. Stein and Mozart

The invention of the "German action" has often been attributed to Johann Andreas Stein of Augsburg, a pupil of Silbermann's. Mozart visited him in 1777, and in a letter to his father spoke of Stein's instrument in terms of the highest praise. Stein's action, which was built in an especially perfect form by his son-in-law, Andreas Streicher, who was a friend of the poet Schiller, and worked in Vienna, is distinguished by its light touch and the small movement of the keys. It favoured a brilliant "pearling" technique, such as is required by Weber's compositions for the piano. Hummel said of the Viennese action: "It readily responds to the most delicate touch. It allows the performer to obtain every possible *nuance* in his interpretation; it speaks clearly and promptly, has a flute-like tone, and does not hamper fluency by requiring an excessive effort." Despite these advantages, the Vienna action was inferior in fullness and beauty of tone to the English. In the Classic period the two actions ranked equally; but the Romantic movement, which called for greater volume of tone, awarded the victory to the English action.

Grand Piano

The original form of the Hammerclavier was that of the Harpsichord (Pl. XLVIII, 1). The Pianoforte was its direct, offspring, and in the eighteenth century many instruments which were originally built as Harpsichords were transformed into Hammerclaviers by changing the action. There

were even instruments of the "grand" form which used
both jacks and hammers together. Sometimes the Hammerclavier was shaped like a Clavichord. After 1750 the small

Square Piano

rectangular *Square Piano* appeared, in which the strings
were parallel with the front of the keyboard. This was
equipped with tiny hammers, which seem very primitive
when compared with the ingenious action of Cristofori's
first instruments; but they fulfilled their purpose perfectly,
as the instrument was played only with the delicate, careful
touch used for the Clavichord. Of course, if to-day we
tried to play on one of the old Square Pianos with the
vigorous touch which is proper to the modern Grand Piano
the result would merely be an unmusical clatter.

Registers

In order to enrich the acoustic possibilities of the Square
Piano, it was soon provided with different stops, which
slightly modified the quality of the tone. The stop that
lifted all the dampers at the same time produced a *forte*.
On the other hand, if the hammers were moved a little to
one side, so as to strike one string only, instead of two,
the result was the softer *una corda* register. Strips of
leather or silk, which were slipped between the hammers
and the strings, produced the *piano* or *pianissimo* effect.
A brush, which was applied to the strings from above, and
made the instrument sound as though the strings were
being plucked, was known as the *Harp* register while a
padded slat, which was pressed against the strings from
below, gave the *Lute* register. Sometimes there was a

shutter swell, as in the Organ and the Harpsichord, in order to produce crescendo and diminuendo effects. The enthusiasm of Mozart's contemporaries for Turkish music led to the introduction of a sort of drum attachment—a mallet, which struck against the sound-board. Lastly, we must not forget to mention an occasional addition in the form of a small enclosed organ attachment, consisting of flue-pipes, which could be employed simultaneously or alternately with the strings.

At first the stops for including or cutting out the registers were contrived above the keys, as in the Harpsichord. But this arrangement had the obvious disadvantage that the player needed his hands to operate them, and had consequently to interrupt his performance; so before long this office was entrusted to the legs of the musician. The registers were now changed by the knees, but as this method of operating the stops often shook the lightly-built instrument, pedals were installed. As yet, however, these pedals were without the wooden lyre-shaped support which they were afterwards given in the Grand Piano, and were not very robustly constructed.

Famous Makers of Square Pianos

Two famous makers of Square Pianos in the second half of the eighteenth century, were Johannes Zumpe, a pupil of the London harpsichord-builder Shudi, and John Broadwood, both of whom were established in London. In Paris there was Sebastian Erard (cf. p. 199), who in 1777 built the first French piano. Of German makers, in addition to Stein and Streicher, there were Johann Schanz, of whom Haydn thought highly, and Anton Walter, preferred by Mozart, both of whom were working in Vienna.

Upright Piano

After the middle of the eighteenth century the Grand Piano and the Square Piano had a rival in the Upright Grand Piano. In 1745 Christian Ernst Friederici, of Gera, built a "Pyramidal Piano" after the pattern of the Clavicytherium; and fifty years later William Stodart, in London, patented a Piano in the form of a book-case. Before long there were "Giraffe" Pianos (Pl. XLVIII, 2) and "Lyre" Pianos, as the instruments were called, in accordance with their outward form. But all these types had the disadvantage of a certain dullness of tone, and they were not very strongly constructed. The problem was therefore attacked from another side. While in all types of Piano hitherto constructed the narrow end of the Piano was uppermost and the wrest-plank underneath, the narrow end was now made to rest on the floor, and the wrest-plank was moved to the upper edge of the sounding-board. This new type, as the *Upright Piano, Pianino,* or *Piano droit,* has survived to the present day. It was first built about 1800. In that year Matthias Müller, in Vienna, built a double Piano for two players, calling it the *Ditanaklasis,* and about the same time J. I. Hawkins, in Philadelphia, made an Upright Piano with an iron frame. The development of the instrument during the following period, especially in England, will be considered in the next chapter.

As regards the wind instruments the Classical period was no more consistent than in the case of the stringed instruments. Individual instruments underwent the most drastic transformation, while others were almost entirely unchanged.

Oboe

The *Oboe* no longer had such a privileged position among the wood-wind instruments as in the Baroque period. In the beginning the Transverse Flute, and later the Clarinet also, disputed the first place. It is characteristic of the period that Mozart rescored his great Symphony in G minor, already completed, in order to include Clarinet parts at the cost of the Oboes. The development of the Oboe during the eighteenth century was correspondingly modest. *The Complete Tutor*, in 1808, teaches its pupils the management of practically the same instrument as that used by Hotteterre in 1708. The Oboe of the eighteenth century was made in three parts, usually of boxwood, more rarely of ebony or ivory. The three keys of the Rococo period were reduced to two, as in the second half of the century it became the rule that the player's right hand was undermost (cf. p. 170). It looked as though the instrument had regressed, by surrendering one of its three keys; but actually there was no real change.

English Horn

In exceptional cases the *English Horn*, standing one-fifth lower than the Oboe, was employed by the classical composers. Jommelli used it in 1741, Haydn in his *Divertimento* in F before 1760, and Gluck in his *Alceste* in 1767. But the peculiarly melancholy and pastoral effect of the instrument was not fully exploited until the Romantic period.

Bassoon

Whereas during the Baroque period the *Bassoon* was used mainly to reinforce the bass strings, and independent parts were seldom written for it, in the Classical period it gradually acquired an independent position. The instrument now assumed its natural function as the bass of the wind instruments. Its tone blended successfully with those of the Oboes, Horns and Clarinets; and it attained a position of ever-increasing importance as a solo instrument. Its characteristic tones, now tender and pathetic, now hollow and mysterious, now grotesquely nasal, recommended it as the interpreter of a great variety of moods and emotions.

The increased interest now taken in the musical qualities of the Bassoon naturally stimulated its technical development, French and German makers rivalling one another in their endeavours to perfect it. While the best instrument of the Baroque period was fitted with only four keys, by the time Beethoven had written the majority of his symphonies, instruments were made with double that number. At the same time the range of the Bassoon was extended upwards, so that the instrument covered more than three octaves (Bb_1-c^2).

Double Bassoon

The *Double Bassoon*, an octave lower than the Bassoon (its parts being written an octave higher than they sound), shared to a certain extent in the success of the parent instrument. Despite its clumsiness and defective intonation—which was partly due to the fact that no adequate tools were available for boring the large billets of wood employed in its manufacture—it was employed by the Viennese composers to obtain certain effects. In Haydn's *Creation*, at the words *"der Tiere Last"* the composer produces the impression of crushing weight (*Last* = might, burden) by a single note of the Double Bassoon. In the prison scene in *Fidelio* the instrument evokes the mysterious atmosphere of the subterranean dungeon.

Clarinet

Of all the wind instruments of the Classical period, perhaps the *Clarinet* had the greatest success. Its warm, vital tones, full and luscious in the lower register, and becoming shrill only in the highest notes, won it an increasing number of friends. About 1740 Handel wrote a so-called "Overture" which included a "Concertino" for two Clarinets and a Horn, and in 1749 Rameau employed the instrument in his *Zoroastre*. In the second half of the eighteenth century the Clarinet gradually made its way in all directions, and Clarinet players were seen with increasing frequency in the various orchestras. Mozart became intimately acquainted with the instrument in 1777, in Mannheim, and promptly conceived a strong affection for it. In addition to symphonies and *divertimenti* he wrote chamber compositions with Clarinet parts (Clarinet Trio and Quintet) and a Clarinet concerto. Weber, too, was among the special admirers of this instrument.

The Clarinet is not an easy instrument to play, for by reason of its predominantly cylindrical bore it behaves, in an acoustic sense, like a stopped pipe (cf. p. 39). In its voice the even-numbered harmonics are only faintly represented, and they cannot be produced by overblowing. The finger-holes and keys must therefore cover not merely an octave—as in the Oboe, for example—but the twelfth lying between the fundamental note and the third partial. Players could therefore play on the Clarinet only in keys closely related to its fundamental key. As a result of this, the instrument had to be built in various sizes. The principal instruments were the Sopranos, in C, B♭ and A, the

Transposing Wind Instruments

fundamental keys of which were C major, B♭ major, and

PLATE XLVI

Haydn's Harpsichord, by Shudi and Broadwood, London, 1775. Vienna,
Society of Friends of Music

PLATE XLVII

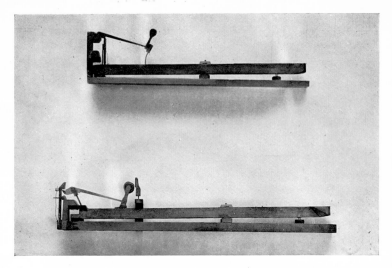

1. English Piano action (*above*); German or Viennese Piano action (*below*)

2. Nail Violin, about 1800. Vienna, Society of Friends of Music

A major. The individual Clarinets do not differ greatly in size, and are constructed in exactly the same manner; but obviously each note of the Bb Clarinet is a whole tone, and each note of the A Clarinet a minor third, lower than on the smallest or C Clarinet. For example, the fingerings which on the C Clarinet produce f^1, g^1, a^1, bb^1, c^2, d^2, eb^2, would give eb^1, f^1, g^1, ab^1, bb^1, c^2, db^2 on the Bb Clarinet, and on the A Clarinet d^1, e^1, $f\sharp^1$, g^1, a^1, b^1, c^2. In order to make the player independent of the pitch of his instrument, and save him the trouble of constant transposition, the notes for the Bb and A Clarinets are written down as though they were to be played on a C Clarinet, and not as they actually sound. The Clarinets belong to the "transposing instruments," which have become more and more numerous since the Classical period. In the case of these " transposing instruments," in the place of the absolute pitch the fingering is scored as it would be on an instrument "in C." The score, therefore, does not represent the actual sound, being written either higher or lower than it is to be read. As a rule a note "in Bb," "in A," "in D," or "in Eb" shows the amount of the transposition. (But in the case of certain instruments in which the key is taken for granted—for example, the English Horn, which is always in F—this direction is omitted as superfluous.) Since only a C-instrument sounds as it is scored, the part for an instrument in the key of Bb must be read a major second lower, that for an instrument in the key of A a minor third lower, and that for an instrument in the key of D or Eb a major second or a minor third higher than it is scored. The relation between the key-letter appended to the name of the instrument and the standard key of C always determines the interval by which the sound must be transposed on reading.

Clarinets were made—in the high register—in *F, E,*

$E^\flat$ and D; in the soprano register, in C, $B^\flat$ and A; and sometimes even in the low G. Although this large variety enabled the musicians to play on each individual instrument only in keys closely related to the fundamental one, the acoustic qualities of the Clarinet, especially in purity and beauty of tone, were at first extremely limited. In 1784 the *Musikalische Almanach* wrote: "Playing this instrument . . . is beset with difficulties which if not overcome can result in the most indescribable coos and squeaks. Run away at such times, if you can!" However, the makers strove indefatigably to improve the instrument. The number of its keys was gradually increased to six or seven, and its range constantly extended in the upward direction until it reached c^4. In order to gain more control over the intonation the instrument was divided into a number of separate parts; and so, little by little, the Clarinet was enabled to satisfy the high demands which were made on it.

Clarinette d'Amour

The *Clarinette d'amour* was an Alto Clarinet in A♭, G or F, fitted with the barrel-shaped bell of the Oboe d'amore; it was occasionally made about 1800. The upper part of the Clarinette was provided with a slightly curved brass tube, which made it possible to hold the rather lengthy instrument closer to the body. The Clarinette d'amour was especially appreciated in Southern Holland, but since it was ultimately discovered that the barrel-shaped bell had no effect on the tone it had only a short career.

Basset Horn

Another kind of Alto Clarinet was more successful: the *Basset Horn*, invented about 1770, possibly by Mayrhofer of Passau. The Basset Horn is an Alto Clarinet in F, whose compass extends a major third, or four semitones, lower than that of an ordinary Alto Clarinet. The deepest note of the Soprano Clarinet in C is E; on an F Clarinet this would sound as A. The Basset Horn, however, went a third lower, to F. On account of its great length the instrument was at first curved like a sickle (whence, perhaps, the description "Horn"), and afterwards its body was bent at an obtuse angle. The lower end of the Basset Horn was twice bent, and enclosed in a wooden box, which sometimes had the shape of a book. This part of the tube serves to produce the four deepest notes, which are controlled by keys. Mozart, a great lover of the Clarinet, made repeated use of the rather cooler and duller voice of the Basset Horn. It is especially effective in certain passages —as in the *Requiem*, the *Magic Flute*, or the *Maurerische Trauermusik*—when the composer wished to avoid the unduly sensuous effect of the Clarinet. The career of the Basset Horn came temporarily to an end with the eighteenth century. Beethoven, who employed the instrument in *Die Geschöpfe des Prometheus*, in 1801, was one of the last to use it.

Flutes

The changes which accompanied the transition from the Baroque to the Classical period may be observed clearly in the Flutes. Whereas in connection with Bach's and Handel's music "Flute" meant usually "Recorder," after the middle of the eighteenth century the Transverse Flute became the predominant instrument. No one would ever think of employing Recorders for the Flute parts of a symphony by Mozart or Haydn. The clear, more expressive, more powerful tone of the Transverse Flute was victorious over the tender and rather monotonous Recorder.

English Flageolet

While the long reign of the Soprano Recorder came to an end about the middle of the century, a smaller type, the *English Flageolet*, continued to play a certain part in England, France and Belgium as a dilettante instrument, at dances and convivial gatherings. This instrument had the finger-holes of the large Recorders and was equipped with two or more keys. It had a narrow mouthpiece of ivory or horn, and its upper portion included a pear-shaped expansion which contained a sponge, intended to catch the moisture. Small ivory studs were often fixed between the finger-holes, to guide the performer's fingers to their proper places over the small holes.

Double Flageolet

Between 1800 and 1820 double and even triple Flageolets were made in England. On the whole they were built like the ordinary English Flageolet. The left-hand instrument usually had six finger-holes, and the right-hand one four, and these were so placed that, when the same fingering was used on both flutes, the instrument on the right always sounded a third lower than that on the left. The two flutes could also be played separately. The popularity of this type is shown by the comparatively large number of examples preserved in collections. However, the mechanical quality of its tone, and its modest compass of less than an octave (it was often d^2–c^3 or bb^1–a^2) prevented its admission to the orchestra.

Transverse Flute

Until late in the second half of the eighteenth century the *Transverse Flute* retained the form which it had assumed in the Baroque period. Only after 1775—that is, about the time when the Classical style was approaching its culmination—was its improvement seriously taken in hand. Since (in the C Flute) only the notes of the scale of D major were really true, keyed holes were made for such other notes as were frequently required. To the already existing D♯ key a G♯, a B♭, and then an F key was added. Moreover, Richard Potter, a London maker, increased the length of the instrument, and gave it, below the fundamental note d^1, a $c♯^1$ and a c^1, which were controlled by two further keys. About 1800 this instrument, with its six keys, was widely distributed. At the beginning of the nineteenth century a key for c^2 was added, and a second key for F, which facilitated the fingering.

So the one-keyed Flute, of which Burney had written in 1772 that it was "natural to those instruments to be out of tune," evolved, in the course of a few decades, into a highly developed instrument with eight keys. But with this the transformation of the Flute was by no means completed; indeed—as we shall see in the next chapter—it had really only now begun.

Although the Discant or Treble Flute in the fundamental key of D major (commonly called the C Flute, since it was not a "transposing" instrument) was that in most general use, it was by no means the only type which existed in the Classical period. In military bands, from the close of the eighteenth century, instruments a semitone or a minor third higher were used (in D♭ and E♭), as they were louder and shriller than the ordinary Flute. On the other hand, just as there was an Oboe d'amore, which was a minor third deeper than the ordinary Oboe, so there was a Flûte d'amour (*Liebesflöte*) in A. There were also—but these

Alto Flute and Bass Flute

were exceptional—an Alto Flute in G, and a Bass Flute an octave lower than the Discant Flute. This, the largest type of Flute, was made more manageable by bending back part of the tube through an angle of 180°, so that it lay beside the main tube.

Piccolo Flute

The smallest Flute is of more importance than the larger types just mentioned. It is an octave higher than the ordinary Flute in C, and reaches almost to the upper limit of recognizable pitch. Of course, the highest notes of the Piccolo, in the fourth octave above middle C, were hardly ever employed, owing to their shrillness. The Piccolo came into use towards the end of the eighteenth century, and its history was thenceforth that of the large Flute. Apart from the absence of the long keys for the deep C# and C, which are superfluous in an instrument whose higher notes are its chief recommendation, the arrangement of the keys is essentially the same as in the ordinary Flute. The Piccolo Flute, on account of its sharp, powerful tones, was especially valued in military bands (in which instruments in Db and Eb were employed as well), but it also found its way more and more rapidly into the opera and symphony orchestras. Gluck, in his *Iphigenia in Tauris*, and Beethoven, in the *Pastoral Symphony*, used its sharp tones in the passages descriptive of a storm.

Organ

During the Classical period the *Organ* was less valued than in the Baroque. Despite all the efforts which the

Baroque period had directed toward making its voice more flexible and capable of expression, it was still regarded as too rigid and lifeless. The Portative and the Positive organs gradually disappeared during the second half of the eighteenth century, and only the great Church Organ remained in general use. It is characteristic of the age that the great Viennese composers wrote for the Organ only in their youth, when they were still influenced by older models. Haydn, between 1756 and 1770, composed an Organ concerto, and two Masses with important Organ solos; Mozart wrote seventeen Organ sonatas, the last of them in the year 1780, and Beethoven, at the age of 11, composed "a two-part Organ fugue in rapid movement," and two years later "Two Preludes for the Fortepiano or Organ." But when they had arrived at full maturity, none of these three masters paid any serious attention to the Organ, and it is significant that Beethoven never fulfilled his declared intention of writing an Organ Prelude to the Mass in C major.

In the history of the tremendous modern development of the Organ the period between 1750 and 1810 was thus comparatively static. One of the most prominent motives at work during this period was the desire, not to enrich and enlarge the instrument, but to simplify it. In 1791 the famous German organist, Abt Vogler, well known even in England through his concert tours, began a thorough transformation of the Organ in accordance with his own ideals. He replaced the large costly pipes by smaller ones which produced the deep fundamental note required by sounding its partials (octave and twelfth). He discarded all registers which he did not regard as indispensable, and enclosed the rest in a chamber which could be closed with the *Venetian Swell* invented by Samuel Green. He also arranged the pipes in a more practical manner, and finally,

he introduced into the Organ the free reeds, borrowed
from the Chinese Mouth-organ, which were afterwards to
play so important a part in the Harmonium. The "simplifications" of Abt Vogler were mainly directed towards
making the Organ cheaper, and easier to manufacture,
repair and maintain, and obtaining a clearer and more
limpid tone, in accordance with the taste of the Classical
period. But as such simplifications gave the Organ a rather
thin and commonplace tone, the early Romantic period
opposed these reforms with all its might, so that they had
little real effect.

French Horn

A great transformation may be noted during the second
half of the eighteenth century in the part played by the
brass instruments. The French Horn, which had been rather
neglected, now received more and more attention. It was
no longer used in the highest register, but the composers
of the Classical period were fond of employing the warm,
soft, deep and middle registers. The Horn plays an important part in the compositions of the time; to some extent
it takes over the rôle of the old *continuo* voices, filling the
gap between the melody and the bass.

Crooks

By the beginning of the eighteenth century, and perhaps
even earlier, circular tubes or *crooks* were coming into use;
these were fitted between the mouthpiece and the main
tube of the Horn, increasing the length of the latter, and
therefore lowering the pitch of the instrument. By means
of a series of crooks of different lengths, of which two or
three might sometimes be used together, it was possible

PLATE XLVIII

2.—Upright "Giraffe" Piano. Early nineteenth century. Vienna, Society of Friends of Music

1.—Mozart's Grand Piano. Salzburg, Museum Carolino Augusteum

PLATE XLIX

3.—Front view of a Balalaika Prima

2.—Octo-bass, by J. B. Vuillaume, Paris, 1849. Vienna, Society of Friends of Music

1.—Arpeggione or Bogenguitarre, 1824

to turn a C Horn into a B♭, A, G, F, E, E♭, D Horn, etc. Since in its deeper register, which was then preferred, the Horn could not produce much more than the notes of the fundamental triad, it became necessary to effect frequent changes of pitch. With the help of crooks this could be done with comparative ease without a change of instrument.

"Stopping"

A further technical innovation introduced about 1750 supplemented the employment of this device. At that time the Horn-player, Anton Josef Hampel, in Dresden, began to "stop" his Horn. He plunged his right hand into the bell of the instrument, closing it more or less completely, which lowered the pitch of the Horn by a semitone or a whole tone. This simple expedient made it possible to obtain more than twice as many notes from the same Horn without altering the pitch; and the new, rather dull and repressed timbre of the "stopped" Horn helped to enrich its range of effects. Very soon, however, it became

Inventions-Horn

apparent that the stopping of the Horn was difficult or impossible if two or more crooks were employed so as to increase the distance between the bell and the player's body. Hampel now hit upon the expedient of replacing the coiled crooks, interposed at the narrow end of the tube, by interchangeable U-shaped tuning slides of different lengths, which were inserted in the middle of the hoop. Now the pitch of the Horn could be altered without increasing the distance of the bell from the player's body. These insertions were known as "Inventions," and the instrument equipped with them was called the *Inventions-Horn*. J. Werner, of Dresden, was the first to make such a Horn in 1753. Crooks and "inventions" were the expedients by which the musicians of the Classic and the early Romantic period were enabled to tune their Horns to the required key; but the more complicated "Inventions-Horn" was seldom employed save by solo performers.

Cornett

The inclusion of the Trumpet among the ordinary instruments of the orchestra, of which more will be said later, was greatly to the disadvantage of the *Cornett*. The interest felt in this little instrument, which was very difficult to play, on account of its small mouthpiece, quickly faded. For the composers of the Classical period the Cornett practically ceased to exist.

Serpent

The larger variant of the Cornett, the *Serpent*, was more favourably situated, for as the contrabass of the wind instruments it was still indispensable; moreover, in the last quarter of the eighteenth century it played an important part in the vigorous development of military music.

Russian Bassoon

Attempts were also made to improve the serpentine form of the instrument, which was troublesome to construct and difficult to manage, by giving it the shape of a Bassoon. This new form, the so-called *Russian Bassoon*, was invented about 1790, in the true home of the Serpent, France, by an orchestral musician, Regibo by name. In construction it closely copied the Bassoon of the period, except that it was more massive, with a much larger bore (Pl. LX, A). The bell was usually of metal, either trumpet-shaped or formed like a grotesquely painted animal's head, an old fancy revived early in the eighteenth century (cf. Pl. XLIII, 1) and remaining in vogue for the larger military instruments, especially the Trombone, for about a century.

(English) Bass Horn

About 1800 a similar instrument, except that it was made of metal, was constructed by a Frenchman who was living in London—Alexandre Frichot (Pl. LX, B). Both were fitted with a curved crook, and soon made their way into all parts of the Continent. However, these new types did not succeed in ousting the parent instrument, the Serpent, which towards the end of the eighteenth century was often fitted with three or four keys in order to improve its intonation.

Trumpet

In the second half of the eighteenth century the *Trumpet* was no longer pre-eminent. The art of "clarino playing," requiring from the performer exceptional endurance and indefatigable practice, gradually declined. The trumpeters were mostly confined to the middle notes of the so-called "principal" register, which had none of the magical quality peculiar to the highest notes. At the same time the social significance of the Trumpet diminished. It lost its exceptional position, and descended to the status of an ordinary and not even very highly esteemed orchestral intrument.

In these circumstances it is not surprising that during the Classical period no important improvements were incorporated in the Trumpet. Substantially, the Trumpet contented itself with taking over the acquisitions of the Horn (for which reason the Trumpet, in this section, does not precede the Horns, as hitherto, but follows them).

In this instrument, which since the middle of the eighteenth century had become rather simpler and compacter in construction, crooks were now employed. Such crooks were known by the beginning of the sixteenth century, but only now came into general use. The F Trumpet, which gradually took precedence of the old D Trumpet, could be transposed into E, E♭, D and C with the help of a single insertion. If two crooks were employed the pitch could be lowered to B, B♭, A and A♭. But since Trumpets provided with crooks were more difficult to blow, owing to the greater number of convolutions, about 1780 "Inventions-Trumpets" were constructed, after the pattern of the French Horn. After 1800 there were even semi-circular or circular stopped Trumpets in use, although the insertion of the hand into the bell infallibly destroyed the pealing tone of the Trumpet.

Keyed Trumpet

All these attempts failed to achieve their purpose of giving the Trumpet the missing notes in the middle register. Recourse was therefore had to the simple expedient which had been employed for centuries in the case of the other wind instruments. Holes were made in the wall of the tube. In order to avoid the defects inherent in the Serpent the holes were not closed by the fingers, but by keys, which made it possible to bore them in the acoustically correct positions. The *Keyed Trumpet* had as a rule five keys, which used in order raised the pitch by successive semitones. They were so arranged that the performer could play upon them with his left hand, holding the Trumpet in his right.

The invention of the Keyed Trumpet has been ascribed by experts to the year 1801 and the Viennese Anton Weidinger. But the instrument is undoubtedly older than this, for Haydn was already acquainted with it in 1796, since in that year he wrote a concerto for the Keyed Trumpet, with orchestral accompaniment. This work reveals the characteristics of the new instrument; one looks in vain for the usual triad-melodies. Haydn's work is predominantly diatonic, and he indulges in chromatic passages even in the deeper register of the instrument. Great demands are made on the nimbleness of the Keyed Trumpet, and in the allegro passages runs of semiquavers are not unusual.

Despite Haydn's efforts, the Keyed Trumpet had no real success. The explanation may be sought in the fact that the holes detracted greatly from the brilliant tone of the Trumpet. The instrument was occasionally used for several decades to come. It did not, however, succeed in obtaining admittance to the symphony orchestra.

Trombone

The *Trombone*, whose employment during the Baroque period was restricted to Church music and special occasions, gradually came into general use during the Classical period. Composers of operatic music—and in this field Gluck was among the pioneers—and of oratorios, made increasing use of the now solemn and now mysteriously menacing tones of the instrument. Moreover, from the end of the eighteenth century military bands employed it with ever-increasing frequency, on account of its powerful voice. But so far it was not accepted as a member of the symphony orchestra.

In the Classical period a Trombone trio was usually employed: the Alto in E♭, the Tenor in B♭, and the Bass in E♭ or F. As a rule all three of these instruments were used in conjunction, though they were by no means equally esteemed. The Tenor was regarded as the principal instrument, being the most perfect in technical and acoustic respects. The Alto, as compared with the Tenor, sounded rather shrill, and was unsatisfactory in the low notes, while the Bass demanded an excessive amount of wind, and made too great demands on the performer's strength.

So far, the technical construction of the Trombone had undergone no essential modification. It is true that for use in military bands instruments were made whose bells were bent backwards, so that the troops marching behind the band could hear them the better. In France and Belgium the bell was sometimes given the form of an animal's head (cf. p. 223), and an instrument so made was known as a *Buccin*. But apart from these externals, the Slide-Trombone of the Renaissance was still in use during the Classical period.

Kettledrum

In the second half of the eighteenth century the use of the *Kettledrum* in the orchestra was becoming more and more frequent. As of old, the drums were always employed in pairs, one being generally tuned in the tonic and the other in the dominant. Like the tuning, the use of the Kettledrum was bound by tradition. It was generally used in *forte* passages, to reinforce the sound of the wind instruments, especially the Trumpets. The mysterious pianissimo effect of the Kettledrums, as obtained by Beethoven, for example, at the close of the slow movement of his Fourth Symphony, was quite exceptional in earlier scores. Until about 1810 the instrument did not undergo any technical modification. As the pitch of the Kettledrums was never varied during the course of a movement, the arrangement of individual screws for tuning the instrument inherited from an earlier period was still adequate.

Since the Turks had ceased to constitute a perpetual menace to Europe, they were regarded, not perhaps with less interest, but certainly with less apprehension. The music of the once so dreaded Janissaries now enjoyed remarkable popularity, and was adopted by the military bands of Europe and also in the Turkish operas of the Classical period.

Bass-Drum

One of the most important components of this "Janissary music" was the great Turkish *Bass-Drum*, with a diameter of two to three feet, and a wooden shell of more than a foot in depth. The skin was stretched by means of cords. The instrument, which was usually played standing on its shell, was beaten with a single drumstick, which sometimes had a head at either end, to facilitate the execution of the roll. The sound of the drum is dull and explosive, indefinite in pitch, and sometimes extremely loud. Mozart was one of the first to use the Bass-Drum, in 1782 in *Il Seraglio*. Haydn employed it in 1794 in his Military Symphony.

Side-Drum

The ordinary *Side-Drum* occurs in the Classical period only as a military instrument. The original wooden shell was more and more frequently replaced by a brass one.

Tambourine

From 1800 onwards, the *Tambourine* also found employment in the military bands of Europe, usually in their "Turkish music."

Cymbals

Other important components of the Janissaries' orchestra were the *Cymbals* and the Triangle. The Cymbals were often sounded by the person who played the Bass-Drum. In this case one Cymbal was fastened to the rim of the Drum; the drummer held the second Cymbal in one hand, and the drumstick in the other. The sharp, strident clash of the Cymbals was often employed in operatic orchestras, in order to produce exotic effects. In 1775 Grétry used the Cymbals in the Gipsy March in *La fausse Magie* and in 1779 Gluck employed them in the Scythian chorus of his *Iphigenia in Tauris*.

Triangle

In both the scores just mentioned the *Triangle* also is utilized. Mozart prescribed the instrument in his *Il Seraglio*. Steadily it made its way from the military band to the orchestra.

Glockenspiel

Small *Glockenspiels* of metal plates, with a keyboard, but without dampers, were sometimes constructed in the eighteenth century. The Glockenspiel which Papageno plays in *The Magic Flute* is such an instrument.

Bells

Dalayrac, in 1791, used real *Bells* in his opera *Camille*, and in 1794 Cherubini did the same in his *Elisa*. Later, they were occasionally employed in the theatre, but they did not gain acceptance elsewhere, owing to their great weight and their extreme loudness.

Gongs

The *Gong*, also known as the Tamtam, bears a certain

PLATE L

[*Photo: Lindsley Barnard*

A player of the Double-action Pedal Harp
(Melville Clark, Syracuse, N.Y.)

PLATE LI

Keyboard and action of a Jankó Piano

relationship to the Bell. It is a bowl-shaped instrument of bronze with an upturned rim, which is pierced to take the cord by which the Gong is suspended. The centre is set in vibration by a mallet or drumstick. The sound of the Gong is dark in colour, mysterious, uncanny. The home of the instrument is the Far East, and it was during the period of the French Revolution that it found its way into European orchestras. In 1791 Gossec used it in the *Marche funèbre* on the death of Mirabeau; and in 1804 Lesueur introduced it into the score of the opera *Les Bardes*.

The sentimentality of the *Sturm und Drang* (Storm and Stress) period, whose culmination coincided with the middle of the Classical period, found expression in the construction of a whole series of curious instruments, which disappeared completely after a few decades. The inventors of these various instruments were mostly non-musicians.

Nail Violin

Some time before 1770 Johannes Wilde, in St. Petersburg, discovered the principle of the *Nail Violin*. As he was hanging up a violin bow, he happened to graze a nail which was projecting from the wall, and produced a penetrating, flute-like note. He thereupon assembled a number of round metal rods of different lengths and pitch, fixed them on a round or oblong sound-box (Pl. XLVII, 2), and stroked them with a bow. The strange, mysterious, nerve-racking tone of the instrument enabled it to achieve a certain popularity until the first few decades of the nineteenth century. It was, of course, never accepted by serious musicians.

Euphon and Clavicylindre

The results of the experiments of the physicist Chladni in Wittenberg were made use of when the *Euphon* was constructed about 1790. Long, thin glass tubes which were set in vibration by stroking them with moistened fingers communicated the vibration to tuned metal rods, which produced a wavering flute-like tone. A more practical instrument was the *Clavicylindre*, invented by Chladni in 1799. In this the tuned rods were pressed against a rotating cylinder by means of a keyboard, and thereby set in vibration. More valuable than these and other related instruments, which will not be mentioned here, as being of no practical importance, were the instruments in which tuned glass bells or goblets were employed. In 1743 and 1744 an Irishman, Richard Pockrich, appeared in Dublin and in England

Musical Glasses or Verrillon

as a performer on the *Musical Glasses*. He was followed by no less a musician than Gluck, who in 1746 played "a concerto on 26 Drinking-Glasses tuned with Spring Water, accompanied with the whole Band" at the Haymarket Theatre, London. The new instrument, also known as the *Verrillon*, was soon extremely popular in England, and Goldsmith, in 1761, records in his *Vicar of Wakefield* that "fine ladies would talk of nothing but high life and high-lived company, pictures, taste, Shakespeare and the musical glasses."

Glass Harmonica

An improvement on this device was the *Glass Harmonica* constructed in 1763 by Benjamin Franklin. His instrument consisted of a number of chromatically tuned, freely vibrating glass bells, which were strung upon a rotating axle. The individual bells were so close together that only the rim of each was visible, the rest being covered by the adjacent bell. The lower edges of the bells were dipped into a basin filled with water. The performer set the axle rotating by means of a treadle, while at the same time he set the wet bells in vibration by pressing on them with a finger. The tones produced in this manner were soft, but peculiarly penetrating, with a lingering, flute-like quality. It was reported that at concerts the hearers were moved to tears by the sound of the instrument, and the celebrated Viennese physician, Franz Mesmer, performed his magnetic cures to the accompaniment of the notes of the Glass Harmonica, since they made the patients peculiarly susceptible to hypnotic sleep. The instrument was soon accepted by the great masters. Mozart wrote a Quintet (K. 617) for Harmonica, Flute, Oboe, Viola and 'Cello, and Beethoven, in his incidental music to Duncker's *Leonore Prohaska*, included a melodrama with Harmonica.

Keyboard Harmonica

Since the friction of the sensitive finger-tips on the glasses led in the long run to nervous disorders, after 1784 Harmonicas were fitted with keyboards. In these, by means of the keys, little pads were pressed against the glass bells. The refined flexibility of tone which was obtained by playing with the finger-tips was naturally lost, and the *Keyboard Harmonica* never succeeded in rivalling the parent instrument, which held its own into the second quarter of the nineteenth century.

VII

FROM THE ROMANTIC PERIOD
TO THE PRESENT DAY

(1810–1940)

1810–1850

The first half of the nineteenth century brought with
it an unprecedented increase of technical possibilities.
Comparable with the great days of violin-making in the
seventeenth and eighteenth centuries, there now began a
period in which special attention was given to the wind
instruments. Many highly-gifted inventors applied themselves with success to the final solution of the problem which
in former ages had seemed to offer insuperable difficulties:
the problem of enabling the wind instruments to produce
in a satisfactory manner all the notes of the chromatic
scale. The final result of their efforts was that most keys
and modulations can be produced on a single wood-
wind or brass instrument.

This technical perfection is due to the fact that the
interest of composers was gradually diverted to the wind
instruments. The bowed instruments still remained the
nucleus of the orchestra; but to the composers of the
Romantic period the colourful tones of the wind instruments were equally indispensable. The endeavour to con-
quer the deeper registers was resumed with renewed zeal.
Giant Contrabass Tubas owe their existence and Contrabass Trombones their revival to the general tendency
toward the ponderous and the superhuman—a tendency
to be observed in the historical paintings of the same

period. Even the delicate wood-wind instruments were drawn into this movement. Clarinets and Oboes were given a conical metal tube of large bore, so that their tone approximated to that of the Trumpets and Horns. The Saxophones and Sarrusophones, which were thus constructed, sometimes even superseded their less robust prototypes. The voice of the softest of the wind instruments, the Flute, was made harder and sharper by giving it the cylindrical bore which since this period has become the rule. Even the Pianoforte, the only keyboard stringed instrument to survive, showed plainly how the musical standpoint had changed. The instrument in use at the close of the eighteenth century had a thin, weak, yet extraordinarily clear tone, and was sometimes so lightly constructed that a touring musician could easily take it with him. But fifty years later the Pianoforte had become the powerful and brilliant Grand Piano, capable of an infinite range of dynamic gradations. The use of three-fold strings for each note, of overstringing, of a heavy cast-iron frame, and Erard's "double escapement" action made it—next to the Organ—the most complicated and yet the most technically perfect instrument of the modern era. This extraordinary expansion of its possibilities went hand in hand with their exploitation by a highly developed virtuosity. Chopin, Schumann, Liszt, Rubinstein, Brahms —to cite only a few names—influenced and developed the technique of the Piano in a decisive manner.

A stronger sense of tone-colour was everywhere apparent. The painters of the Romantic school ruthlessly sacrificed careful drawing to a purely chromatic effect, and music, too, sought for means of enriching the range of colour at its disposal. Many new instruments appeared, while the groups and families of the sixteenth century were revived with a view to obtaining more harmonious effects. When

Adolphe Sax in Paris made his Saxhorns and Saxophones in various sizes, and when—as Richard Strauss records—a performance of Mozart's Symphony in G minor was given at the Brussels Conservatoire, in which all the parts, from the highest to the lowest, were taken exclusively by variously proportioned members of the Clarinet family, this signified a revival of some of the conditions of the late Renaissance.

1850–1900

After the seventeenth century and the first half of the eighteenth had laid the foundation of the string orchestra, and the first few decades of the nineteenth century had worked on the improvement of the wind instruments, the exaggerated "colourism" of the following period gave special attention to the percussion, and also included the keyboard instruments in the orchestra.

The "Impressionist movement" which prevailed during the last quarter of the nineteenth century found new means of expression in instruments which either had not been known before or, although familiar, had not been employed in this way. The Xylophone, the Celesta, the Tubular Bells, the Castanets, the Rattle, as well as the Pianoforte, Organ and Harmonium owe their incorporation in the orchestra to this tendency.

1900–1930

In the twentieth century there have been decisive changes in the musical sphere, as elsewhere. Avoidance of the romantic, a preference for sobriety and objectivity, characterize the standpoint of the twentieth-century composers, especially since the first World War. Their striving for clarity and lucidity has essentially diminished the stress laid on the element of colour, while their efforts are directed toward the plastic elaboration of the musical outline. The listener should be able to follow each part of the composition, so that instruments have to be assembled whose voices are refractory to a blending of colours. Stravinsky, in the *Petit Concert* of his *Histoire du Soldat*, employs a combination of Violin, Clarinet and Cornet-à-pistons, and Schönberg, in the sixth part of the *Pierrot Lunaire*, accompanies a melodrama with Flute, Bass Clarinet and Violoncello. In both cases colour is subordinate to polyphony. The melody of each individual voice must be given its full value, and to this end the voices are allotted to instruments of contrasting tone. Here is a surprising revival of the conditions of the late Middle Ages (cf. p. 90).

Economic Considerations

In the period after the War of 1914-18 economic considerations co-operated with artistic principles to effect the gradual replacement of the huge instrumental *ensembles* of the late romanticism (of which a characteristic example is Gustav Mahler's *Symphony of the 1,000 Executants*) by small chamber orchestras, often comprising hardly more than a dozen performers; and this not only in the concert-hall, but even in opera. This extreme restriction is also more in accordance with the less solemn and more playful approach to musical problems, and with the far shorter works of this period.

Jazz

Following the ever more frequent infraction of the limits that of old were so carefully drawn between serious and light music, the gradually increasing influence of "jazz" upon Occidental music may be observed. The dance-music of America, which soon became predominant also in Europe, made many discoveries in the use of colour. It employed executive methods which had hitherto been unusual (*vibrato* and *glissando* of the wind instruments) and introduced many new instruments borrowed from popular or exotic sources (such as the Banjo, Musical Saw, Vibraphone, Marimba, etc.). This new and rich colour-scale was in itself enough to arouse the interest of the young generation of composers; besides, there is a certain conformity between jazz and the novel principles of musical structure: first, in the marked preference of the wind to the stringed instruments; then in the subtly differentiated treatment (as in chamber music) of the percussion; and lastly, in the partiality for the combination of primitive sounds which do not blend together. The result of all this has been that the influence of jazz has extended beyond the narrow circle of dance-music proper, to the instrumentation and coloration of such composers as Stravinsky, Milhaud, Satie, Weill, Grünberg, etc.

Influence of Radio

The introduction of radio at the beginning of the '20's was accompanied by a tremendous revolution in the musical world. No other institution brings music to so many listeners as the radio, or employs so many artists. The specific nature of the compositions for which it calls is in keeping in many respects with the musical tendencies of the post-war period. The highly-developed colourism of the Romantic period, and of Impressionism, is not suitable for broadcasting, since tone-colour is apt to be distorted in transmission. On the other hand, a small number of

PLATE LII

[Photo: A. Fischer, Wiener-Neustadt

Members of the Vienna Philharmonic Orchestra at the performance of an Oratorio

In the last row a Kettledrum player, in the middle row (from left to right) players of Bassoon, Trumpet, Trombone, Bass-Tuba; in the front row players of Flute, Oboe and Horn

PLATE LIII

Two Oboe players and an English Horn player of the **B.B.C.** Orchestra

voices which are sharply differentiated in *timbre* are transmitted extremely well. Moreover, since the radio addresses itself to the widest public, the pieces to be broadcast should not be too intellectually profound, nor too serious, nor unduly long. But these qualities are also those of post-war music. Although the influence of radio is so revolutionary in a sociological sense, it has not evoked any essential changes in the direction followed by the composers of the day. The number of compositions written especially for the radio is small, and their significance slight. Orchestral technique has been influenced by it only in so far as is compatible with the tendencies of the period.

Electric Instruments

In the train of radio there have come a number of electric instruments, which either increase and improve the qualities of the stringed instruments in a hitherto unprecedented manner, or produce new sounds by electro-acoustical means. The invention of these instruments has for the most part been the work of physicists. The musical world proper has not taken great note of their existence. They have hardly found a place in the orchestra, nor have composers written for them works of any importance.

The Last Decade

In the political and cultural spheres the last decade has abrogated many of the unduly forthright tendencies of the second and third decades of the century. Objectivity and progressiveness are by no means in such high repute as in the years following the first World War. They have made way for a pronounced idealism and for retrospective tendencies. In the latest works of the modern composers, elements now Romantic, now Classic, now pre-Classic or Baroque are to be noted. Historical tendencies are constantly gaining in strength, one consequence being that the old instruments, such as the Harpsichord, Clavichord, Spinet, Viola da gamba and Recorder are manufactured in ever-increasing numbers for the purpose of historical recitals. How far this development, which is only in its beginnings, will finally lead us cannot yet be estimated; especially as the outbreak of the second World War can hardly fail to have a decisive influence on the artistic and musical life of our time.

Bowed Instruments

If we take a general survey of the bowed instruments from the Romantic period to the present day, we find that the resulting picture does not differ in its main features from that of the preceding period. The Violin, Viola, 'Cello and Double-bass are still, not indeed the only bowed instruments, but the only ones of any importance. On the whole the nineteenth and twentieth centuries found as little need as the eighteenth century to alter their classic form. Constant progress has been made, but it has been in the technique of the performer, not in the technique of construction. One of the greatest virtuosi of the violin, Niccolò Paganini, whose career fell in the Romantic period, and the Contrabassist Domenico Dragonetti, who made light of playing works written for the 'Cello on his great, ponderous instrument, evoked storms of applause from thousands of listeners. But of even greater importance than the supreme achievements of individual artists is the fact that during the nineteenth century the general standard of orchestral performers was enormously improved. The difficult tasks which Liszt, Wagner and Richard Strauss required of the whole body of the strings were far more arduous than those demanded of the solo instruments in the Violin concertos of Haydn and Mozart. The two classical masters hardly ever took the solo violin higher than a^3; but Berlioz, in his *Traité d'instrumentation* (1844), asserts that the Violins of the orchestra can go a third higher—that is, to c^4—and Richard Strauss declares, in his supplement to this work (1909), that even this assertion is out of date, since the members of a symphonic or operatic orchestra can play up to g^4. With the help of tremolos, trills, arpeggios, pizzicatos, and *col legno* (when the strings are set in vibration by the wood of the bow instead of the horsehair) new effects are always being obtained, and it seems as though after a history of more than 300 years the possibilities of the stringed instruments are by no means exhausted.

Violin

To the Violin (tuned in g, d^1, a^1, e^2) is assigned the undisputed leadership of the strings. The number of violinists in the orchestra is usually as great as, or even greater than, that of all the rest of the strings together. In tutti and solo passages alike the most important tasks are allotted to them, and they also provide the basis of chamber music no less than of orchestral music. Following the example of Bach, Max Reger has written sonatas for the unaccompanied Violin.

Viola

The *Viola* (tuned in c, g, d^1, a^1) was employed as a solo instrument by Berlioz in his symphony *Harold en Italie*. It was the favourite instrument of Brahms, and among the more recent composers Hindemith has a special predilection for it.

Violoncello

It is characteristic of the important position allotted to the *Violoncello* (tuned in C, G, d, a) in the Romantic period that Rossini, in the Overture to *William Tell* (1829), introduced a quintet for five solo 'Cellos, which were accompanied by the pizzicato of the rest of the 'Cellos. Beethoven wrote a triple concerto for Violin, 'Cello and Piano and Brahms a double concerto for Violin and 'Cello. Solo concertos were written by Schumann, Dvořák, d'Albert, and other composers; and it is assuredly no mere accident that one of the greatest living instrumentalists—indeed, perhaps the greatest of all—Pau Casals, should be a 'cellist.

Double-Bass

The long-standing conflict between the three-stringed Double-bass tuned in fifths (G_1, D, A) and the four-stringed instrument tuned in fourths (E_1, A_1, D, G) was decided, in the course of the nineteenth century, in favour of four strings. Recently instruments are occasionally seen which have, in addition, a fifth, deepest string in C_1. The music for Double-bass is always written an octave higher than it actually sounds. The thick, heavy strings of the instrument are generally tuned with the help of steel cogwheels. We have evidence of the high opinion which was held of the capabilities of the Double-bass even at the beginning of the nineteenth century in the great unaccompanied bass recitative in the finale of Beethoven's Ninth Symphony; while Wagner, in Act III of *Tristan*, and above all, Verdi, in

Act IV of *Othello*, have given proof of the impressive quality of a solo Double-bass. A celebrated example of the naturalistic effect of the instrument is that obtained by Richard Strauss in his opera *Salome*. In order to represent the death-rattle of the murdered Jochanaan a string of the Double-bass is bowed *below* the bridge, instead of above it, as is usual. It is interesting to note that the greatest living exponent of the Double-bass, Sergeï Koussevitzky, is also one of the most celebrated conductors in the United States.

Effective though the supremacy of Violin, Viola, 'Cello and Double-bass was in practice, it was by no means uncontested. In the last 130 years, which were marked by greater progress in the matter of instrument-making than any previous period of equal length, many experiments were made in the construction of stringed instruments. As a matter of fact, none of the "improvements" made was really successful; the old-established instruments were not excelled, and their pre-eminence has been undisturbed.

Variants of the Violin

Some of the "improved" forms may be mentioned here, though to deal with them all would require a special chapter. Chanot (of Mirecourt, France) believed that the sharp corners of the Violin inhibited the diffusion of the tone, and from 1817 onwards he accordingly built instruments which had somewhat the shape of a Guitar. Contemporaries of Chanot's declared that in the quality of their tone these violins could rival the creations of Guarneri and Stradivari, and the famous violinist Viotti is said to have played on them occasionally. However, the Chanot Violins had no more enduring success than the trapezoid Box-Fiddle of the French physician Felix Savart (1819), or the elliptical instrument of the Dresden composer Dr. Alfred Stelzner (*circa* 1890). Practical tests subsequently established their acoustic inferiority. An interesting experiment was made by Stroh in London. At the close of the nineteenth century he was building Violins in which the sound-box was replaced by a diaphragm and a trumpet like that of the old gramophones. His instruments had a powerful tone, but a grotesque appearance. Quite recently—especially in Germany—Violins have once more been made without sound-boxes. They are provided with microphone and loud-speaker, and with the help of a pedal any desired loudness of tone can be obtained, from the softest *ppp* to the most powerful *fff*.

Variants of the Viola

Attempts were made to combine the characteristics of the Viola and the Violin; the Viola being given, as a fifth string, the highest string of the Violin (e^2). Instruments of this kind were the *Alto Violin* of the Frenchman Woldemar (d. 1816) and the great *Viola alta* of Hermann Ritter of Würzburg, produced in 1876.

Baritone Violins

As a connecting-link between Viola and 'Cello various *Baritone Violins* were constructed, tuned an octave lower than the Violin (*G, d, a, e*^{1}). In 1847 Carolus Henry, in Paris, made a Baritone Violin, and about 1900 Valentino de Zorzi, in Florence, produced his *Controviolino*. The elliptical *Violotta* of Alfred Stelzner (1891), which had a fine, full tone, was employed by Max Schillings, among other composers, in his opera *Der Pfeifertag*. All these three instruments were held like the Violin, but the

Tenor-Geige, made by Hermann Ritter, and by A. von Glehn in Reval (1912), was held between the legs like a 'Cello.

Variants of the Violoncello

A 'Cello in the cornerless form devised by Chanot was the *Arpeggione* or *Bogenguitarre* (Pl. XLIX, 1) invented by G. Staufer in Vienna (1823). This had the frets and the six strings of the Guitar, and was tuned like it in *E, A, d, g, b, e*[1]. Franz Schubert wrote an admirable sonata for this instrument. A larger variant of the Violoncello was the elliptical *Cellone* of Alex. Stelzner (*circa* 1890), which was a fourth deeper than the 'Cello and therefore two octaves deeper than the Violin (G_1, *D, A, e*). This was especially intended to replace the all too unwieldy Double-bass in chamber music. Stelzner himself and A. Krug wrote compositions for this instrument.

Variants of the Double-Bass

An enlarged variant of the Double-bass was the *Octobass*, invented in 1849 by J. B. Vuillaume in Paris. It was thirteen feet in height, and had three strings, in C_1, G_1, C; they were tuned from the tail-piece and were shortened by means of a key mechanism (Pl. XLIX, 2). The performer had the choice of operating this mechanism with his left hand or with his feet, for a system of pedals was provided. Berlioz, who was an enthusiast for all innovations, praised the Octo-bass in his *Traité d'instrumentation*. I myself have had the opportunity of hearing this instrument, and I was surprised by the weak tone of its rather loosely stretched strings. This defect, no less than its unwieldy dimensions, must have hindered any wider use of the instrument. As far as I know, in all only three Octobasses have been made. Even this mammoth instrument was overtopped in America by the *Grand Bass* of John Goyers (1889), which was fifteen feet in height.

While all these instruments were devised as innovations and improvements—even when unsuccessful—the historical tendencies of the period led to a conscious reversion to old forms. The *Bass-Viola da gamba* (tuned to *D, G, c, e, a, d¹*) and the *Viola d'amore* (tuned to *d, f♯, a, d¹, f♯¹, a¹, d²*) were not infrequently constructed, and there are many schools of music in which a student can learn to play them. In particular, the Viola d'amore has never become entirely obsolete. Of the Romantic composers Meyerbeer employed it in *Les Huguenots* (1836) and Wilhelm Kienzl in *Der Kuhreigen* (1911). Paul Hindemith has composed a sonata and a concerto for the Viola d'amore.

Guitar

Like the bowed string instruments, the *Guitar* (tuned to *E, A, d, g, b, e¹*, and scored an octave higher than its pitch) has undergone no structural alteration since the beginning of the nineteenth century. Up to the middle of the century its popularity was very great. C. M. von Weber wrote songs with Guitar accompaniment. Berlioz was a Guitar-player; so was his friend Paganini, who wrote some masterly chamber music for the Guitar. In Southern Germany particularly the Guitar holds its own to this day as the people's instrument for accompanying song. In its native Spain, however, the Guitar actually serves as a substitute for the Piano. Individual masters, such as Miguel Llobet, Andrès Segovia and Emilio Pujol have attained a mastery

PLATE LIV

Bassoon players of the B.B.C. Orchestra

PLATE LV

A Serpent; a group of Bassoons and a Baritone Oboe

From the collection and with the kind permission of Mr. John Parr, Sheffield

Behind the player (left to right) four Bassoons; Double Bassoon by Heckel, Biebrich;
Tenoroon by Morton, London; another by an unknown maker. In front: Alto Bassoon
by Hawkes, London, and Baritone Oboe by Piarttet and Benoit, Lyons

which reminds us of the art of the old lute-players. The leader of the modern Spanish composers, Manuel de Falla, has written his profoundly emotional *Homenaje*, dedicated to the memory of Claude Debussy, for the Guitar.

The Guitar also finds employment in jazz music; and here it is accompanied by two of its variants.

Ukulele

The *Ukulele* is really of Portuguese origin. In the nineteenth century this little four-stringed Guitar was introduced into the Sandwich Islands by the Portuguese; in the twentieth century it was exported from the Sandwich Islands to the United States as an original invention, and from there it was brought back to Europe.

Hawaiian Guitar

The Hawaiian Guitar is a large Guitar with a high bridge and metallic strings. A metallic pressure-bar laid over the finger-board serves to shorten the strings.

Banjo

One of the principal instruments of Jazz music is the *Banjo*. For sound-box it has a shallow metal drum, open at the back. This instrument, which is made in various sizes, used to be provided with from five to nine strings, the highest lying immediately beside the lowest. At the present time the Tenor Banjo with four metal strings in Viola tuning is preferred. The Banjo, which when wire-strung is played with a plectrum, has a hard, metallic tone, admirably fitted for the production of rhythmical effects.

Electric Guitar

In 1936 an *Electric Guitar* was invented in America. In this—as in the Electric Violin—the sound-box is replaced by a microphone and a loud-speaker. With the help of this device the tone of the instrument can be reinforced until it is audible above the loudest orchestra.

Mandoline

The *Mandoline* (tuned to g, d^1, a^1, e^2) is to this day diligently cultivated in Italy and South Germany. Whole orchestras are formed of Mandolines and their larger relatives, which perform light music with an often astonishing display of technical skill. Even in symphonic and operatic music the Mandoline sometimes appears in serenades and the like. It is thus that Verdi employs it in *Othello*, and the same use is made of it by the Viennese composers Mahler, Schönberg and Schreker. Hans Gál has written a quartet in which the Mandoline figures.

Balalaika and Domra

Russian folk-music relied largely on the use of three primitive instruments with plucked strings. Two of these, the *Balalaika* and *Domra*, are guitar-like; the third, the *Gusli*, is a kind of Psaltery or Zither.

Late in the last century V. V. Andreev modernized these instruments and made them the basis of an All-Russian orchestra, with which he toured Europe.

The Balalaika (Pl. XLIX, 3) has a triangular body, with a central "rose" in the table, and a fretted neck carrying three strings. At first the modern instrument was made in five sizes, which with their tunings are: *Prima* (e^1, e^1, a^1),

Secunda (*a*, *a*, *d*^{1}), *Viola* (*e*, *e*, *a*), *Bass* (*E*, *A*, *d*), *Contrabass* (*E*$_1$, *A*$_1$, *D*), the last standing on the ground when in use. Soon a sixth instrument, the *Piccolo* (*b*^{1}, *e*^{2}, *a*^{2}), was added. The Balalaika is usually strung with gut strings and played by being plucked with the fingers, or swept by the open hand; but it has recently become the practice among professional players to use wire strings and pluck them with a piece of leather. This adequately reproduces the effect of the gut strings while saving the wear and tear inseparable from their use.

The Domra resembles a mandoline in having a rounded-oval table and convex back. It also has three wire strings, which are played with a hard plectrum. The player produces a tremolo similar to that employed on the Mandoline, but with the difference that it has to be made on single and not on paired strings. The six sizes of the Domra correspond with those of the Balalaika, the *Prima* being tuned *e*^{1}, *a*^{1}, *d*^{2}, and the others to the same intervals at different pitches.

To complete his orchestra, Andreev used a Double Flageolet (*Svirely*) and a kind of Shawm with a single beating reed (*Brelka*), both developed from rustic originals, and for percussion Kettledrums (*Nakri*) with earthenware bodies, the Tambourine, and wooden Tablespoons, used as castanets in a manner familiar to street-musicians.

Harp

It was not before the second decade of the nineteenth century that Sebastian Erard in Paris succeeded after long experiments (cf. p. 199) in building a Harp which satisfied the highest requirements. His new *Double-action Pedal Harp* had a range of C♭$_1$–*g*♭^{4}; that is, of 6½ octaves (Pl. L). Like the older Harp, it was furnished with seven pedals.

Each pedal could be pushed right down or depressed to an intermediate position. When half-way down it raised the pitch of all the strings connected with it through all the octaves by a semitone; when fully depressed it raised them by a whole tone. The mechanism of the double-action pedal is shown schematically in Fig. 12. In Fig. 12a

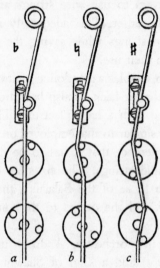

FIG. 12.—Diagram of the action of a Double-action Pedal Harp.

we see an unshortened string, the pedal being in the resting position. At 12b the effect of depressing the pedal half-way down is shown. The upper disc has rotated, and the pins attached to it have shortened the string by such an amount that it is now tuned a semitone higher. Fig. 12c shows the result of depressing the pedal fully. The lower disc and the fork have also rotated, and the string is so far shortened that it sounds a whole tone higher. The depression of a pedal produces this effect not merely in the case of a single string, but of the strings tuned to the same note through all the octaves. Since the pedals can be fixed in either position, it is possible, in a Harp tuned to the key of Cb major, by depressing the pedals through half their range, or through their full range, to obtain all the major and minor keys.

The Harp was so far perfected by Erard's invention of the double-action pedal that it was able to gain admission to symphonic and operatic orchestras. Not only chords and arpeggios, but also harmonics of a peculiar charm can be played upon it. Since the neo-Romantic period the timbre of the Harp has been blended most successfully with the tone of the wind instruments, especially with the brass, and it is indispensable for the expression of solemn pageantry and radiant refulgence. A Wagner score—to take only one example—would be unthinkable without the Harp. The effect is enhanced, in passages where the tonally weak instrument has to assert itself against a great ensemble, by multiplying the Harps. At Bayreuth the Harp parts are often quadrupled.

The Harp is also often employed in chamber music, or as a solo instrument. Louis Spohr wrote a fantasia for the Harp, as well as sonatas and rondos for Harp and Violin; Nicolas Bochsa, harper to Napoleon I, enjoyed international celebrity as a virtuoso and composer for the Harp, as did his pupil Elias Parish-Alvars.

The Double-action Pedal Harp, although it was by far the most important, was not the only Harp of the nineteenth century. G. C. Pfranger's *Chromatic Harp* needs no pedal, since it has a string for every note of the chromatic scale; the strings for the notes of the C major scale are white, while the rest are dark blue. More efficient than this instrument, in which all the strings lie in the same plane, is the Chromatic Harp invented by Jean Henri Pape in 1845, in which those strings which correspond to the white keys of the Piano lie in one plane, while the rest of the strings form a separate series. The two sets cross each other at the level of half their height. This instrument was still further improved in America, and more particularly by Gustave Lyon, the director of the firm of Pleyel in Paris (1903). It has found many exponents in France, Belgium and Switzerland. The fact, however, that in *forte* passages the strings collide with one another where they cross, and the rather poor tone of the instrument, militate against its wider diffusion.

Aeolian Harp

Aeolian Harps were in use even in the second half of the nineteenth century, and inventors made structural improvements in these instruments. Following the tremendous advances effected in keyboard instruments, the Aeolian Harp, although certainly less adapted for such a device, was provided with a keyboard (Anémocorde, 1789).

Aeolian Piano

Working upon the old invention of the Anémocorde, Isouard and Herz in Paris, about the middle of the nineteenth century, built the *Aeolian Piano*. In this the strings were differently tuned, and the depression of a key directed a current of air, compressed by bellows, against the strings. Since the notes took some time to build up, this ingenious instrument failed to hold its own against the more primitive basic form.

Zither

In the folk-music of Scandinavia, Denmark and Holland, and above all of Central Europe, the *Zither* plays to this day the same important rôle as in the past. It is often most artistically finished, and for use in dilettante circles is provided with all sorts of devices to facilitate the technique of the instrument. In order to make it available to exponents of the bowed instruments, Petzmayer (in Munich) invented in 1823 the *Streich-Zither* or Bowed Zither.

Bowed Zither

This heart-shaped instrument is usually provided with a fretted finger-board and four wire strings, tuned as in the Violin, though the order is the reverse of that found in the Violin. The instrument is played with the bow. In England a related instrument was known under the name Sultana or Cither-Viol. It had a form similar to that of the Violin and had four short legs, so that it could be placed on a table.

Electric Zither

Recently, in America, *Electric Zithers* have been employed, in which a microphone and loud-speaker replace the sound-box. This device makes it possible to produce tones of any desired strength. But in the case of the Zither, as with other instruments, the simple basic form evinces far more vitality than all the "improvements."

Cimbalom

The Dulcimer has come down to our days as the *Cimbalom* of the Hungarian gipsy orchestras. In the form improved by Schunda of Budapest the instrument has a compass of four octaves (E–e^3) and is fitted with dampers, which can be lifted by means of a pedal, as in the Piano. The metallic strings are set in vibration by two mallets. The Cimbalom players, most of whom play without notes, attain to an astonishing degree of virtuosity on this simple instrument.

Pianoforte

The upward career of the Pianoforte during the nineteenth century was quite unprecedented. Steadily advancing, it became one of the most important instruments of the period. While in Haydn's work the compositions for the Piano take a comparatively modest place, Mozart, who was twenty-four years his junior, wrote pieces for the instrument which are among his very finest achievements. In the work of Beethoven, born fourteen years after Mozart, the compositions for the Piano play an even more considerable part; while Chopin, Liszt, Schumann and Brahms not only were distinguished pianists, but their whole creative output is based on composition for the Piano.

It is obvious that this increasing interest in the Piano was bound to be accompanied by an enlargement of its technical possibilities. Many excellent Pianoforte manufacturers, in England, France, the U.S.A. and Germany, contributed to transform the delicate, fragile instrument of the eighteenth century into the powerful Grand Piano of the present day.

England

English makers, at whose head was the firm of Broadwood, must be credited with the perfecting of the English action, with its beautiful tone, whose superiority over the German action was admitted by Beethoven. They were also largely responsible for the wider compass and more robust construction of the Piano. The Parisian manufacturer,

France

Sebastian Erard, who had also improved the Harp by his ingenious inventions, gave the Piano thicker and therefore more sonorous strings, with hammer-heads of corre sponding dimensions. Above all, his improvements of the action of the Piano were of decisive importance. In 1821 he patented the Double Escapement, which made it possible

Double Escapement

to repeat the same note as often and as rapidly as the performer pleases. As long as the finger remains on the key, the hammer, having struck its blow, does not fall back into quite the initial position, but only half-way, so that it is ready for another quick blow. Hummel and the young Liszt were not slow to realize the importance of the new invention; yet almost twenty years were to pass before it gained general acceptance. Then, indeed, it was adopted by almost all the manufacturers of Pianos, though naturally with various modifications of detail.

U.S.A.

In America, where such makers as Meyer, Chickering, and above all, Steinway were working, decisive improvements were made in another important respect. The adoption of heavy, thickly-felted hammer-heads, and the consequent employment of thicker and more tensely stretched strings, together with the constant extension of the compass, which sometimes exceeded eight octaves, resulted in an enormous increase of the tension which the frame of the

Cast Iron Frame

instrument had to withstand. Even as early as 1862 it amounted to no less than sixteen tons, while in our days tensions up to thirty tons are to be found. After various experiments, in which European makers also played an important part, a heavy cast-iron frame was produced in

R

America by Babcock of Boston, of the kind in use to this day. Babcock and other American makers also adopted

Over-Stringing

the practice of over-stringing, in which the bass strings run diagonally above the rest. Thanks to this compacter arrangement of the strings, the over-strung Piano is shorter than the older type. At the same time—if the pedal is raised—the close proximity of the strings increases the wealth of overtones, and therefore the volume of sound. The tone of the over-strung Piano has not, however, the limpidity of the older instruments. It is less well adapted for polyphonic playing, and chords in the lower octaves, such as occur in the classical compositions, may assume the character of a buzz or growl. Such chords were, therefore, avoided by composers of the Romantic period.

Germany and Austria

Not only England, France and America, but also Germany and Austria, where experts of the standing of Bechstein, Blüthner and Bösendorfer were at work, made contributions to the structural development of the Piano. But Central Europe no longer played so important a part as in the days of Silbermann, Stein and Streicher.

The various forms of case adopted in the Classical period were retained in the Pianos of the Romantic period. The prevailing form of the instrument, now as then, was that of the Grand Piano or *Flügel*, adopted from the Harpsichord. It underwent a gradual increase in size, weight and structural solidity. The keyboard projected from the case, and was covered with a lid of its own, which could be opened independently of the lid closing the case of the Piano. Three heavy legs with baroque protuberances replaced the many thin legs of a former day. The pedals were given a strong wooden lyre-shaped support. Their number was now reduced, since the Romantic period began to regard the many subtly differentiated registers of the Classical period as a sort of toy. One pedal served to lift all the dampers, and the other to shift the keyboard, so that the hammer-heads no longer struck all three strings of the unisons. The Piano of the Late Romantic period, and still more the modern Concert Grand, can easily make itself heard against a full orchestra, and fill a big concert-hall with its powerful notes. For music in the home, however,

Baby Grand

the smaller Baby Grand Pianos are preferred, as better adapted to the rooms of a twentieth-century dwelling-home. The same conditions are fulfilled by the *Neo-Bechstein*, built in 1936 by the physicist Nernst in Berlin. In

Neo-Bechstein

place of the usual three strings for each note, only one is employed, or two at most, while the iron frame and the sound-board have disappeared. In their place the Neo-Bechstein is furnished with microphone and loud-speaker, which effect the necessary amplification of tone. The instrument possesses as usual two pedals. The right-hand pedal performs the traditional function of lifting the dampers and allowing the strings to vibrate freely; but the left enables the performer to regulate the volume of sound from the most powerful fortissimo to the softest pianissimo. Both a crescendo and a decrescendo can be obtained without moving the fingers; while chords can be long sustained with the greatest facility. Whereas in a normal Piano the resistance to be overcome on depressing the keys is from $2\frac{1}{2}$ to 3 ounces, and sometimes even more, in the Neo-Bechstein it is only a fraction of this amount. Whether the undeniable qualities of the instrument will make up for the mechanization of the tone only experience can determine.

Square Piano

The *Square Piano* underwent the same development as the Grand Piano in its more important phases. The strings were thickened, the compass was extended, and in America it even preceded the Grand Piano in the adoption of the iron frame and over-stringing. Large and powerful instruments were built, which were hardly smaller than a Grand Piano; but they were inferior to the latter in beauty of tone, and this sealed the fate of the Square Piano. It disappeared first in Europe, and the '80's of the last century saw the last of it in the U.S.A.

Upright or Cottage Piano

France and England had the greatest share in the development of the *Upright* or *Cottage Piano*. In England Thomas Loud (1802), W. Southwell (1807) and above all Robert Wornum the younger (from 1811) worked at the improvement of the instrument. Wornum's "Piccolo Piano" of 1829 already contained the essential features of the modern Upright. In France Henri Pape in particular made important improvements in the structure of the instrument. America, where the necessity of saving space was less urgent than in Europe, did not embark upon the manufacture of Upright Pianos until the second half of the nineteenth century, though it had done much to further the development of the instrument by the introduction of over-stringing.

It is impossible, within the limits of this survey, to note all the many more or less unsuccessful attempts to modify the structure and the technique of the Piano. We will men-

Jankó Keyboard

tion only the "Reformed Keyboard" of Paul von Jankó (1856–1919) (Pl. LI). This consisted of six rows of short keys, arranged in terraced form, which made it possible to strike any note in three different places. The advantage of this keyboard is that all major and all minor scales can be played with the same fingering, while the execution of large intervals and great leaps, as well as of interesting *glissandi*, is possible.

Moór Keyboard

Like Jankó, Emanuel Moór (1863–1931) was a native of Hungary. His "Duplex Coupler" was suggested by the structure of the Harpsichord. Moór placed two keyboards, of which the upper sounded an octave higher than the other, so close together that it is possible to play on both simultaneously with one hand; or if desired the upper can be coupled to the lower. Among the advantages of this device is again the ease with which octaves and large intervals and leaps can be played. However, the tenacious conservatism of the pianist has prevented any wide diffusion of either invention.

Mechanical Pianos

Mechanical Pianos have been employed since the beginning of the nineteenth century. Modern instruments, such as the "Duo-art" or the "Player-piano" have an electro-pneumatic mechanism and are able to reproduce the performance of a pianist with great fidelity in every detail. However, in consequence of the development of the Gramophone the interest in mechanical Pianos has greatly declined.

Keyboard instruments, in which the strings are not struck with a hammer, but are set in vibration by means of a bow, have been built since the year 1600; indeed, Leonardo da Vinci examined the problem more than a century earlier. More than fifty types have been constructed—the latest in the twentieth century—but none has been able to take its place among serious musical instruments, for the effect of a mechanically-operated bow is always rigid, lifeless and unsatisfying.

Clavichord, Spinet, Harpsichord

Clavichords, Spinets, and above all Harpsichords have often been built of recent years by Dolmetsch, Pleyel, Neupert and others. The modern Harpsichords are sometimes equipped with a third manual; in order to leave the hands free the change of stops is usually effected by means of pedals; and the strings are plucked by tags of leather instead of by quills, which results in a more powerful though a harsher tone. The modern Harpsichords are not infrequently employed for concert performances of ancient music (the old instruments, though far more beautiful in tone, are seldom used for such purposes, on account of their great delicacy), and recently Fr. Poulenc, M. de Falla, Hugo Hermann, H. W. von Waltershausen, Kurt Thomas and others have written original compositions for the "Clavicembalo."

While only a certain proportion of the stringed instruments suffered any important modifications during the Romantic period, all the wind instruments underwent a decisive development. Their construction was completely revolutionized, for the makers had the courage to shake off the bonds of tradition. Every least detail was carefully investigated; nothing was accepted without criticism; and the result was a richness and purity of tone that were quite unknown in the preceding period.

We shall now consider the wood-wind instruments, in an order approximating to that in which they commonly appear in a modern score.

Flute

The life-history of Theobald Boehm, the reformer of the Flute, who was born in Munich in 1794, and died in that city in 1881, may be cited as a confirmation of the proverb *Nemo propheta in patria*. He brought to the manufacture of the Flute a new impulse of decisive importance, and the results of his efforts were received with enthusiasm in France, England and America; while his native Germany always regarded his innovations with a certain degree of aversion. Boehm, who was himself a distinguished flautist, had felt, even as a youth, that his instrument suffered under a very great disadvantage, inasmuch as even with the eight-keyed Flute, which was then without a superior, certain passages and keys—as, for example, the scale of E major—could be played only with difficulty, while their intonation was far from perfect. Taking advantage of the previous achievements of the English flautist Nicholson and Captain W. Gordon, Boehm constructed a Flute whose holes were bored with the acoustically correct diameter and in the acoustically correct positions. The possibility of covering the holes with the fingers, which hitherto had played an essential part in the arrangement of the holes, was from the first wholly disregarded. Then, and only then, Boehm proceeded to equip his instrument with a rational system of keys to cover his correctly-placed holes. Here a difficulty was immediately apparent: there were more holes in the Flute than fingers on the human hand. In order to overcome this defect Boehm employed a device which was equally ingenious, clever and effective. He covered certain of the holes with ring-keys which were connected by rod-axles with key-covers which closed those holes for which no finger was available. How this was done is shown in

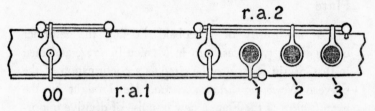

Fig. 13.—Action of the Boehm-Flute.

Fig. 13. The performer covers the hole 3 with the third finger of his right hand, hole 2 with his second finger, and hole 1 with his first finger. When these holes are closed the ring-keys over the holes are depressed at the same time, and these, by means of the connecting rod-axles r.a.1 or r.a.2, also close the key-cover over the o hole, for which no finger is available. If the third finger is raised, while the two other fingers are pressed upon their holes, 2, 1 and o are kept closed and the note e^1 is sounded. If the third and the second fingers are raised, while the first finger is pressed upon its hole, 1 and o are kept closed and the note f^1 is sounded. In order to play the note $f\sharp^1$ the hole 1 has to be uncovered while o must still be kept closed. This is done by raising the first and second fingers and depressing the third finger. The closing of the hole 3 is practically ineffective, as two holes lying higher up on the Flute are kept open, but it is important, inasmuch as the ring-key over 3 also closes the key-cover over o, for

PLATE LVI

A Clarinet player

Clarinets in A and B♭, Basset-horn, and Bass Clarinet in B♭ with extension to low C

PLATE LVII

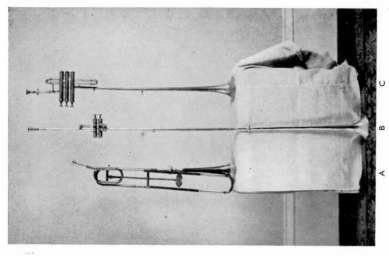

2.—A. English Slide Trumpet   B. Bach Trumpet in A, by Silvani, London, 1885. C. Bach Trumpet in D, by Mahillon, Brussels, ca. 1894.

A   B   C

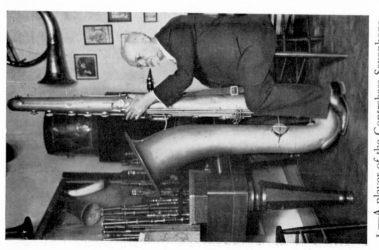

1.—A player of the Contrabass-Saxophone

which no special finger is available. By raising all three
fingers, the four holes 3, 2, 1 and 0 are uncovered and the
note g^1 is produced. While the ring-cover over 3 controls
two holes, the ring-key over 1 controls three; i.e., the
holes 1, 0 and 0 0. The hole 0 0, producing the note b^1,
lies farther up the Flute, among the holes controlled by the
fingers of the left hand. But the first finger of the right hand,
which would be idle as soon as notes above g^1 are played,
assists them by opening and closing this hole, for which
no finger of the left hand is available. This and similar
ingenious devices of the Boehm Flute were naturally bound
to revolutionize the fingering and therefore the whole
technique of the performers, which explains why, in spite
of its enormous advantage, Boehm's method of construction
met with violent opposition from many circles of flautists.
The first model, which Boehm produced in 1832, had still
the traditional and predominantly conical form of bore.
However, Boehm continued his improvements. Working
on the basis of exhaustive experiments undertaken in
conjunction with his friend, the physicist K. F. E. Schaf-
häutl, in 1846–47 Boehm produced a new model, which
was now cylindrical in bore, apart from the head-piece
containing the embouchure, which was parabolic. The
new Flute was remarkable for its great purity and evenness
of tone throughout its compass. The thin, delicate, ethereal
tone of the older Flutes was replaced by a much fuller,
more robust and powerful tone; which is perhaps the
reason why the cylindrical Flute has never been completely naturalized in Germany. Nevertheless, recent
instrument-makers have been obliged to equip even the
traditional conical Flute with many of Boehm's devices.

In its present form the Flute has a chromatic range of
b–c^4 (though Richard Strauss, in his opera *Ariadne on Naxos*,
requires it to play $c\#^4$). It is made of wood or metal; the

wooden Flutes are considered to have greater beauty of tone, while the metal instruments are reputed to "speak" more easily. The deepest tones are of course rather dull, and the highest extremely hard and shrill. The Flute is one of the most nimble and versatile instruments in the orchestra, being capable of the greatest variety of emotional nuances.

Giorgi Flute

Since Boehm's time there have been no really important changes in the structure of the Flute. But mention should be made of the instrument built by Giorgi in Florence, in 1888. The material of this Flute was ebonite; and it dispensed with keys altogether, having a separate hole for every semitone of the octave. But since only ten fingers were available for the eleven holes of this instrument, the left forefinger had to cover one hole with the tip and one with the second joint of the finger. Giorgi's Flute is not held transversely before the face, but in the same position as the Oboe and Clarinet, the embouchure being pierced in a separate bulbous headpiece. The difficult fingering and the wide intervals between the holes, which can be compassed only by performers with unusually large hands, have prevented any general adoption of this instrument.

Alto Flute

The powerful, mellow, expressive *Alto Flute*, a fourth deeper than the ordinary Flute (compass g–e^3, scored a fourth higher), has gained an ever-increasing number of devotees since its structural reformation by Boehm. Among other composers, Weingartner uses it in *Die Gefilde der Seligen*, Pfitzner in *Palestrina*, Rimsky-Korsakov in *Mlada*,

Holbrooke in *The Children of Don*, and Holst in *Phantasies*.

Bass Flute

Bass Flutes (which should really be called Tenor Flutes) made their appearance in the nineteenth and twentieth centuries, pitched an octave below the ordinary Soprano Flute; but in practice they are very rarely employed. Special mention should be made of the *Albisiphone*, constructed by Abelardo Albisi in 1910, whose metal tube, on account of its great length, is twice doubled on itself near the embouchure; the body of the instrument—as in the Oboe and the Giorgi Flute—points downwards and away from the performer. Another form of Bass Flute with the tube bent back was made by Rudall, Carte & Co., Ltd. (London), in 1932.

Piccolo Flute

Since the Romantic period the *Piccolo Flute* (compass d^2–b^4, best performance g^2—g^4, scored an octave deeper) has attained a position of almost greater importance than it held in the Classical period. For the expression of wild passion and moods of riotous emotion, or the description of storm and tempest, its hard, sharp utterance, which is unpleasantly shrill only in the highest register, is extremely valuable. It is an indispensable component of the Romantic and the modern orchestra. Wagner employed two Piccolo Flutes in the smithy scene of *Siegfried*, and three in the storm scene of *Der Fliegende Holländer*.

In this description of the various kinds of Flute only the more important types are included. The Flutes, which were among the favourite instruments of the eighteenth and nineteenth centuries, were made, about 1830—as is shown by the price-list of a Belgian instrument-maker—in twenty different sizes, and even since 1900 they are to be obtained in more than a dozen different keys—some of them only for use in military bands.

Recorder

In the Romantic period the *Recorder* was ignored. But since 1912 or thereabouts the late Arnold Dolmetsch, who earned our gratitude by his revival of ancient instruments, paved the way for a revival of the Recorder, which in England, and still more in Germany, has attained considerable dimensions. Recorders in various sizes—mostly without keys—are now made for revivals of old music, for use in schools of music, and for performances of folk-music. During the last few years various exercises and original compositions for the Recorder have been published.

Ocarina

The *Ocarina* is a sort of flageolet which belongs to the cheap instruments of amateur music. It has a hollow body of terra-cotta or metal, made in the shape of an egg, and is played by means of a mouthpiece similar to that of the recorder. Its sound is hollow, sweet and rather dull. These characteristics might be responsible for the unusual names of the instrument (the Italian word *ocarina* meaning "little goose"; the French sometimes call it *cou-cou*). The Ocarina is supplied with 9–10 finger-holes, and occasionally also with keys and tuning-slides; it has a compass of more than an octave. The instrument was first made in 1860 by Donati at Budrio (Italy) after the model of the ancient Flutes, closed at the end, which from the Stone Age onwards were known all over the world.

Oboe

The development of the *Oboe* during the nineteenth century was such as to make it all but the equal of the Flute. No new methods of construction were adopted; the improvements introduced consisted mainly of adaptations of Boehm's devices to the reed instrument. Even before 1800 Grundmann and Grenser of Dresden began to experiment with the Oboe, fitting it with keys in order to obtain the chromatic scale. During the first quarter of the nineteenth century the number of keys was rapidly increased, until at last there were ten. About 1825 the leading maker was the Viennese Koch, who was guided by the advice of the celebrated Oboe-player Sellner. The instrument was constantly improved, and by 1840 the number of keys had increased to fourteen. But now the example of Boehm's Flute began to influence the Oboe. French makers—above all F. Triébert—took the initiative, and we may trace through several decades a period of reformation in the construction of the Oboe. The climax and conclusion of these efforts were represented by an instrument (Pl. LIII) which was made about 1880, and which to this day has never been excelled: the Parisian "Conservatoire Model" (compass b–a^3), an instrument equipped with a key-mechanism as complicated as it is ingenious, which facilitates execution by offering the player two, three, and sometimes even four ways of obtaining the same note. Oboes are no longer made of boxwood, as of old, ebony or rosewood being more frequently selected. Recently, as an exception, metal or ebonite has been employed.

Since the middle of the nineteenth century the difference between the French Oboe, used in England, America, Belgium and Italy, and the German-Austrian instrument has become increasingly marked. The French Oboe has a thinner and more delicate tone; the German is harder and more powerful. The reasons why the French Oboe found an enthusiastic advocate in Richard Strauss are not without interest. In his supplement to Berlioz' work on instrumentation he praises it for its finer workmanship, its more equable voice in the various registers, and its greater flexibility and power of expression, while he criticizes the thick, trumpet-like voice of the German Oboe, and the incompatibility of its tone with that of the Flutes and Clarinets. Since this criticism was uttered in their own camp, there has been no lack of German makers who copy the French model. But on the whole Central Europe has remained true to its own ideal of the Oboe.

Oboe d'Amore

The Oboe d'amore, which is a third lower in pitch than the ordinary Oboe, was unknown to the early Romantic period. In the '70's of the nineteenth century, however, V. C. Mahillon, in Brussels, resuscitated the instrument for historical performances, and since then it has again been produced—equipped with the mechanism of the modern Oboe—by a number of different makers. Richard Strauss employed the instrument in his *Domestic Symphony* for the melody associated with the innocent child. The compass of the instrument as scored is $b-e^3$; but it sounds a third deeper, so that the actual range is $g\#-c\#^3$.

English Horn

While the Oboe d'amore is a rare member of the orchestra, the *English Horn*—at all events since Wagner's day—is very often to be found in the great *ensemble*. Until about the middle of the nineteenth century the body of the instrument showed the sickle-shaped curve or the obtuse angle of the eighteenth century. After this date, however, both the English Horn and the Oboe d'amore were given the straight body (Pl. LIII) and the key mechanism of the Oboe. Apart from its greater length and its pear-shaped bell, it now exactly resembles the parent instrument. Moreover, the English Horn is always blown by Oboe-players, who use the same fingering as on their usual instrument. It is therefore scored as a transposing instrument, on which every note sounds a fifth lower than it is written. Its written compass is b–f^3; its actual, e–b^{b2}. The instrument is in special request for the description of languorous pastoral moods. Schumann so employed it in his *Manfred*, Wagner in *Tannhäuser*, and above all, in the tragic passages of *Tristan und Isolde*. In fact the English Horn, with its tender and noble utterance, has been successfully employed, since the days of the Romantics, for solo passages of a melancholy and expressive character, and in conjunction with other wood-wind instruments.

Baritone Oboe and Heckelphone

Yet another fourth lower than the English Horn, and therefore an octave below the Oboe, is the *Baritone Oboe*, constructed by several makers, and finally in 1889, after various experimental attempts, by Lorée in Paris. It is more than three feet in length, has the pear-shaped bell of the English Horn, and is blown, like the Bassoon, through an S-shaped tube (Pl. LV). The voice is akin to that of the English Horn. A German attempt to solve the problem of the Baritone Oboe is the *Heckelphone*, constructed in 1904 by Wilhelm Heckel, of Biebrich-am-Rhein. This instrument, with its wide, conical bore, is made of maple-wood and has a barrel-shaped bell with a lateral opening. Despite its considerable length of more than four feet it has the same key mechanism as the Oboe. Its compass is A–g^2, and it is scored as it sounds. The rich, noble voice of the Heckelphone has been employed by Richard Strauss in his opera *Salome* and his *Alpine Symphony*, and also by M. von Schillings in *Der Moloch* and *Mona Lisa*. A small variant of this instrument is the *Piccolo-Heckelphone*.

Piccolo-Heckelphone

in F, with the compass e^1–a^3 (written a fourth lower).

In our survey of the Oboes of the Romantic period and the present day we have been able—as in our survey of the Flutes—to mention only the most important forms. Various other sizes, most of which have been made for use in military bands, are omitted by reason of their comparative rarity.

Bassoon

The voice of the *Bassoon* (Pls. LIV, LV), now mysterious, now grotesquely nasal—heroic and menacing in the *forte* passages, in the *piano* intimately tender—is one of the favourite means of musical expression in the music of the nineteenth and twentieth centuries. Hardly any composer of this period has neglected the rich possibilities of the instrument, which, apart from its other qualities, has a compass of three octaves and a fourth (B_1–eb^2). As regards the constructive development of the instrument, we may note the same difference between the French and the German method of construction as we have already noted between the French and the German Oboes. The efforts of the French builders were directed mainly toward improving the mechanism and the technical possibilities of the instrument, while at the same time they were anxious to preserve its individual tone quality, which is characterized by distinct contrasts of colour between the different registers. The Germans, however, were not content with producing a purer tone; they also endeavoured to give the instrument a softer and more equable voice, which is less characteristic than that of the old Bassoon, though it blends better with the tone of other wind instruments. Up to the present time each country has remained faithful to its own ideal of the Bassoon. Belgium and Italy prefer the French type, while in England and America both types are found.

In France the Parisian manufacturers, F. G. Adler, G. Triébert, and above all J. N. Savary *fils*, were the first to work at the improvement of the Bassoon. In their hands the eight-keyed instrument developed, by the middle of the nineteenth century, into a seventeen-keyed instrument, which in technical respects was greatly superior to the old type. An attempt of Triébert's in 1855 to apply the entire Boehm system to the Bassoon was unsuccessful, since the technical improvements could be carried out only at the cost of its traditional tone. Although this radical transformation was rejected, small and repeated improvements were made in the Bassoon during the third quarter of the century, and additional keys up to five were fitted. The Bassoon constructed at this time in accordance with Jancourt and Buffet's system—which had twenty-two keys, and was usually made of maple or rosewood—represents the highest achievement of the French manufacturers.

The German instrument-makers were working on other lines. The Bassoon-player, conductor and composer, Karl Almenräder of Nassau (1786–1843), guided by the researches of the musical theorist, Gottfried Weber, rearranged the finger-holes of the Bassoon in accordance with acoustical requirements, thereby doing for the Bassoon what Boehm was presently to do for the Flute. The fifteen-keyed Bassoon made by Schott, in Mainz, in 1820, in accordance with Almenräder's data, was distinguished by greater purity of intonation and a more uniform utterance

S

through all its compass. After Almenräder his friend
Johann Adam Heckel, of Biebrich, and Johann's son
Wilhelm, continued to work at the improvement of the
German Bassoon. After 1880—that is, about the same time
as the French makers—they discontinued their efforts.
Apart from minor improvements, the German Bassoon
of to-day is still in essentials the practically-planned, even-
sounding, tonally true instrument of the Almenräder-
Heckel type.

Double Bassoon

In the days of Haydn and Beethoven the *Double Bassoon,*
an octave lower than the Bassoon, was greatly valued in
Germany and Austria for the production of special effects.
In the finale of his Ninth Symphony Beethoven has
employed it in a most impressive manner. But the necessity
of having the holes small and close together, in order that
they might be covered by the finger-tips, as well as the
reasons stated on p. 211, made true intonation on the
Double Bassoon quite impossible, so that even in the
German-speaking countries this instrument steadily lost
ground during the second quarter of the nineteenth century,
whilst in other parts of Europe, even during the Classical
period, its employment was restricted to military music.
It is characteristic of the opinion held of the Double
Bassoon that in 1830 Parke derisively compared its long
tube to the funnel of a steamer. During the following
decades various attempts were made, in the interests of the
military band, to solve the problem of the Double Bassoon;
in 1839 Schöllnast, for example (in Bratislava, Slovakia),
produced his Universalkontrabass, and in 1855 L. Muller
(in Lyons) the Mullerphone; but such attempts were unsuccessful. Not until the '70's was a practical instrument
constructed, in which the tube was bent upon itself several

times, and a modern key mechanism was fitted. A wooden model with metallic bell, having the compass B_2–f, was made by Heckel in Biebrich (Pl. LV). The English and French models are rather shorter and larger in bore than the Heckel type so widely employed in Germany. They have a more powerful tone and a wider compass (C_1–c^1) than Heckel's Double Bassoon. They owe their various features to two Englishmen, Stone and Morton, a Frenchman, Thibouville, and a Belgian, Mahillon.

Tenoroon, Soprano Bassoon, Subkontrafagott

It may be noted that the Bassoon has occasionally been made in other sizes than the two described. The *Tenor Bassoon* or *Tenoroon* is pitched a fourth or fifth higher than the usual bass instrument, while the *Alto Bassoon* is pitched a sixth and the *Octave* or *Soprano Bassoon* an octave higher (Pl. LV). Perhaps the most interesting of the rarely employed types is the Subkontrafagott, produced in 1873 by the Czech instrument-maker Červený, which was an octave below Heckel's Double Bassoon, so that it went down to B_3.

An interesting attempt to replace the various types of Oboes and Bassoons—mainly for use in military bands—by a single new type is deserving of mention.

Sarrusophone

In 1856 the French military bandmaster Sarrus patented the *Sarrusophone*, which he had constructed in collaboration with the Parisian instrument-maker P. L. Gautrot. The Sarrusophone is a brass instrument of pronouncedly conical form, which is blown with a double reed. No less than nine different sizes are made, from the small Sopranino in high Eb to the Contrabass in deep Bb, all of which can be played with the same fingering. The written compass for all types is $b-g^3$; but the Sopranino sounds a third higher, and the Contrabass three octaves and a whole tone lower. The other sizes are transposed correspondingly. The two highest types are straight, the others doubled back. The Sarrusophone, which has a powerful but rather coarse and common tone, has not gained any real footing outside the military band. Only the Contrabass is sometimes employed in the place of the Contrabassoon. Saint-Saëns has frequently used it, and Jules Massenet employed it in *Esclarmonde*. Recently the conductor-composer F. L. Casadesus has written a solo for the Sarrusophone.

Clarinet

As with all the rest of the wood-wind, so with the *Clarinet*: the beginning of the nineteenth century saw it provided with a number of additional keys, which were added in the attempt to remedy the unreliability of the chromatic semitones produced by cross-fingering. In 1812 the clarinettist Ivan Müller (1786–1854) appeared in Paris with a thirteen-keyed instrument, which showed great acoustic improvement, and had a separate key for every semitone in the fundamental that was not already provided with one. But Müller was evidently in advance of his time. A commission which was appointed to examine the new type gave an unfavourable opinion of Müller's instrument, and it was only in the years 1825–35 that the thirteen-keyed Clarinet really established itself. In 1840 a new type appeared in the form of the so-called *Boehm Clarinet*, which was produced by Hyacinthe Klosé, professor at the Paris Conservatoire, and the instrument-maker Auguste Buffet, and patented in 1844. In this Boehm's improvements were fully adapted to the Clarinet, and the result was an instrument distinguished by great uniformity of tone, on which trills and legato passages could be executed more perfectly than on any Clarinet hitherto constructed. Of course, the inventors were subjected to the same opposition as Boehm himself. Since the new instrument often necessitated a modification of the traditional fingering it was a long while before the French clarinettists would accept it. In Germany, also, where in 1867 R. Mollenhauer had constructed a Boehm Clarinet, and where in 1890 the German *Normalklarinette* made its appearance (based largely on Buffet and Mollenhauer's invention), the opposition to the Boehm Clarinet has never been completely overcome. The cheapness and simplicity of the old Müller Clarinets, with their thirteen or fourteen keys, have always been appreciated, especially by military bands.

To-day Clarinets are usually made of cocus wood or some other hard, dark wood, or of ebonite, or metal (Pl. LVI). The written compass of the instrument is e–c^4, but the upper fourth is extremely sharp and strident, while, on the other hand, the deepest notes have a particularly warm and noble utterance. The instrument is made in about twenty different sizes, of which a few are here described.

Octave-Clarinets

The *Octave-Clarinets* in C, B and A♭, one octave above the usual Soprano-Clarinets, are to-day rare, even in military bands. Their tone is extremely shrill, and on account of the small size of the instruments the finger-holes are so close together that these Clarinets are difficult to play. The largest instrument of the group, the A♭ Clarinet, plays an important part in gipsy music.

Fourth-Clarinets

Among the high *Fourth-Clarinets* in F, E♭ and D, a fourth higher than the principal Clarinets in C, B♭, and A, the extremely shrill F Clarinet has always been virtually restricted to military music and German dance music. On the other hand, the E♭ Clarinet, since its classic employment in the caricature of the *idée fixe* in Berlioz's *Symphonie fantastique*, has found its place in operatic and symphonic orchestras. Modern composers are fond of employing its clear, penetrating tones to give sharpness to the wood-wind registers. The effect of the brilliant D Clarinet was cunningly employed by Liszt in *Mazeppa*, and by Wagner in the *Feuerzauber* of his *Die Walküre*, where it flashes out against the restless surging and crackling of the flames. Richard Strauss uses it with coruscating effect in his *Till Eulenspiegel*.

Soprano Clarinets

Of the *Soprano Clarinets* in C, B♭, and A the highest is in C. It is particularly suitable for strong and brilliant or convivial effects. Beethoven uses it in the finale of the Fifth Symphony, and Mendelssohn at the end of the Reformation Symphony. On the other hand, Richard Strauss employs it in the tavern music in the *Rosenkavalier*. Apart from such special effects, the C Clarinet has its place to-day in military and dance bands. The standard instruments are the B♭ and A Clarinets. Until late in the nineteenth century, the choice between them was made according to the easier way of fingering. Generally speaking, the A Clarinet was prescribed for sharp keys and the B♭ Clarinet for flat keys. Many players use both Clarinets when indicated, even in our days. The improvements in the key mechanism have made it possible, however, to play in all keys on the same instrument, so that the performer no longer has to drag two instruments about with him. This being the case, for use in the orchestra the clarinettist will prefer the more powerful and robust Bb Clarinet, which is equally capable of heroic strains and of tender and dreamy passages. The gentle, intimate A Clarinet is perhaps better suited for chamber music. It was for this instrument that Brahms wrote his Clarinet Quintet and his Clarinet Trio.

Alto Clarinets

Alto Clarinets in F and Eb are sometimes made a fourth and a fifth respectively below the ordinary Bb Clarinet. They are essentially like the Soprano Clarinet in their construction, but are provided with a metallic bell. The Eb Clarinet (usually called the *Tenor Clarinet*) was until recently employed in British military bands, but to-day it has been almost entirely replaced by the Saxophone.

Basset Horn

The *Basset Horn* is an Alto Clarinet in the key of F, or more rarely, the key of Eb. It is, however, narrower in bore, and has a thinner wall. Its tone is duller and cooler; also being furnished with extra keys, its compass extends a third deeper. The written compass is not, as in the Clarinet, e–c^4, but c–c^4; the sound is a fifth or a sixth deeper. The instrument is made to-day in the straight form, and possesses the mechanism of the modern Clarinet, while the characteristic book-shaped box near the bell is omitted (Pl. LVI). It is employed mainly in performances of Mozart's music, though Richard Strauss has used it in *Elektra* and *Frau ohne Schatten*. A *Kontra-Bassethorn*, an octave below the Basset Horn, was sometimes made in Germany.

Bass Clarinet

Bass Clarinets, an octave below the Soprano Clarinets, have been made since 1772, and have varied in shape. However, the instrument first achieved importance in the

'30's of the nineteenth century. In 1836 Meyerbeer introduced the Bass Clarinet in *Les Huguenots*, and in 1839 Adolphe Sax made a model which attracted attention by its efficiency and its beauty of tone. Since then the Bass Clarinet has been made in the straight form, or with the metallic bell turned upwards, and with the same key mechanism as the Soprano Clarinet. In the nineteenth century instruments in C, B♭ and A were in use. To-day we are content with the Bass Clarinet in B♭ (Pl. LVI). It is scored in the treble clef (compass e–g^3), the actual sound being a ninth deeper. Owing to the soft, expressive tone of the instrument, it seems even more fitted to form the bass of the woodwind than the Bassoon. It is also greatly esteemed as a solo instrument. Wagner, above all, has made use of its noble voice in passages of a peculiarly expressive character.

Contrabass Clarinet

Contrabass Clarinets, an octave lower than the Bass Clarinets, were made for use in military bands as far back as the first half of the nineteenth century; but it was only in 1890 that Besson, in Paris, succeeded in constructing an efficient Contrabass Clarinet in B♭, which consisted of three wooden tubes of unequal length. This powerful instrument, whose sonorous tone is like that of an organ, and goes down to A_2—that is, deeper than the Double Bassoon and Contrabass-Sarrusophone—has also been made in Belgium, America and Germany. Vincent d'Indy employed it in 1897 in his opera *Fervaal*. The costliness, weight and sensitiveness of the instrument—which moreover, makes tremendous demands upon the lungs of the performer—have hitherto prevented its extensive use.

Saxophone

In 1840 Adolphe Sax (*fils*), in Brussels, constructed

PLATE LVIII

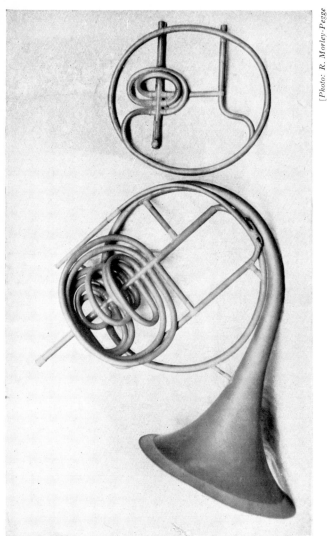

[Photo: R. Morley-Pegge

Cor ommitonique by Charles Sax, Brussels, 1824. Paris, Conservatoire National de Musique

All the crooks needed in the orchestra are carried on the instrument and can be successively brought into use by means of a slide. On the right is an alternative mechanism carrying the tubing for F, E and E♭ only, which can be substituted for the use of a soloist

PLATE LIX

[By kind permission of the British Broadcasting Corporation

Horn players of the B.B.C. Orchestra

(The instruments of French type)

metallic Clarinets of conical bore, the *Saxophones*, which
when overblown sounded not the twelfth, but the octave.
All the holes are closed with keys, and the mechanism is
akin to that of the Oboe. The instrument is easier to play
than the Clarinet, since fewer keys are required, and its
voice is more brilliant and powerful. Sax gradually built
up a family of six members, all of which are scored in the
treble clef, their compass being from bb–eb^4. The highest
instrument, the Sopranino, in the high Eb, sounds a third
higher (db^1–g^3), while the lowest, the Bass in Bb, sounds
two octaves and a tone deeper (compass A_1b–db^1). Besides
this group, intended for use in military bands, all the
members of which are keyed in Bb or Eb, he made the
same series of six instruments for use in operatic and
symphonic orchestras, all keyed in F and C. Later a
Contrabass in Eb was added (compass Db^2—g) (Pl. LVII, 1)
and C. G. Conn, of Elkhart, Indiana, produced a Sub-
contrabass in Bb (compass Ab_3–d). At the same time many
improvements were made in the construction of the instruments. The two highest members of the Saxophone family
(Sopranino and Soprano) are straight; the others have a
curved mouth-pipe and an upturned bell.

Kastner, in 1844, was the first to introduce the Saxophone
in opera (in his *Le dernier roi de Juda*). After him Ambroise
Thomas, Bizet and Verdi employed the instrument, and
the military bands of the Latin countries adopted it with
enthusiasm. Germany alone was at first extremely averse
to the instrument, and for a long while the Saxophone
quartet which Richard Strauss introduced *ad lib.* in his
Domestic Symphony could not be performed. The situation
is very different now, since jazz music has cast the Saxophone
for the leading part. To-day, in all parts of Europe as in
America, the Saxophone is one of the most familiar and the
most extensively employed wind instruments.

Tárogató

A relative of the Saxophone is the *Tárogató*, an instrument frequently employed in Hungary; it is a straight wooden Saxophone with a sombre tone-colour. It was first made in Budapest, in the year 1900, by W. Schunda, by transforming a popular Hungarian wooden Shawm.

Oktavin

Here, too, mention must be made of the *Oktavin*, invented in 1894 by J. Jehring in Adorf (Germany): a wooden Saxophone with a straight or bent body (compass g–e^3), which has been used in America. The firm of Heckel (Biebrich) makes two different varieties of Saxophone,

Heckelphone-Clarinet, Heckel-Clarina

the wooden *Heckelphone-Clarinet* (compass d–c^3), and the *Heckel-Clarina* with Oboe mechanism, which is sometimes employed for the execution of the joyous shepherd's tune in *Tristan und Isolde*.

Brass Wind-Instruments

In the nineteenth century the construction of the brass wind-instruments underwent an almost more decisive change than that of the wood-wind. Neither the crooks nor the "inventions" of the Classical period proved equal to the increased demands made upon them by music of the Romantic period. Skilful performers could, of course, change the key of their instruments in the midst of a composition. Haydn, for example, in the Second Sonata of his *Sette ultime parole*, composed in 1785, required the E♭ Horn to change its key to C, and allowed it for that purpose only $3\frac{1}{2}$ bars rest. But it would obviously have been impossible to make this change in the course of a passage, and the expedient which was sometimes employed of using simultaneously Horns in different keys, so that, for example, the notes which were difficult to obtain on the first Horn were played on the second, was not really satisfactory.

Cors Omnitoniques

In 1818 Dupont in Paris, and in 1824 Charles Sax (the elder), in Brussels, attempted to fasten all the crooks for the various tunings to the instrument, and to include them at will in the windway by means of a valve (Pl. LVIII). The *Cors omnitoniques*, which were so constructed, and on the improvement of which both French and German instrument-makers laboured for decades, did not find acceptance, as the attachment of many crooks made them unduly heavy and unwieldy. Moreover, simultaneously with the production of the Cors omnitoniques, another ingenious invention was made, which solved the problem of the chromatic Horn in a simpler and more practical manner. In the second decade of the nineteenth century

The Valve Mechanism

Blühmel, in Silesia, and Stölzel, in Berlin, constructed the valve mechanism, which they patented in collaboration in the year 1818—the same year that saw the appearance of the Cor omnitonique. The principle on which it is based is essentially a development of the old "Inventions." The valves are devices which make it possible by a single touch to intercalate in the main tube of the Horn short lengths of tube which increase the total length of the instrument, and so deepen its pitch. At first only two valves were employed, but a third was soon added. As a rule the first valve lowers the pitch of the instrument by a tone, the second by a semitone, and the third by a tone and a semitone. An F Horn, by the use of the semitone valve, becomes an E Horn; by the use of the whole tone valve an E♭ Horn; by the use of the tone-and-a-half valve, a D Horn. The employment of the tone-and-a-half valve plus the semitone valve makes it a D♭ Horn. The tone-and-a-half valve and the whole tone valve used together change it into a C Horn, while the tone-and-a-half plus the whole tone plus the semitone valve converts it into a B♮ Horn. The instrument which thus unites these seven different tunings in itself—as we see on page 49—would be able to play a chromatic scale through the whole of its compass of $3\frac{1}{2}$ octaves, and would need a much smaller length of tubing than a Cor omnitonique.

The mechanism by which the supplementary tubes are included or cut out takes many forms, but it can all be referred to two basic types: the *pistons*, which had already been employed by Blühmel and Stölzel, and which are still

Pistons and Rotary Valves

—in an improved form—preferred in France and England, and the *rotary valves*, which were invented about 1830 in Vienna, probably by Josef Riedl, and are particularly favoured by German performers. The effect of both these devices is shown in schematic form in Fig. 14. When the piston-valve is in the resting position (Fig. 14*a*) the wind passes through the main tube as shown by the arrow, without traversing the supplementary tube. But if the piston is depressed (Fig. 14*b*) the wind is compelled to pass through the additional length of tube. The same effect is produced by the rotary valve, by which the wind is diverted when a cylinder is rotated. In the resting position (Fig. 14*c*) the wind passes only through the main tube; but if the cylinder is rotated (Fig. 14*d*) by pressing the key the wind has to pass through the additional length of tubing.

It is impossible to mention in these pages even a fraction of the great number of instrument-makers who have done good work in the improvement of the valves, and especially of the pistons. Here only a few can be named: Uhlmann, of Vienna, who in 1830 produced the "Wiener Ventil" or Viennese valve, based probably on John Shaw's (of Glossop) transverse Spring Slides of 1824; Wieprecht and Moritz, of Berlin, who in 1835 introduced the Berlin "Pumpen-

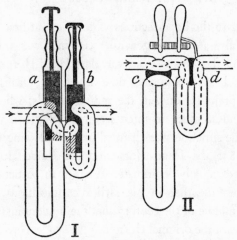

FIG. 14.—Mechanism of Valved Brass instruments.

I. Piston system.   II. Rotary system

a and *c*. Valves in resting position.   *b* and *d*. Valves in action

(*Note.*—In I the wind-channels through the pistons are not shown in detail)

ventil"; Périnet, of Paris, who in 1839 invented the excellent "Périnet valves"; Halary, Besson and Adolphe Sax, also of Paris; Embach, of Amsterdam; and the Englishmen Dr. Oates and Henry Distin. Thanks to the efforts of these and many others, it has been possible gradually to overcome the serious faults of the oldest models, which affected both beauty of tone and accuracy of pitch. The sharp corners and narrow passages of the oldest models detracted from the quality of the tone, while the simultaneous employment of several valves put the instrument slightly but unpleasantly out of tune. This defect was finally overcome by automatically-operated compensating valves. In France what are known as ascending valves have often been used instead of the original descending valves—that is, devices by which lengths of tube are cut out, thereby raising the pitch, instead of lowering it.

French Horn, Hand and Valve

Owing to the imperfections which were at first inherent in the Valve Horn, its general acceptance was very slow. Until after the '30's the old valveless Hand Horn held the undisputed lead, and the new invention was accepted without prejudice only in the military bands, where tonal beauty and accuracy of pitch were not of the first importance. The situation was changed in the following decades. About 1850 the Hand Horn and the Valve Horn were considered equally legitimate. Wagner in particular used both types together in his earlier compositions. It was after the middle of the century that the modern instruments began to cast the original Horn into the shade. Nevertheless, in 1865 Brahms still employed the Hand Horn for his Horn Trio, as he thought the Valve Horn too coarse for chamber music. The unqualified victory of the Valve Horn towards the close of the century also put an end to the old multiplicity of horn tunings. The favourite instrument was now the F Horn (compass $B_1\text{–}f^2$), on which the performers played almost any part, even if it was originally written for an instrument in quite another key. It is blown by means of the traditional long and funnel-shaped mouthpiece.

The national difference to be noted in respect of the woodwind instruments may also be observed in connection with the Horn since the latter half of the nineteenth century.

German and French Types of Horn

The French instruments have retained the slender shape of the older Horns. They are distinguished by a peculiar nobility of timbre, for the sake of which the performer is willing to put up with the greater difficulty of playing. The Horn preferred in Germany and Italy is somewhat larger in bore, which makes it rather easier to play, although the tone is somewhat less refined (Pl. LII). In Germany the first and third Horn players are sometimes equipped with a valve Horn in B♭ alto, the better to produce the higher notes. Central Europe also favours the "Double Horn" (*Doppelhorn*), which by means of a fourth valve changes an instrument in B♭ alto into an F Horn. This Double Horn is provided with a separate set of valves for each tuning, or else the length of the valve-tubing is changed automatically, as that used on the B♭ Horn would be too short for the F Horn. The Anglo-Saxon countries originally favoured the French type of the Horn (Pl. LIX), though now it looks as if they are inclined to prefer the German-Italian model, which is now exclusively used in the United States.

Stopping the Horn

The practice of stopping the Horn, which is inevitable in the case of the Hand Horn, is also applied to the Valve Horn. This Horn, however, is no longer stopped in order to alter its pitch, but because the stopped tones, with their dull, repressed timbre, have an absolutely different colour to the natural tones. The stopping is effected either with the right hand, or with the help of a damper or mute, a wooden or metal cone inserted in the bell. In all cases, the valves are so placed that they can be operated with the left hand. in order to leave the right hand free for stopping.

Keyed Bugle

Horns with finger-holes occasionally made their appearance as early as the latter half of the eighteenth century; but they played no important part until the Irish bandmaster Joseph Halliday supplied the English Bugle with keys. This *Keyed Bugle* looks externally like a keyed Trumpet; however, the bore is not cylindrical, but conical. The Keyed Bugle was at first fitted with five keys; later, more commonly with six, or even seven, and in exceptional cases, up to twelve. Its compass is *b–c³*; it is made in C, B♭ and A, and sometimes, as a Sopranino, in E♭ and F. It used to be employed principally for the soprano parts in military music; and in the second and third decades of the nineteenth century it was often entrusted with solo parts. In 1831 Meyerbeer used it in his opera *Robert le Diable*. But in consequence of its hard and rather common tone, and its unreliable pitch, the instrument suffered increasing neglect after the middle of the nineteenth century. Its successors were the Flügelhorn and the Cornet-à-pistons, both of which were made with valves.

Serpent

The *Serpent*, which even in the Classical period seemed a little out of date, surprisingly enough survived through half the nineteenth century. It was employed principally in churches—but also in military bands; and it was even prescribed in works by Rossini (*The Siege of Corinth*, 1826), Mendelssohn (*Meeresstille*, 1828, and *St. Paul*, 1836) and Wagner (*Rienzi*, 1842). In order to overcome at least in some degree the defects of unreliable pitch and poor quality of tone, resulting from the too small finger-holes, the Serpent was given an ever-increasing number of keys. On the Continent, particularly in France, it expanded into a remarkable variety of forms, with still more remarkable names. Two, the *Serpent militaire* (1806) and the *Serpent Forveille* (1822), are shown on Plates LX and LXI. Both were used in military music until displaced by the Ophicleide. By about the middle of the nineteenth century the Serpent disappeared from general use, and the annihilating attack which Berlioz made upon this instrument shows how little the progressive composers of his day esteemed it. Berlioz, who had himself employed the instrument in a youthful Mass, wrote in his *Traité d'instrumentation* (1848): "The essentially barbaric timbre of this instrument would have been far more appropriate to the ceremonies of the bloody cult of the Druids than to those of the Catholic religion. There is only one exception to be made—the case in which the Serpent is employed in the Masses for the Dead, to reinforce the terrible plainsong of the Dies Irae. Then, no doubt, its cold and abominable howling is in place."

English Bass Horn

The improved Serpent, the English *Bass Horn*, was even more quickly discarded than the Serpent itself. It survived only in military bands until the fourth decade of the nineteenth century.

The Ophicleide

A more successful rival of the Serpent was the *Ophicleide*, a sort of bass Keyed Bugle (Pl. LXI, 1). (The unusual name is derived from the Greek words *ophis*, snake, and *kleides*, keys, *ophicleide* meaning "Keyed Serpent.") This instrument, which is really an improved form of the English Bass Horn, was first constructed in 1817 by Jean Hilaire Asté, better known under the name of Halary. The Ophicleide is shaped somewhat like the Bassoon; it is

T

conical in bore and is usually made entirely of metal. It was at first fitted with eight to nine, and later eleven keys, which replaced the open holes of the English Bass Horn. It was usually made in C or B♭, with the compass B_1-c^2, or A_1-b^1 respectively. Halary made also Contrabass Ophicleides, an octave below the main instrument, the (Bass) Ophicleide, and Alto Ophicleides in F or E♭, a fourth higher than the standard instrument; these Halary called "Quinticlaves," because they are one fifth lower than the Keyed Bugle. The (Bass) Ophicleide is distinguished by its easy utterance and its suitability for legato playing. In view of its slightly raw, rough tone, and the fact that its accuracy of pitch is not entirely satisfactory, it seemed more suitable for use in the military band than elsewhere. However, it played a not insignificant part in the romantic orchestra. Spontini employed it in his opera *Olympie*; Meyerbeer in *Robert le Diable* and *Les Huguenots*; Wagner introduced it in *Rienzi*, and Berlioz in *La Damnation de Faust*. Most delightful is the burlesque way in which Mendelssohn used the Ophicleide in his *Midsummer Night's Dream* overture.

The career of the Ophicleide did not greatly outlast that of the superseded Serpent. By 1850 it had been largely displaced by the far more efficient Bass Tuba, which was equipped with valves, but it lingered in the hands of a few performers down to the last quarter of the century.

The number of Horns of various dimensions, furnished with valves, which are employed in addition to the French Horn, is extraordinarily large, and is far in excess of the number of Horns fitted with finger-holes and keys.

Cornet-à-Pistons

In France, in the late '20's, the Cornet (known also as the *Cornet de poste*), a small instrument with a narrow, conical bore, was fitted with two and then with three valves. The new *Cornet-à-pistons* has the form of a short, rather broad Trumpet, and is blown by means of a cup-shaped mouthpiece (Pl. LXI, 3). It is now made in various sizes, of which the Cornet in B♭ (compass $e-bb^2$) and A (compass $eb-a^2$) are the most frequent. The Soprano in E♭, a fourth higher than the B♭ Cornet, is employed as the highest voice of the English brass band.

France, England and Belgium gave the new instrument a very ready welcome; for it is easy to play, is very mobile, and has a far better tone than the Keyed Bugle. Germany and Austria, however, accepted it with some reserve, since in those countries the *Flügelhorn*, which we shall presently describe, was widely distributed. In Western Europe the Cornet is employed mainly in military and brass bands, and as a solo instrument in light compositions and dance music. However, it not infrequently makes its appearance in the romantic orchestra. It is a favourite instrument of the composers of French opera, and was employed by Rossini, Meyerbeer, Bizet and Gounod. Elgar introduced it into his *Cockaigne*, and recently Hindemith employed it in his Violin Concerto.

Formerly, in point of tone the Cornet was midway between the Trumpet and the Horn. It was less brilliant than the Trumpet, but its sound was fuller, and it blended excellently with the tones of other instruments. Berlioz, and many more recent writers after him, complained that the Cornet was a trivial instrument, and that its tone was shrill and vulgar, yet it may well be that they were unconsciously attributing to the instrument itself the qualities of the light music in which it was most frequently employed. Because it is easy to play the Cornet has been eagerly accepted as a substitute for the Trumpet, and one consequence of this has been that it has more and more frequently been given the cylindrical bore of the Trumpet; to-day, indeed, the two instruments are sometimes indistinguishable.

Flügelhorn (Valved Bugle)

The *Flügelhorn* (valved Bugle), which came into existence in Austria at about the same time as the Cornet-à-pistons in France, represents the direct offspring of the Keyed Bugle, being made with valves instead of keys. The Flügelhorn has the same compass as the Cornet; it is, however, rather larger in bore, has a deeper mouthpiece, and a somewhat wider bell, so that its tone is fuller, softer, and less brilliant than that of the Cornet. The instrument is employed mainly in military bands. It has been in especial favour in Germany and Austria; but also in many other countries, as for instance in England, where it is a much appreciated constituent of the brass band.

Alto and Tenor Horns

Before long deeper members of the Horn family were added to the Flügelhorn: the *Alto Horn* or *Alto Cornet*, also known as the *Clavicor alto*, in F or E♭ (compass e–g^2), and the Tenor Horn or *Tenor cor* in C or B♭ (compass B♭–bb^1). The latter instruments have the conical bore and the deep mouthpiece of the Flügelhorn and also its full, soft tone. Their form is not subject to any rule; they are made in a trumpet-like form, or else in the form of the Ophicleide, or in the circular form of the French Horn. The instruments of this type, which since 1830 have been made in most countries, are intended principally for military bands.

While on the valve instruments of the Soprano, Alto and Tenor registers hitherto described, the fundamental note cannot be sounded, owing to their narrow bore, the deeper members of the family are so wide in bore that their compass reaches to the fundamental tone. In order to bridge the interval of the octave between this and the second partial tone most of them are fitted—in addition to the usual three valves—with a fourth valve which deepens the notes by a fourth; during the last quarter of the nineteenth century even a fifth valve was added, enabling the player to correct the tonal falsity resulting from the simultaneous use of several valves. The *Euphonium* was invented

Euphonium

in the '40's of the last century, probably by Sommer of Weimar. Its key is Bb or C, and it has a compass of Bb_1—bb^1. It is employed above all in military and brass bands, the notes of its high register being often used for solo passages. This instrument is known in Germany as the *Baryton*, but not in Britain, where the narrower bored Tenor Saxhorn in Bb is known as the Baritone.

Bass Tuba

The principal instrument of the group is the *Bass Tuba*, in F or Eb, invented in 1835 by Wieprecht and Moritz. In military bands it is often called the *Bombardon*. It has a compass of A_1—e^b, is generally provided with five valves, sometimes with three, four or six, and is blown by means of a cup-shaped mouthpiece. The Bass Tuba is sometimes made for the use of troops on the march in a circular form, to be carried round the shoulder (the usual name for this form is the *Helicon*, from the Greek *helikos*, winding). But the most frequent shape is the Bassoon-like "Tubaform" shown in Plate LII. Since the middle of the nineteenth century *Contrabass Tubas* or Bombardons in Bb or C

Contrabass Tubas

have been made. Their compass is Bb_2–bb^1. Even bigger

instruments have been built—mainly in America—but their effectiveness is to some extent imaginary. Their mighty bells, which are up to thirty inches in diameter, or more in freak specimens, offer an impressive spectacle, but since the human mouth and lungs can no longer cope with these overgrown instruments, and since, moreover, the human ear cannot perceive excessively low notes, the purely musical effect of such instruments is comparatively poor. As an example of this gigantic type the *Contrabass-Sousaphone* in Bb, built for J. P. Sousa's orchestra in the U.S.A., may be cited. This instrument, with its monstrous bell, is employed in jazz orchestras as well as in military bands.

Wagner-Tubas

In the score of the *Ring* Wagner included, in addition to a Contrabass Tuba proper in C, two Tubas made to his own design, a Tenor in Bb and a Bass in F. These instruments of Wagner's, which were first built about 1870, are much narrower in bore than the ordinary Tubas, although they are not so narrow as the French Horn. They are blown with a funnel-shaped French-horn mouthpiece, and since they are usually entrusted to French-Horn players their valves are operated with the left hand. The voice of these instruments is full of unction and majesty. Since Wagner's day they have been employed, in particular by Bruckner and Richard Strauss, for the expression of quiet majesty.

Cornophones

In France the Wagner-Tubas were replaced by the related Cornophones, made by the firm of Fontaine-Besson and patented in 1890.

Saxhorns

In 1845 the celebrated Parisian instrument-maker, Adolphe Sax (*fils*), the inventor of the Saxophone, took out a patent for the family of *Saxhorns* which he had created. This comprised some ten members of different size, from the tiny "Saxhorn Sopranino" to the mighty "Saxhorn Bourdon." They are all scored in the violin clef between $f\sharp-c^3$, while the actual sound varies according to the size and tuning of the instrument. The Saxhorns were by no means an original invention, for they had borrowed their principal features from the Flügelhorn (Bugle); and in consequence Sax's right to name his instrument after himself was hotly disputed. Adam Carse reports that when the Italian maker Pelitti was asked "if he made Sax's instruments at Milan," he replied: "It is Sax who is making my instruments in Paris." Sax's real merit consisted in the fact that he built, instead of all the innumerable varieties of Horn and Tuba instruments, one uniform family, the members of which were all carefully made, and of excellent tone.

Sax owed not a little of his success to the British family of Distin, a father and four sons, who between 1838 and 1849 toured Europe as a brass quintet, perhaps the first of its kind. They began by using a mixed group of instruments, cornet, slide-trumpet, trombone and two hand-horns, and attracted little attention in France until 1844. In that year Sax made a set of instruments for them, graduated in size and uniform in tone-quality. Plate LXII shows the quintet with four of Sax's instruments, the fifth player being provided with one of a different pattern, probably by a German or Austrian maker.

With this set of horns the Distins created a sensation; they appeared before Louis Philippe and his family, and were presented by the king with a second set made, accord-

ing to one of the sons, of solid silver. The success of the
Distins in England and the extensive adoption of instruments made in accordance with Sax's principles were
powerful factors in furthering the growth of the brass-
band movement.

English Slide Trumpet

In the English *Slide Trumpet* (Pl. LVII, 2) we see an
assimilation of the Trumpets to the structure of the Trombones. While in the case of the Slide Trumpet of the
Baroque Period the whole instrument approached or
receded from the player, in the nineteenth century instrument the U-shaped portion lying next to the mouthpiece
is made to draw out. A spring returns the draw-tube to
the resting-point after use. The slide makes it possible to
correct faults of intonation and to lower the pitch of the
whole instrument by a semitone, and sometimes even by
a whole tone. The instrument is usually made in the key
of F, and provided with crooks for lower keys. According
to tradition the English Slide Trumpet was invented by
John Hyde in 1804. In its native country it held its own
during much of the nineteenth century, and was until
recently employed for Handel performances. However, it
never gained general acceptance out of England.

Valve Trumpet

Of incomparably greater importance than the Slide
Trumpet is the Valve Trumpet (Pls. LII, LXIII), which
originated in Germany in the third decade of the nineteenth
century. From Germany it spread with the greatest rapidity
to all parts of Europe and America. The exacting technical
demands which were presently made on the Trumpet
led to the gradual replacement of the Alto Trumpet in F

PLATE LX

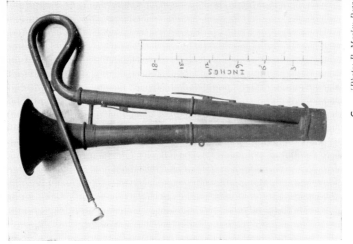

[*Photo: R. Morley-Pegge*]

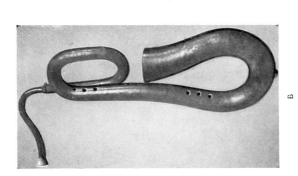

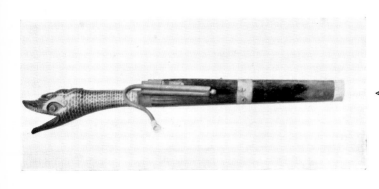

A. Russian Bassoon B. Serpent militaire, Paris, 1806 C. English Bass Horn

In the collection of the Conservatoire National de Musique, Paris.

With kind permission of Messrs. Boosey & Hawkes, Ltd.

PLATE LXI

3.—Cornet-à-pistons, Vienna, Society of Friends of Music

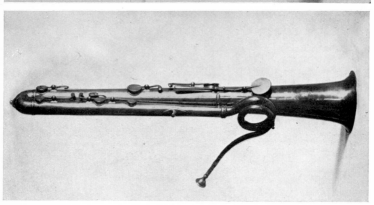

2.—Ophicleide, Vienna, Society of Friends of Music

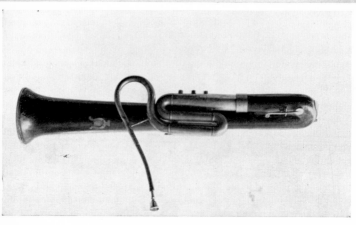

1.—Serpent Forveille, Paris, 1822 Morley-Pegge collection

(or sometimes E♭ and D), which at first was in most general use, by the smaller and more flexible Soprano Trumpet in B♭ (or sometimes C and A), whose compass (scored a tone higher) is *e-bb²*. This instrument is easy to play, though it has not the noble and vigorous tone of the larger Trumpets.

Bass Trumpet

Richard Wagner introduced the *Bass Trumpet*, which was employed in the military bands of the Austrian cavalry, to the operatic orchestra. This instrument is usually made in C, an octave or a seventh below the ordinary Soprano Trumpet, and its bore is so wide that its fundamental tone is obtainable. Its sounded compass is *F♯-e²* (noted in the violin clef an octave higher). In point of timbre the Bass Trumpet approximates to the Trombone. After Wagner, Richard Strauss, Schönberg, Stravinsky, and Janáček have made use of this instrument, with its noble and solemn utterance. In England, however, it has never become naturalized.

Bach Trumpet

Smaller instruments than the Soprano Trumpet are occasionally built—above all, for the Clarino parts of Bach and Handel. In order to give these instruments an antique appearance they are sometimes made in the straight form (Pl. LVII, 2). These so-called *Bach Trumpets* were first constructed in the '80's of the nineteenth century by the German trumpeter Julius Kosleck.

Muted Trumpets

As long ago as 1707 Alessandro Scarlatti employed muted trumpets in his opera *Mitridate*. But the first com-

poser to make a really significant use of the effect of the
damper was Richard Wagner, who in his scores repeatedly
directed the muting of the Trumpets; this was effected
by means of a hollow, pear-shaped piece of wood placed
in the bell of the instrument. The Trumpet so treated
has a strongly nasal, discontented sound, which is emi-
nently suitable for the characterization of Mime and Beck-
messer. Of recent years the muted Trumpet has very often
been employed, and jazz bands in particular are fond of
using it for humorous effects.

Trombone

In the Romantic period the *Trombone* (Pl. LII) was
an important and highly esteemed member of the symphony orchestra. While hitherto it had been restricted
to Church music, oratorio and opera, it now began to make
its way into the symphony orchestra. The chief instrument
of the family, the Tenor Trombone in B♭, has the compass $E-bb^1$ (which is written as played), to which must
be added three rough, muffled notes, which are obtainable
only with difficulty: the so-called pedal notes $B♭_1$, A_1 and
$A♭_1$, being in fact the fundamental notes of the instrument.
Berlioz employed these pedal notes for special effects in
his *Requiem*; Hérold in *Zampa*, and Elgar in *Cockaigne*.
As a rule, however, they are avoided.

The Tenor, in the course of the nineteenth century,
usurped the place of the Alto, which in its highest notes
was extremely shrill and unsatisfying. The Bass also,
which was a third, a fourth, or a fifth lower than the Tenor,
was cast into the shade by the latter. In Germany it was replaced by the Tenor-Bass-Trombone, which by means of an
extra valve changed a B♭ Tenor into a F Bass Trombone.

In 1816 Gottfried Weber suggested the construction of
Trombones with a double slide, in which the effect of the

draw was increased, since four instead of two tubes were involved. In 1830 Halary in Paris built a *Contrabass Trombone* on this principle, and similar instruments have also been constructed in England (Pl. LXIV, 1).

Contrabass Trombone

This instrument achieved a special importance, since in the '60's Wagner introduced it in the score of the *Ring*, and had it built for this purpose by C. Moritz in Berlin. His *Contrabass Trombone* in B♭ was an octave below the Tenor Trombone, and had a compass of E_1-d^1 (scored as played). The tremendous demands which this powerful instrument makes upon the lung-power of the performer are of course an obstacle to its wide distribution.

Valve Trombone

Although the Trombone is inherently chromatic, so that the application of valves is hardly necessary, yet several makers have provided it with such a mechanism. The new *Valve Trombones*, in which the valves are sometimes made to lengthen the tube, and sometimes to shorten it, have found employment mainly in military bands, though they are occasionally used in symphonic and operatic orchestras. In shape they often differ completely from the Slide Trombone, so that the bond which connects them with the parent instrument is a very loose one (Pl. LXIV, 2). The Valve Trombone may be technically more efficient than the Slide Trombone; but it is decidedly inferior in beauty and purity of sound, so that it cannot really replace the older instrument. The Slide Trombone is the only wind instrument which from the beginning of the modern era to the present day has retained its historic structure essentially unaltered. But as with the stringed instruments, of which the same thing may be said, the manner in which it is played has undergone decisive changes. In the seventeenth and eighteenth centuries it was played in unison with the human voice, with a delicacy that would almost befit chamber music. Its mighty, menacing fortissimo was the discovery of the nineteenth century. Recently it has been employed in jazz bands with *vibrato* and *portamento* effects, and is even played with a mute, which gives it a completely new and by no means attractive quality of tone.

Organ

Hardly any other instrument has undergone such decisive changes during the nineteenth and twentieth centuries as the Organ. Compared with the modern giant instruments of America and England the small Organs of the classical period seem to be mere toys. In power of tone and variety of sounds the modern Organ can hold its own against a large orchestra, and sometimes even excel it. The theatre and cinema Organs of our days are used to imitate a modern dance orchestra with its abundance of different effects. Little remains of the old Organ's simplicity and austerity.

The process of enlargement and modernization has brought forth changes in all parts of the Organ. While a discussion of all the details would fill a whole book, some of the essential changes will be described in the following pages:

Bellows

Until the beginning of the nineteenth century the bellows were operated by man power. It became, however, more and more evident that the immense quantity of wind required by the nineteenth and twentieth-century Organs could not be produced in such a way. F. Haas of the

Convent Muri, Switzerland, was the first to have the bellows operated by machinery. His invention was taken up more especially in England and America. Steam, hydraulic power, gas, and in later years mainly electric motors, have been used to obtain the necessary wind pressure.

To provide the evenness of wind pressure needed for the satisfactory working of the instrument, the great single "feeder" (as the outer part of the bellows is called) has been replaced by several small feeders, which work alternately. Moreover, there are devices which automatically put the feeders out of action as soon as the necessary pressure is reached in the reservoirs.

Action

The organist often wishes to connect one key with several pipes. To do this, he has to overcome a considerable wind pressure. To depress simultaneously several of the valves or "pallets" which allow the wind to enter the pipes, requires a strong effort. It is reported of the organists of the early nineteenth century that they stripped almost completely before their concerts, and nevertheless, after playing for a little while, they were bathed in perspiration. To facilitate the depression for the deepest organ-notes, Joseph Booth of Wakefield used little bellows (or "puff-valves"), which, with the aid of wind pressure, relieved the player of some part of the effort required to depress the pallets. An improvement of this idea is shown in the "pneumatic lever" invented in 1832 by Charles Spackman Barker, and used for the first time in 1841 by the famous French organ-maker, A. Cavaillé-Coll, for the organ of St. Denis, France. With the pneumatic lever the depression of a key opens the valve of a small auxiliary bellows, which in its turn opens the valve proper of the pipe. Using Barker's invention in 1867, Henry Willis constructed the "tubular pneumatic action," in which the wind actuating the tiny auxiliary bellows is led through tubes of sometimes considerable length. The tubular pneumatic action was used successfully in 1874 in the organ of St. Paul's Cathedral, London. Almost simultaneously with this device the "electro-pneumatic action" was invented in 1868, again by Barker. Here the attempt was made for the first time to operate the pneumatic lever by electricity instead of air. A decade later this system was considerably improved by Schmöle & Mols of Philadelphia, Pa. Recently all-electric organ actions have been built.

Keyboards and Console

While the older Organs were usually equipped with two to four manuals, modern instruments may be provided even with five or six. The manual known as the *Great Organ* operates the greatest number of registers and the largest stops. The pipes of the keyboard which is known as the *Choir Organ* were in the past often situated behind the player (the German name for this manual then being *Rück-Positiv*). There is the *Solo organ*, whose stops are used mainly for playing of solo melodies, and the *Echo Organ*, with soft-toned stops which are frequently fixed at some distance from the bulk of the other pipes. The pipes of the *Swell Organ* are enclosed in a wooden box which can be opened and shut by means of a "Venetian swell," thus producing a crescendo or decrescendo. Moreover the Solo, Echo and Choir Organs are often fixed in swell-boxes with shutters. Some instruments are provided also with a *Tuba Organ*, comprising stops played with a high wind-pressure.

Towards the middle of the nineteenth century the *double touch* was invented in England. Here the keys of the Organ are constructed in such a way as to produce the normal power of tone when lightly depressed; but if the player exerts a greater effort, a more powerful combination of stops comes into action. This device makes it possible to bring a certain part of the music into relief, or suddenly to produce a brilliant fortissimo.

In modern Organs, especially in Cinema Organs, frequent use is made of the *extension system*. This means that the compass of the pipes extends both higher and lower than that of the keyboard, so that it becomes possible to sound on one manual, together with the original 8' stop, a 16' stop, a 4', and even a 2' stop. The simultaneous playing of several octaves adds greatly to the brilliancy of the sound.

Old organs were sometimes fitted with two tiers of pedals. This was subsequently abandoned as uncomfortable for the player and musically superfluous. To-day tonal colour as well as power can be altered immediately on a single tier, thanks to the *combination pistons*. The organist is able to prepare a certain combination of registers in advance, so that when he is playing a single touch on the combination piston suffices to bring the whole group of registers into action.

Another feature of the modern Organ is the *crescendo-pedal* invented in the second half of the nineteenth century. It consists of a cylinder, which, when set in rotation by the foot, brings in further stops of increasing power. By rotating the cylinder backwards these stops are again disconnected. Most effective *crescendi* and *decrescendi* can be achieved by this device.

J. F. Schulze of Paulinzelle invented the *concave pedal* in the middle of the nineteenth century. In order to bring the keys for the highest and the lowest notes within easier reach of the player's feet they are slightly raised, thus giving the whole pedal a concave form. Many modern Organs are equipped with the concave pedal.

The consoles of Cinema Organs are sometimes built in such a way as to make their appearance, even when the performance has already started, from a trap, into which they return at the end. In the case of some Organs in concert-halls the console can be placed on any part of the platform. The modern electric actions make it possible to connect the console with the rest of the Organ merely by electric cables.

Pipes and Stops

The Organs of the nineteenth and twentieth centuries frequently employ devices for varying the wind pressure, whereby pressures from three to fifty inches and even more are produced. A. Cavaillé-Coll introduced over-blowing flue-pipes, such as the *Flûte harmonique*, which sound a harmonic instead of the fundamental note. They require a very high wind pressure, but the result is an uncommonly full and powerful tone.

As far back as in Bach's Cantata *Schlage doch gewünschte Stunde*, little bells, affixed to the Church organ, were pre-scribed; and certain devices for imitating percussion instru-ments have always been included in the modern Organ. The Cinema Organ in particular makes ample provision for triangle, xylophone, timpani, drums, and many others. I shall never forget what a well-known English organist told me of a misfortune which he had experienced when inaugurating a big Cinema Organ. The action of the stops and combination-stops had not been fully explained to him, and when he had intended to play the roll of the drums introducing the anthem "God save the King," he heard, to his dismay, a voice calling "Cuckoo, cuckoo."

Cinema Organs also make ample use of the tremolo effect. The *tremulant*, giving a fluttering quality to any note, had already been invented in the Baroque period,

PLATE LXII

[From a lithograph dated 1845

The Distin Family, John Distin and his four sons. The four players from the left have instruments of Sax's earliest pattern and graduated in size. The player on the right has an instrument of a different pattern, with "Viennese valves", probably by some other maker.

PLATE LXIII

[By kind permission of the British Broadcasting Corporation]

Trumpet players of the B.B.C. Orchestra

but its excessive employment has been reserved for the instruments of our own day.

Praetorius Organ

During the present century the efforts of organ-builders directed to enlarging and modernising the instrument have coincided with a movement in historically-minded musical circles aiming at the reconstitution of the simple organ of the early Baroque period. Thus in 1921 in Freiburg (Breisgau) Dr. Willibald Gurlitt, supervised the construction of an organ according to the specifications given by Praetorius in his *Syntagma Musicum* (1618). Similar instruments have been built in the United States of America by the Aeolian Skinner Organ Company of Boston, Mass., which erected a *Praetorius Organ* in the Germanic Museum of Harvard University in 1937, and a similar instrument in 1939 in the Westminster Choir School of Princeton, New Jersey.

Radio-Synthetic Organ

This instrument, built in 1934 by Abbé Pujet in the Church of Notre-Dame de Liban of Paris, applies the principles of radio-technique to the construction of an Organ. The *Radio-synthetic Organ* is equipped with four manuals and one pedal. For its more than fifty stops some four thousand pipes would be required by an ordinary organ. Abbé Pujet, however, manages with little more than one fourth of this number, by arranging that the harmonics of the pipes are picked up by microphones. These harmonics are mixed synthetically into new tone-colours, and finally sounded over loud-speakers. A far greater variety of tone-colours can be obtained in this way than by sounding the pipes of the organ directly.

U

Harmonium

The Harmonium, the Accordion and the Mouth Organ belong to a special group of free-reed instruments which were not employed in Europe before the nineteenth century. The free reeds owe their name to the elastic tongue which vibrates freely within a frame and by its vibrations causes a stream of air to sound (cf. p. 44). The shape and material of the tongue determine the pitch and quality of the tone. The tube of the ordinary wind instruments is superfluous.

Experiments with free reeds, which had already been used by the Chinese in their Mouth Organ or *Cheng*, were made in the early nineteenth century in various parts of Europe. The versatile Sebastian Erard, in conjunction with Grenié in Paris, experimented in the use of free reeds in a keyboard instrument of the organ type. In 1816 two Germans, Eschenbach and Schlimbach, constructed the *Aeoline*, a keyboard instrument with a compass of six octaves, whose bellows were operated by the knees of the player. Improvements of this instrument were the *Physharmonica* produced in 1818 by Haeckl of Vienna, and the *Aeolodicon*, constructed from 1820 onwards by different makers. In England John Green of London produced the *Seraphine* in 1833. Although its sound was rather harsh, the public was attracted by the novelty of the instrument, and it was sold at the considerable price of forty guineas. These experiments culminated in 1840 in the construction of the *Harmonium* by Auguste Debain, of Paris. His instruments were built much more carefully than most of the older free-reed Organs, and were provided with several registers of different tone-colour. Later inventors found reason to alter only a few details in the construction of the instrument. In 1843 the Harmonium was built with the "expression" stop—a slide enabling the player to cut out the wind reservoir, so that the air travels directly from the feeder to the sound-board. The player can control the wind-pressure and consequently the strength of the tone with his feet. Even crescendi and decrescendi can be produced in this way. About the same time another Frenchman, L. P. A. Martin, invented the "Percussion"; as soon as the key is pressed, a small hammer hits the tongue, making it "speak" more promptly. The "Prolongement," also invented by Martin, makes it possible to hold certain notes after the finger has left the key. The 'Melody attachment" of W. Dawes, London (1864), enables the player to give prominence to the highest voice by making it sound more strongly than the rest of the notes, while the "Pedal Substitute," introduced by Dawes and Ramsden, does the opposite, by emphasizing the lowest part of the composition.

While the European instruments work mainly with pressure-bellows, the *American Organs* built in U.S.A. are operated by suction. The air is drawn in through the reeds, producing a softer and more organ-like sound. The invention of the American Organ was due mainly to Mason and Hamlin, Boston, who, making use of earlier European experiments, produced the first reliable instruments in 1860.

The American Organs are sometimes constructed with two manuals and one pedal. They have various stops, which usually bear names adopted from the Organ. The newer instruments are provided with a swell and the inevitable device for producing a tremolo effect.

As a far cheaper substitute for the Organ, and one which incidentally is much easier to play, the Harmonium and the American Organ are still popular on both sides of the Atlantic.

Accordion

The *Accordion* is a small portable Organ of the free-reed type. Its reeds are often arranged in such a way as to produce one note as the bellows are expanded and another when they are compressed. One key can therefore sound two different notes. The left hand works the bellows and a large number of "touches" or studs, which are used mainly for the bass parts and the accompaniment. The melody is usually played with the right hand, for which the larger instruments provide a keyboard with a compass of four or more octaves.

The instrument was first built in 1822 by Friedrich Buschmann of Berlin, under the name of the "Handäoline." It was improved in 1829 by Demian of Vienna (who gave it the name Accordion). In the same year Sir Charles Wheatstone in London constructed the *Concertina*, in which drawing and pressing produced the same note. The Concertina was then provided with a complete chromatic scale. Chamber-music works and concert pieces with orchestral accompaniment were written specially for this instrument, and virtuosi on the Concertina are numerous.

An American relative of the Accordion is the *Rocking Melodeon*, which before the 1850's enjoyed great popularity. At the present time the Accordion is frequently in use for popular and dance music. Its wide diffusion is illustrated by the fact that it holds a place in American Jazz music, and in the traditional "Schrammel" Quartets of Austrian folk music.

Mouth Organ (Harmonica)

The smallest member of the free-reed family is the *Mouth Organ*, also called the *Harmonica* in Germany, the U.S.A., etc. It consists of a box containing sometimes scores of reeds, which can be played both by blowing and by suction.

The instrument was invented in 1821 by Buschmann, the constructor of the Accordion. His *Mundäoline* or *Aura* had a length of only 2¼ inches. To-day Mouth Organs are constructed either in quite a primitive form, as a sort of toy, or as a rather elaborate and expensive instrument. In both forms the Mouth Organ belongs to the instruments of folk-music, and even the best performers, who sometimes achieve a quite surprising virtuosity, are mostly amateurs.

Orgatron

A kind of Harmonium based on modern electro-acoustic principles was built in America in 1934 under the name of *Orgatron*. It is a free-reed instrument with two manuals, one pedal and twenty-four stops. By an electric device those harmonics are picked out from the tones of the reeds which are needed to build up the voices of the different stops. The resulting tone-colours differ completely from the usual sounds produced by a Harmonium. Surprisingly enough, the Orgatron sounds more like a Pipe-Organ than a reed instrument.

Kettledrum

The vast improvements which the first half of the nineteenth century made in the wind instruments were extended to the most important of the percussion instruments—the *Kettledrum*. The significance which the Romantic period attributed to this instrument is shown by the fact that Berlioz, for example, in 1837, employed eight pairs of Kettledrums in his *Requiem*. The manipulation of six or more screws, which in the Classical period had to be undertaken whenever the instrument was re-tuned, proved to be much too laborious directly it became necessary to alter the pitch not merely between movements, but sometimes during the course of a movement.

This difficulty was overcome by the device of a crank fitted at the side of the drum, which made it possible to tighten all the screws simultaneously. It was first applied in 1812 by Gerhard Cramer of Munich, then, in 1837, by the English maker, Cornelius Ward, and in 1840 by the Italian, C. A. Boracchi. Even to-day this method is preferred by many. Another device was adopted by J. C. N. Stumpff in 1821. In his Kettledrums the whole frame of the instrument was revolved in order to stretch or relax the skin, and thereby to alter the pitch. From Paris, about 1830, came Kettledrums in which the pitch was altered by means of pedals. But here two different principles were applied. In the older Pedal Kettledrums the area of the vibrating skin was reduced by pressing rings or cylinders against it, while in the later type the tension of the skin was altered. Kettledrums with pedals are so efficient that within a compass of at least an octave all semitones can be quickly and accurately obtained. In slow tempo a whole melody may be played upon a single instrument.

Beethoven was one of the first to depart from the tuning of the Kettledrums in fourths or fifths, as was usual in the Classical period; for example, in the Seventh Symphony his Kettledrums are tuned in sixths, and in the Eighth and Ninth Symphonies in octaves. To-day a set of three Kettledrums is favoured; the compass of the highest drum being *B-f*, that of the intermediate instrument *G-d*, and that of the deepest *Eb-Bb*. The instruments are scored as played. In exceptional cases, however, even this compass is exceeded; for example, in his Ninth Symphony Mahler has a Kettledrum going down to D, whereas Elgar, on the other hand, in the *Enigma* Variations, has a small Kettledrum going up to *g*, while Stravinsky, in the *Sacre du Printemps*, goes up to *b* and Rimsky-Korsakov, in *Mlada*, reaches *db'*.

Muffled Drums

Occasionally the Kettledrum is damped or muffled by laying a cloth over the skin or "head" of the drum. Mozart was one of the first to prescribe the effect of "Timpani coperti" in *The Magic Flute*.

Snare or Side Drum

The *Snare* or *Side Drum* was greatly improved in the nineteenth century, so that it was able to make its way from the military band into the orchestra. In 1837 the English maker, Cornelius Ward, patented "a mode of dispensing with the use of cords to all drums." Instead of the troublesome stretching of the skin or head by means of a cord he introduced the method of applying tension by screws, as in the Kettledrum. The Drum which before long was in general use is small and shallow, with a brass shell and tuning-screws. Across the lower skin one or more catgut strings or *snares* are stretched, which rattle when the drum is played. This pattern of drum, which is similar to the French *Tarolle*, has, however, not ousted the deep-shelled Side Drum, tightened by cords, either in most military bands, or some orchestras.

As a rule the roll is sounded, or single short taps are given on the instrument, producing a rattling, banging sound of indeterminate pitch, which has been employed, since the days of the Romantics, as an important means of expression in opera, oratorio and symphonic music. If the snares laid across the lower skin of the instrument are wrapped in cloth the Drum has a dull sound, which is peculiarly appropriate for funeral marches.

Tenor Drum

Another survivor of the old eighteenth-century Drum

is the larger Tenor Drum. Tenor Drums with deep wooden shells and cord tension and without snares, were employed, for example, by Wagner in *Rienzi, Die Walküre* and *Parsifal.* Their tone is much duller and heavier than that of the Side Drum, and, like the latter, is of indeterminate pitch. A French variety somewhat resembling the Tenor Drum, which possesses a snare, and is beaten with a single large drumstick, is known as the *Tambourin de Provence.* It was

Tambourin de Provence

used specially to accompany the *Galoubet* (the Provençal Tabor-pipe). Bizet employed the instrument in his second *L'Arlésienne* Suite, and William Wallace in *Villon.*

Bass Drum

Like the small Side Drum, the big *Bass Drum,* without snare, has come down to us both in the older form, with wooden body and cord tension, and in a modern form with brass body and screw tension. In this case the wooden Drum certainly ranks first, for its tone is fuller. The Bass Drum is usually beaten with a single drumstick with a felted head, or with a double-headed drumstick. For the roll Kettledrum-sticks are often used. In some of Richard Strauss's compositions, and in Mahler's Second Symphony, one head of the Bass Drum or even the wood of the rope-hoop is beaten with a birch rod, just as Mozart prescribed in his *Il Seraglio.* The sound of the Bass Drum is hollow and resounding in *fortissimo,* but gloomy and mysterious in *pianissimo.* Its pitch is indeterminate. Since the early nineteenth century the Bass Drum has been employed for the expression of exceptional power and energy, and also for mournful and mysterious effects.

PLATE LXIV

1.—Contra-Bass Double-Slide Trombone in CC. by Boosey, London

2.—Trombone with seven ascending pistons by Lebrun, Brussels

The instrument, with the pistons at rest, stands in E, and the pistons used in succession raise the pitch by semitones up to B♭. The seventh piston bridges the gap between E♭ and B♭ below the bass stave.

PLATE LXV

[Photo: Hedrich-Blessing Studio, Chicago, Ill.

Hammond Organ

Gong Drum

A variant of the Bass Drum is the English *Gong Drum*, with a shallow metal body and only one head. In the modern dance music big Drums are used, the sticks of which are operated by a pedal.

Tambourine

The *Tambourine*, a small wooden Drum with only one head, in whose hoop little jingling metal discs or small bells are inserted, adopted screw tension, like the rest of the Drums, in the nineteenth century. This instrument, which is beaten with the bare hand, without a drumstick, has been employed not only in military bands, but also in symphonic and operatic orchestras, in wild dances and scenes of carnival. Thus Weber used it in the overture to *Preciosa*; Berlioz in the *Carnaval Romain* overture, Elgar in *Cockaigne*; and Tchaikovsky in the *Nutcracker Suite*.

Cymbals

Like the Drums, the *Cymbals* won the freedom of the orchestra in the nineteenth and twentieth centuries. The two plates are softly clashed together in the mediaeval manner, so that a gentle vibration results, or they are violently swept past each other in the Turkish fashion, producing a sharp hissing sound. Frequently, too, a single plate, hanging freely, or supported underneath by a special spring, is played by means of a Kettledrum-stick. Wagner uses this mysterious ringing sound to describe the glitter of the *Rheingold*. The custom formerly observed—for reasons of economy—of fastening one plate of the Cymbals to the wood of the Bass Drum, so that one performer can deal with both instruments, is now fortunately restricted mainly to bands of minor importance, and is rarely to be observed in the symphony orchestra. The Cymbals, however played, yield a sound of indeterminate pitch.

Antique Cymbals

Tiny tuned Cymbals, on the pattern of the Greek and Roman Cymbals preserved in various museums, were resuscitated by Berlioz. He required them in *Les Troyens* and *Roméo et Juliette*. Following his example, Debussy used them in *L'Après-midi d'un Faune*. Most orchestras, however, replace these instruments, which are difficult to obtain, by the Glockenspiel.

Castanets

Castanets are the Spanish instrument of the national dances, and as such are known throughout Europe. No composer, of whatever nationality, will write a Spanish dance without introducing the Castanets. One of the best known examples of their use is in the second act of Bizet's *Carmen*. The Castanet parts in modern scores are generally executed, not with the real Castanets, fastened to the fingers, which are very difficult to use, but with a more convenient substitute. This consists of a staff, to one or both ends of which the plates of the Castanets are loosely attached, with an intermediate plate between them. The desired rhythm is produced by shaking the staff.

Triangle

In the course of the nineteenth century the *Triangle* became a most important and frequently employed member of the Percussion family. It now has the form of an equilateral triangle, and is set in vibration with a small metal rod. The sound is clear, penetrating, and of indeterminate pitch.

Jazz bands make use also of elastic sheets of metal, which the player bends more or less in order to alter the pitch.

Musical Saw

The *Musical Saw* is an ordinary handsaw, which is usually set in vibration by a violoncello bow or a mallet with rubber head. Its tone is tremulous, and bell-like in the deep notes, and it is employed mostly for the performance of slow melodies, allowing for slurring from note to note.

Xylophone and Marimba

The *Xylophone* consists of small tuned bars of wood, which—for the convenience of the player—are mostly arranged in two rows like the keys of a piano and are played with little mallets. The usual compass of the instrument is c^1–c^4, but Xylophones are also made with compasses of 2, $2\frac{1}{2}$ and 4 octaves. Thanks to its peculiar dry, hollow timbre the instrument has quite recently found its way into the symphonic and operatic orchestra. Saint-Saëns employed it in the *Danse macabre* to describe the clatter of skeletons; Mahler has introduced it in his Sixth Symphony, and Holbrooke in his *Queen Mab*. The Xylophone is frequently employed also in jazz bands, when very great demands are made upon the technical skill of the performer.

The *Marimba* was originally a kind of Xylophone common among the native Africans, in which the sound was reinforced by gourds placed under the bars to act as resonators. Brought to America by slaves, it was developed and became extremely popular, especially in Central America. The present Marimba is really a large Xylophone with a compass of $4\frac{1}{2}$ or 5 octaves. The bars are of rose-wood and under each one is suspended a tubular metal resonator, accurately tuned so as to reinforce the sound of the bar. It may be played by two or more players, and this is commonly done in Central and South America.

Glockenspiel

The *Glockenspiel* of the nineteenth and twentieth centuries consists as a rule of small tuned metal bars, arranged in a row, or in two rows, like the keys of a piano, and struck with hammers. To-day the compass of the instrument is commonly c^2-c^5, or perhaps only bb^2-c^5. Wagner uses it in the Fire Music of *Die Walküre*, and in the Apprentices' Dance of the *Meistersinger*; Puccini in *La Bohême*; and Mahler in his Eighth Symphony. The Glockenspiel with a keyboard, as used by Mozart in his *Magic Flute*, is rare to-day.

Celesta

Its place has been taken by the *Celesta*, a Keyboard Glockenspiel, the bars of which are rested on wooden resonators. The tone of the Celesta is soft and almost harp-like. The instrument has a compass of c^1-c^5, and is usually scored an octave lower than it sounds. The Celesta was invented in 1886, by Victor Mustel, in Paris. Since then it has often been prescribed in modern compositions. Richard Strauss has very beautifully blended its tones with those of the wood-wind in the second act of *Der Rosenkavalier*.

Typophone

A forerunner of the Celesta is the *Typophone* or *Dulcitone*, which employs tuning-forks instead of metal laminae.

This instrument, which Mustel had constructed more than twenty years before the Celesta, was employed by Vincent d'Indy in *Le Chant de la Cloche.*

Tubular Bells

In the modern orchestra *Tubular Bells*, hung in a frame, and struck with a hammer, serve as a substitute for the real bells, which are heavy and costly. Unlike the real bells they are tuned to definite pitch—commonly from *g* to *g*²—and have a full and round, though not very powerful tone. Among composers who have used them are Sullivan in his *Golden Legend*, Stanford in *Much Ado about Nothing*, Schreker in *Vorspiel zu einem Drama*, and Bittner in *Bergsee*.

Vibraphone

The *Vibraphone* must be numbered among the few valuable achievements of the jazz orchestra. It consists of tuned metal bars which are fitted over resonators. Above the openings in these resonators are tiny electrically-driven fans, which impart a peculiar vibrato to the full, soft tones of the instrument. Alban Berg made effective use of the Vibraphone in his *Lulu* Suite.

The Gong

The dark, persistent clangour of the *Gong*, now mysterious, now ominously solemn, found ready acceptance in the dramatic compositions of the nineteenth and twentieth centuries. Meyerbeer employed it in *Robert le Diable*, Saint-Saëns in *La Princesse jaune*, and Puccini in *Madame Butterfly*. The Gongs made and employed in Europe—unlike some of those manufactured in Asia—are generally of indeterminate pitch.

Rattles

Wooden *Rattles*, in which an elastic tongue is caused to vibrate by the rotation of a toothed wheel, were used of old in Catholic churches in Easter Week as a substitute for bells. Their clattering tone is sometimes employed in the symphony orchestra, as in Richard Strauss's *Till Eulenspiegel*.

Wind Machine

The *Wind Machine*, which is used on the stage to represent the voice of the storm, consists of a barrel covered with silk, which is stroked as it revolves by a piece of pasteboard. This curious sound was employed by Richard Strauss in *Don Quixote* and in the *Alpine Symphony*.

Electric Instruments

In the past two decades various instruments have been constructed which use electricity for the production of sound (see p. 53). Their inventors are mainly physicists and technicians, not musicians, and the composers of our time treat them with an admiration which is not altogether free from suspicion. For all this, some advanced masters, like Honegger and Milhaud, have written for electric instruments.

In the following some of them will be described; we shall, however, confine ourselves to those in which the sound is produced by electricity. Mention has been made already of violins, pianos, organs, etc., which, although making wide use of electro-mechanical methods, produce the sound by means of vibrating chords, oscillating air, etc.

Aetherophon

The *Aetherophon* (see p. 53) invented in 1924 by

Professor Thérémin, Leningrad, is a pure melody-instrument on which not more than one note can be played at a time. It makes a quaint and rather magical impression, as the player regulates the pitch simply by movements of his arm. The nearer the hand approaches an upright rod connected with a valve, the higher is the resulting note; the farther the hand recedes, the deeper. The sound of the Aetherophon is soft and attractive, but the technique of the instrument allows only for legato playing, and the change from one note to the next can be effected only by producing a rather unpleasant glissando. Various efforts have been made to improve the principle of this instrument.

Ondes musicales

In the *Ondes musicales* built in 1928 by the Paris composer Maurice Martenot the player wears on his finger a ring which is fastened to a cord. The instrument is provided with a sort of manual which indicates to the player the exact place for his hand in order to obtain a given note. Moreover, a key makes it possible to cut off the electric current whenever desired, so that the wailing glissando between the different notes is avoided. Martenot arranged recitals in which as many as eight *Ondes musicales* were played in concert. So far about fifty works have been composed for the *Ondes musicales*, and Martenot himself wrote a Tutor for the instrument.

Hellertion, Trautonium, Emicon

Relatives of the *Ondes musicales* are the *Hellertion*, constructed in 1930 by Helberger and Lertes of Leipzig, and the *Trautonium*, built in the same year by Trautwein, Berlin, the latter offering special possibilities for varying the sound-colour. In 1931 America produced the *Emicon*, equipped with a proper keyboard, on which a special key is provided for each note.

An instrument suited not only for one-part music but also for the production of chords and polyphony is the *Givelet-Coupleux Organ* constructed in 1932 in Paris. Here a separate, carefully tuned valve is provided for each note. The instrument has three manuals, one pedal, and thirty-four stops. As is generally the case with electric instruments, the dynamic scale, revealing countless shades from the most delicate *pp* up to the most powerful *ff*, is very effective.

More successful still is another pipeless organ, the *Hammond Organ*, invented in 1934 by Laurens Hammond, Chicago. Here the tone is produced by an electro-magnetic method (see p. 53). This comparatively small and movable instrument has two manuals and one pedal (Pl. LXV). It is provided with combination registers, and also with a species of stops, which can be drawn out to eight different positions, whereby harmonics varying in intensity can be produced. Votaries of the Hammond Organ claim that by mixing and combining all its possibilities no less than 25 millions of different sound-colours can be produced.

Wave-Organ, Midgley-Walker Organ, Electrone

Similar to the Hammond Organ are the *Wave-Organ* built in 1937 in Ontario, and also the *Midgley-Walker Organ*, and the *Electrone*, both constructed in 1939 in London. The tone of the Electrone is particularly effective and brilliant, its sounds being built up from natural instead of tempered harmonics.

Superpiano, Rangertone

The photo-electric method (see p. 53) is used for

the *Superpiano* invented in 1927 by the Austrian Spielmann and for the American *Rangertone*. The first-named employs rotating discs, the latter vibrators for the production of sound. Both instruments are regarded as very promising experiments.

At present we cannot even hazard a guess as to the direction in which these electric instruments will develop in the future. What we can assert to-day is that they are accurate, durable, and often cheaper and easier to transport than the older instruments. Apart from these practical advantages, the electric instruments can both imitate the sounds of other instruments and create perfectly new sounds. Great possibilities are available in this direction, and a positive revolution in our traditional and rather petrified system of sound-colours does not seem at all impracticable.

X

BIBLIOGRAPHY

ADLUNG, J.: Musica mechanica organoedi. 1768.

AGRICOLA, M.: Musica instrumentalis deudsch. 1529. (Reprint as Vol. 20 of *Publikationen der Gesellschaft f. Musikforschung.*)

ALMENRÄDER, K.: Abhandlung über die Verbesserung des Fagotts. 1820.

ALTENBURG, J. E.: Versuch einer Anleitung zur heroisch-musikalischen Trompeter- und Paukenkunst. 1795. (Reprint, 1911.)

ALTENBURG, W.: Die Klarinette. 1904.

ANDERSSON, O.: Strakharpan. 1923.

The Bowed Harp, transl. by K. Schlesinger. 1930.

ARMSTRONG, R. B.: Irish and Highland Harps. 1904.

ARNOLD, E. T.: Die Viola pomposa, in *Zeitschrift für Musikwissenschaft* XIII, 1930.

AUERBACH, C.: Die deutsche Clavichordkunst des 18. Jahrhunderts. 1930.

BACKOFEN, J. G.: Anweisung zur Klarinette. 1803, 1824.

BAKALENIKOFF, V.: The Instruments of the Band and Orchestra. 1940.

BARESEL, A.: Das Jazzbuch. 1926

BARNES, W. H.: The Contemporary American Organ. 1933.

BARON, E. G.: Untersuchung des Instruments der Lauten. 1727.

BECHLER and RAHM: Die Oboe. 1914.

BEDOS DE CELLES: L'Art du facteur d'orgues. 1766–78. (Reprint, 1849.)

BERLIOZ, H.: Traité d'instrumentation. 1848, 1856.

Instrumentationslehre, revised by R. Strauss. 1905.

BERMUDO, J.: Declaracion de instrumentos musicales. 1555.

BERNHARD, P.: Jazz. 1927.

BESSARABOFF, N.: Ancient European Musical Instruments. 1941.

BIERDIMPFL, K. A.: Die Sammlung der Musikinstrumente des bayerischen Nationalmuseums. 1883.

BLANDFORD, W. F. H.: The Bach Trumpet. *Monthly Musical Record*, March–April, May, June, 1935.

Handel's Horn and Trombone Parts, *Musical Times*, Oct.–Dec., 1939.

BOEHM, T., and MILLER, D. C.: The Flute and Flute-Playing. 1908, 1922

BONANNI, F.: Gabinetto armonico. 1722.

BOTTÉ de TOULMON, A.: Dissertation sur les instruments de musique au moyen-âge. 1833 and 1844.

BRÜCKER, F.: Die Blasinstrumente in der altfranzösischen Literatur. 1926.

BUHLE, E.: Die musikalischen Instrumente in den Miniaturen des frühen Mittelalters. Bd. I. Die Blasinstrumente. 1903.
Die Glockenspiele in den Miniaturen des frühen Mittelalters. 1910.
Verzeichnis alter Musikinstrumente im Bachhause zu Eisenach. 1913.

CARSE, A.: The History of Orchestration. 1925.
Musical Wind Instruments. 1939.
The Orchestra in the XVIIIth Century. 1940.

CHAVEZ, C.: Toward a New Music. 1937.

CHLADNI, E. F. F.: Beyträge zur praktischen Akustik. 1821.

CHOUQUET, G.: Le Musée du Conservatoire national de musique. Catalogue. 1884 ff.

COEUROY, A., and SCHAEFFNER, A.: Le Jazz. 1926.

COUSSEMAKER, E. H.: Essai sur les instruments de musique au moyen-âge. 1845 ff.

CROSBY BROWN Collection of Musical Instruments. Catalogue. 1904–5.

DAY, C. R.: Catalogue of the Musical Instruments in the Royal Military Exhibition. 1891.

EICHBORN, H. L.: Die Trompete in alter und neuer Zeit. 1881.
Das alte Clarinblasen auf Trompeten. 1894.
Die Dämpfung beim Horn. 1897.

ENGEL, C.: Descriptive catalogue of the Musical Instruments in the South Kensington Museum. 1870.

EUTING, E.: Zur Geschichte der Blasinstrumente im 16. und 17. Jahrhundert. 1899.

FLOOD, W. H. G.: The Story of the Harp. 1905.
The Story of the Bagpipe. 1911.

FORSYTH, C.: Orchestration. 2nd ed. 1922.

GALPIN, F. W.: Notes on a Hydraulus. *The Reliquary* 1904.
Old English Instruments of Music. 1910, 1911, 1932.
A Textbook of European Musical Instruments. 1937.

GEIRINGER, K.: Die Flankenwirbelinstrumente in der bildenden Kunst des 14.–16. Jahrhunderts. Thesis, 1923.

Der Instrumentenname Quinterne. *Archiv für Musikwissenschaft,* 1926.

Musikinstrumente. Adler's *Handbuch der Musikgeschichte,* 1927.

Das Engelkonzert von Gaudenzio Ferrari im Dome von Saronno. *Zeitschrift für Musikwissenschaft,* 1927.

Vorgeschichte und Geschichte der europäischen Laute. *Zeitschrift für Musikwissenschaft,* 1928.

I Ritratti Musicali Fiamminghi e Ollandesi del secolo XVII. *Il Pianoforte,* 1929.

Alte Musikinstrumente. (A catalogue of instruments in the Salzburg Museum.) 1933.

GERBERT, M.: De cantu et musica sacra. 1774.

GERLE, H.: Musica Teusch. 1532.

GEVAERT, F. A.: Nouveau Traité d'instrumentation. 1885.

GRANOM, L. C. A.: Plain and Easy Instructions for playing on the German Flute. 1766.

GREETING, TH.: The Pleasant Companion or New Lessons for the Flageolet. 1661.

GRILLET, L.: Les Ancêtres du violon et du violoncelle. 1907.

GROVE, G.: A Dictionary of Music and Musicians. 4th ed. 1940.

HAMMERICH, A.: Musikhistorik Museum. 1909 ff.

Les Lurs de l'âge de Bronze. 1894.

HARDING, R. E. M.: The Pianoforte. 1933.

HAYES, G. R.: The Viols and other bowed instruments. 1930.

HECKEL, W.: Der Fagott. 2nd ed. 1931.

HEINITZ, W.: Instrumentenkunde. 1929.

HERTZ, E.: Johann Andreas Stein. 1937.

HICKMANN, H.: Das Portativ. 1936.

HIPKINS, A. J.: The Pianoforte and Older Keyboard Instruments. 1896.

HIPKINS, A. J., and W. GIBB: Musical Instruments Historic, Rare and Unique. 1888.

HORNBOSTEL, E. M. v., and C. SACHS: Systematik der Musikinstrumente. 1914.

HOTTETERRE-LE-ROMAIN: Principes de la flûte. 1707.

HOWARD, A.: The Aulos or Tibia. *Harvard Studies.* 1893.

HUCHZERMEYER, H.: Aulos und Kithara. 1931.

HUTH A.: Les Instruments radio-électriques, in *La Nouvelle Encyclopédie française.* 1935.

JACQUOT, A.: Dictionnaire pratique et raisonné des instruments de musique anciens et modernes. 1886.

JAHN: Die Nürnberger Trompeten und Posaunenmacher im 16. Jahrhundert. *Archiv für Musikwissenschaft,* 1925.

JAMES, P.: Early Keyboard Instruments. 1930.

JEANS, J.: Science and Music. 1938.

KASTNER, G.: Traité général de l'instrumentation. 1837, 1844. Manuel général de musique militaire. 1841. Cours d'instrumentation. 1848. Les Danses des morts. 1852.

KINKELDEY, O.: Orgel und Klavier in der Musik des 16. Jahrhunderts. 1910.

KINSKY, G.: Katalog des musikhistorischen Museums von Wilhelm Heyer in Köln. 1910 ff. Doppelrohrblatt-Instrumente mit Windkapsel, in *Archiv für Musikwissenschaft,* 1925. A History of Music in Pictures. 1930.

KIRCHER, A.: Musurgia universalis. 1650.

KLOSÉ, H. E.: Méthode de la clarinette. 1844.

KOCH: Abriss der Instrumentenkunde. 1912.

KOERTE, O.: Laute und Lautenmusik bis zur Mitte des 16. Jahrhunderts. 1901.

KOOL, J.: Das Saxophon. 1931.

LABORDE, B. DE: Essai sur la musique. 1780.

LANGWILL, L. G.: The Bassoon. Its Origin and Development. *Proceedings of the Musical Association.* 1939.

LAVOIX, H.: Histoire de l'instrumentation. 1878.

LEFÈVRE, J. X.: Méthode de clarinette. 1802.

LEWIS, W. and TH.: Modern Organ Building. 3rd ed. 1939.

LÜTGENDORFF, A. L. V.: Geigen- und Lautenmacher vom Mittelalter bis zur Gegenwart. 1904 ff.

LUSCINIUS, O.: Musurgia. 1526 ff.

MACE, T.: Musick's Monument. 1676.

MAHILLON, V. C.: Éléments d'acoustique. 1874. Catalogue descriptif et analytique du conservatoire royal de musique. 1893 ff.

MANDYCZEWSKI, E.: Katalog der Sammlung alter Musikinstrumente der Gesellschaft der Musikfreunde in Wien. 1912.

MATTHESON, J.: Das neu-eröffnete Orchester. 1713. Der vollkommene Kapellmeister. 1739.

MENDE, R. W.: The Appeal of Jazz. 1927.

MENKE, W.: History of the Trumpet of Bach and Handel.   1934.
MERSENNE, M.: Harmonie universelle.   1636.
MUSTEL, A.: L'Orgue expressive.   1903.

NEF, K.: Katalog der Musikinstrumente des historischen Museums
in Basel.   1906.

PANUM, H.: Middelalderens Strengeinstrumenter.   1915–31.
PARENT, D.: Les Instruments de musique au XIVe siècle.   Paris,
1925.
PEDRELL, F.: Emporio cientifico é historico de organografia musical
antigua española.   1901.
PEGGE, R. MORLEY: The Evolution of the large bore Bass Mouth-
piece Instrument.   *Musical Progress & Mail*, 1940,
March–July,
PIERRE, C.: La Facture instrumentale à l'exposition de 1889.   1890
Les Facteurs d'instruments de musique.   1893.
PIERSIG, F.: Die Einführung des Hornes in die Kunstmusik.   1927.
POHL, C. F.: Zur Geschichte der Glasharmonika.   1862.
PRAETORIUS, M.: Syntagma Musicum.   2nd vol.   1618.   Reprint
Kassel, 1929.

QUANTZ, J. J.: Versuch einer Anweisung die Flöte traversière zu
spielen.   1752.   (Reprint 1906.)

RAVEN-HART, R.: The Development of Electrical Music in 19th
Century.   1932.
RENDALL, F. G.: A Short Account of the Clarinet in England
during the eighteenth and nineteenth Centuries.   *Proceedings
of the Musical Association*, 1942.
RICHARDSON, E. G.: The Acoustics of Orchestral Instruments.   1929.
RIMSKY-KORSAKOV, N. A.: Die Grundlagen der Instrumentation.
1913 ff.
RÜHLMANN, A. J.: Geschichte der Bogeninstrumente.   1882.

SACHS, C.: Reallexikon der Musikinstrumente.   1913.
Katalog der Sammlung alter Musikinstrumente bei der Staatlichen
Hochschule für Musik zu Berlin.   1922.
Die modernen Musikinstrumente.   1923.
Das Klavier.   1923.
Die Musik des Altertums.   1924.
Geist und Werden der Musikinstrumente.   1929.
Handbuch der Musikinstrumentenkunde.   1920, 1930.
Die Musik der Antike.   1929.
The History of Musical Instruments.   1940.

SAUERLANDT, M.: Die Musik in fünf Jahrhunderten der europäischen Malerei. 1922.

SCHAD, G.: Musik und Musikausdrücke in der mittelenglischen Literatur. 1911.

SCHAEFFNER, A.: Origine des instruments de musique. 1936. D'une nouvelle classification méthodique des instruments de musique. *Revue Musicale*, 1932.

SCHILLINGER, J.: Electricity, a Musical Liberator. *Modern Music*, 1931.

SCHLESINGER, K.: The Instruments of the Modern Orchestra and Early Records of the Precursors of the Violin Family. 1910.

SCHLOSSER, J.: Alte Musikinstrumente. 1920.
Unsere Musikinstrumente. 1922.

SCHULTZ, H.: Instrumentenkunde. 1931.

SEEWALD, O.: Beiträge zur Kenntnis der steinzeitlichen Musikinstrumente Europas. 1934.

SKINNER, E. M.: The Modern Organ. 1917.
The Belle Skinner Collection of Old Musical Instruments 1933.

SONNECK, O. G.: Benjamin Franklin's Musical Side. 1916.

STRAETEN, E. VAN DER: La Musique aux Pays-Bas. 1867.

TERRY, C. S.: Bach's Orchestra. 1932.

TEUCHERT, E., and E. W. HAUPT: Musikinstrumentenkunde. 1910 ff.

TROMLITZ, J. G.: Kurze Abhandlung vom Flötenspielen. 1786.

VIDAL, F.: Galoubet et Tambourin. 1869.

VIRDUNG, S.: Musica getutscht. 1511. Reprint 1882.

VOLBACH, F.: Die Instrumente des Orchesters. 1913.

WALTHER, J. G.: Musikalisches Lexikon. 1732.

WARMAN, J. W.: The Hydraulic Organ of the Ancients. *Proceedings of the Musical Association*, 1903–4.

WELCH, C.: History of the Boehm Flute. 1883, 1892, 1896.
Six Lectures on the Recorder. 1911.

WELLESZ, E.: Die neue Instrumentation. 1928.

WHITWORTH, R.: The Electric Organ. 1936.
The Cinema and Theatre Organ. 1936.

WIDOR, C. M.: Die Technik des modernen Orchesters. 1904.

WILLIAMS, C. F. A.: The Organ. 1903.

ZACCONI, L.: Prattica di Musica. 1596.

ZUTH, J.: Handbuch der Laute und Gitarre. 1926 ff.

INDEX OF PERSONS

INDEX OF SUBJECTS